THE TWENTIES IN AMERICA

BAAS Paperbacks

Series Editors: Simon Newman, Sir Denis Brogan Chair in American Studies at the University of Glasgow; and Carol R. Smith, Senior Lecturer in English and American Studies at King Alfred's College, Winchester.

Titles in the series include:

The Cultures of the American New West
Neil Campbell

Gender, Ethnicity and Sexuality in Contemporary American Film
Jude Davies and Carol R. Smith

The United States and World War II
Martin Folly

The Sixties in America: History, Politics and Protest
M. J. Heale

The United States and European Reconstruction
John Killick

American Exceptionalism
Deborah L. Madsen

The American Landscape
Stephen F. Mills

Slavery and Servitude in North America, 1607–1800
Kenneth Morgan

The Civil Rights Movement
Mark Newman

The Twenties in America: History and Politics
Niall Palmer

The Vietnam War in History, Literature and Film
Mark Taylor

Jazz in American Culture
Peter Townsend

The New Deal
Fiona Venn

Animation and America
Paul Wells

Political Scandals in the USA
Robert Williams

The Twenties in America
Politics and History

NIALL PALMER

EDINBURGH UNIVERSITY PRESS

For my friend,
Paul Michael Taylor

Alis volat propriis

© Niall Palmer, 2006

Edinburgh University Press Ltd
22 George Square, Edinburgh

Typeset in Fournier by
Koinonia, Manchester, and
printed and bound in Great Britain by
Antony Rowe Ltd, Chippenham, Wilts

A CIP Record for this book is available from the British Library

ISBN-10 0 7486 2037 0 (paperback)
ISBN-13 978 0 7486 2037 1 (paperback)

Published with the support of the Edinburgh University
Scholarly Publishing Initiatives Fund

Contents

Ackowledgements

Thanks to Edinburgh University Press and to Stuart Midgley and Simon Newman for their patience and help throughout this project. Particular thanks go to Martin Folly, for encouraging me to start *and* finish this book. Thanks also to David Hornsby, for his eagle eye, to Maisey and Sophie and to Stuart Boydell and Roger Wilson who, in various ways, created space.

Introduction

This book attempts to present an examination of American politics and society during the decade of the 1920s. Inevitably, the treatment of any ten-year time-span as a cohesive historical period has its problems. 'Decades' are artificial, chronological divisions. Important events and cultural patterns rarely stay within their margins but spill over the edges. The heated political arguments of one decade mostly have their origins in the past, whilst their resolution lies somewhere in the future. Similarly, the social and economic developments of a particular decade result from many factors, including demographic change and world trade patterns. Both of these influences are usually in evidence before the opening of one decade and may continue long after it has passed into history.

It is also important to note that academic assessments of a decade are strongly influenced by the disciplinary tools employed for the analysis. Cultural and sociological analysts, for example, consider the 'Sixties' to have opened with the advent of the Beatles and the first stirrings of the 'counterculture' around 1964. Using this yardstick, the years 1960–3 are represented merely as 'holdovers' from the previous decade. Political historians are divided, however, in their treatment of the Sixties. Some perceive the inaugural speech of John F. Kennedy in January 1961 as the decade's curtain-raiser, whilst others focus upon Kennedy's assassination in Dallas as the Sixties' 'true' beginning. Similarly, the Fifties are often identified by historians and political scientists with the eight-year presidency of Dwight Eisenhower, which does not begin until 1953. Consequently, the last Truman years (1950–2), slip into a historical limbo.

Approaches to the 1920s do not usually diverge so significantly. Political scientists and historians are in the habit of using the tag 'Twenties' to refer to the period of economic prosperity between 1924 and 1929, years which also encompass most of the Calvin Coolidge administration. The period 1920–3 is often referred to as the 'post-war period', years when American society and its economy recovered from the shocks of war and recession. These were the years *before* the 1920s became the 'Roaring' Twenties of popular memory. Cultural historians reflect this view, identifying the decade with prosperity, materialism, jazz, 'flappers' and 'crazes', phenomena mainly associated with the middle or late Twenties.

What is, perhaps, most interesting about history's treatment of the 1920s is the way in which the decade has been left largely in the hands of literary critics and sociologists. Published works on popular culture in the Twenties are in plentiful supply, but serious scholarly analyses of the *politics* of the period are less numerous. In part, this is because political historians, writing since the Twenties, were 'united in condemning the era for its ideological sterility' and 'myopia'. Its political leaders were often depicted as 'pygmies' in comparison with the 'giants' of the pre-1917 and post-1933 eras. These historians were, by and large, liberal in their political sympathies and were in the habit of skating over the politics of the Twenties in order to pass immediately from the fall of Woodrow Wilson in a heroic battle for the League of Nations, to the glorious reign of Franklin D. Roosevelt and the New Deal.

The points made above provide an indication of the principal aims of this book. First, it offers a treatment of the Twenties which is mainly *political* in focus and attempts to bring to life some of the major political debates of the period. Second, it offers a more detailed analysis of President Warren Harding and his 1921–3 administration than is usually available in standard histories of the decade. Third, this work tries to assess the years 1920–9 on their own terms and in their own socio-economic and political context, rather than following the more traditional, liberal, school of thought which regards the Twenties as one long prologue to the Great Depression. For that reason, this book does not deal with the Wall Street Crash of October 1929. It reaches back to 1917 in evaluating the dominant political and social trends of the Twenties, but ends on 4 March 1929. Its analysis focuses primarily upon the political programme of the Harding and Coolidge administrations, traditionally referred to as 'normalcy'. The hypothesis put forward in this book is that the era of normalcy ended, to all intents and purposes, with the inauguration of Herbert Hoover in 1929.

Few eras in US history have confronted changes of the force and scale which confronted American citizens in the 1920s. Even at the decade's apogee, as 'Coolidge prosperity' gave the nation a sense of tranquillity it would not know again for at least thirty years, there were comparatively few areas of its economic, social and cultural identity which were not undergoing profound alteration. Most of these changes had their roots in earlier times – in the 'great migration' of black Americans from the southern states and the flood of immigrants into the country in the late nineteenth century; in the spread of Charles Darwin's theory of evolution; in the growth of powerful industrial monopolies; in the campaigns of the Anti-Saloon League; and in the first, rudimentary experiments conducted by Thomas Edison and Henry Ford. Their convergence began during the second decade of the twentieth century, as cars started to replace horses on America's roads; as state Prohibition laws moved the country inexorably towards its 'dry decade'; as religious doctrines came under greater scrutiny; and as women campaigned for social and legal equality. The coming of war, far from damping down change, accelerated its pace. Women and black migrants flooded into factories and offices to replace those workers now fighting in Europe. Labour unions, black civil rights organisations and groups advocating equality for women all gained new adherents and fresh determination as a result. New technology was deployed to help boost industrial and agricultural production. The federal government swelled to unprecedented proportions, spending more money, accruing more authority over all sectors of the economy and regulating freedom of speech and assembly. Abroad, as the war ended, the United States emerged as a powerful economic and military force, the only nation to emerge strengthened by the ordeal.

When the bubble burst, American society was rent with anxiety and disillusionment. The economy fell into a deep recession, thousands of farmers fell into bankruptcy, anti-communist paranoia poisoned political debate, strikes were met with brutality and lock-outs, white racial violence was met with equally violent black resistance, the Ku Klux Klan reappeared as a social and political force and unemployment stirred nativist anger towards immigrants. Unable to agree upon a workable formula for involvement in the new 'League of Nations', a body designed to arbitrate international disputes and prevent a second world war, Republican and Democratic politicians bickered amongst themselves and a cynical electorate turned its back on idealistic 'crusades'.

In this bitter, dysfunctional environment, American voters turned decisively to the political right. In the three presidential elections of the 1920s, conservative Republican candidates won sweeping victories and, throughout the period, the party never lost the majority in Congress that it had gained in 1918. Yet the nation itself did not appear to embrace conservatism in all its forms. As the post-war dislocation faded, American society entered upon an age of experimentation and iconoclasm, an age which venerated its past but was simultaneously preoccupied with the 'now' and the 'new'. Change was embraced, often unthinkingly, but also with a sense of excitement. Radio and mass advertising campaigns raised, in every sense, the volume of national communication, whilst car and air transportation eroded old geographical boundaries. The accumulation of material goods became a national obsession and their availability, even to lower-income earners, seemed to justify the faith of many Americans in capitalist entrepreneurship. The first 'youth rebellion' took place during the Twenties. Though by no means as sullen or as political as the rebellion of the 1960s, it was, perhaps, more lasting in its impact upon society. The young of the 1920s were the first to push against the barriers of gender, class and race discrimination. White youths mixed with black in the jazz clubs of New Orleans and Chicago, whilst young women experienced a greater degree of economic and sexual freedom. The impatience of the younger generation with the morals and beliefs of the older was palpable throughout the decade.

Equally palpable, however, was a sense of unease and dissatisfaction which pervaded the Twenties. Nativist organisations such as the Klan were simply the most extreme manifestations of a widespread, underlying fear that '100 per cent Americanism' was under threat as blacks and non-Anglo Saxon Protestant immigrants 'mongrelised' the white race. Christian fundamentalists issued dire warnings against, variously, 'petting parties', alcohol, Hollywood, materialism, Darwinism, socialism and Freudianism. Many regarded the Twenties as an era of arrogance and self-indulgence and bemoaned the apparent decline of religiosity.

Progressives and liberals spent most of the 1920s on the political sidelines, thinking wistfully of Theodore Roosevelt and Woodrow Wilson, or fighting guerrilla actions against the conservative-dominated government apparatus in Washington. Led by 'Fighting Bob' LaFollette, they attacked conservative economic policies as the gap between rich and poor grew wider and corporations grew larger and more powerful. Liberal critics of the Republican administrations in Washington, quite naturally, disparaged any evidence of progress which failed to address the issues of social welfare and wealth redistribution. Farmers, black activists and union leaders were also disappointed by their lack of progress in advancing their agendas during the Twenties.

Despite growing economic prosperity, many in the white upper and middle classes also appeared insecure and cynical – feelings given voice by the 'lost generation' of writers and poets, including Hemingway, Fitzgerald and Dos Passos. It would be their voices, not those of the brash, upwardly mobile advertising executives, which echoed down the years – transmitting to future generations the impression of the 'Roaring Twenties' as a spiritually empty and directionless era. Ironically, the one great 'crusade' of the 1920s, rooted in high moral purpose and backed by segments of both conservative and progressive opinion, deeply *divided* American society and drove ordinary citizens to break the law. Prohibition may not have been solely responsible for the rise in organised crime and gangsterism which is closely associated with the Twenties, but its influence was crucial.

The 1920s ended in financial calamity, with the Wall Street Crash of October 1929. The Depression which followed swept away the policies and the brash self-confidence of the old era. Subsequently, what once appeared exciting, colourful, innovative or amusing about the decade was depicted as gaudy, trivial, pointless and myopic. Historians competed with each other to devise derogatory labels, such as 'The Lawless Decade', 'The Aspirin Age', 'The Age of Anxiety', 'The Mad Decade', 'The Retrograde Years', 'The Years of Reaction' and even 'The Age of the Golden Calf'. The 1920s, according to Henry Bamford Parkes, were 'an extraordinary period in which the American people seemed to be engaged in a collective effort to evade realities.'[1] For Stevenson, the Twenties were a 'flimsy, juvenile and doomed age' during which the American public lived in 'massive, dumb affirmation' of capitalist and conservative values.[2]

Such labels are all too characteristic of standard historical approaches to the Twenties. They give an oversimplified and misleading impression of a complex era which began and ended in socioeconomic and political chaos but which laid the foundations of modern American society. To those studying the United States from the vantage point of the early twenty-first century, the America of Harding and Coolidge is instantly recognisable, with its Hollywood films and celebrity scandals, motels and highways, giant sporting arenas, pop psychology, radio phone-ins and supermarkets. The impact of the Twenties stretches far beyond the legacy of the Wall Street Crash but the tendency has been to interpret the entire decade as one long march towards the economic precipice. Consequently, as Henry F. May, in his polished review of Twenties historiography, observes, the prophets of abundance are denied credit for good intentions, the approach of the depression becomes something that nearly anybody could have foreseen and the decade's many advances in science, social science, medicine and even government are left out.[3]

The politics of the Harding-Coolidge era attract little attention, since the general consensus of historians was that the Depression and Second World War were the inevitable consequences of conservative political 'shortsightedness'. The truth is more complex, as this book seeks to demonstrate. In the fractured political atmosphere of the Twenties, neither the twenty-ninth nor the thirtieth Presidents were able to maintain control of the national political agenda and it is unlikely that any other potential president could have succeeded where they failed.

In oversimplifying the politics of the decade, historians also tend to present broad-brush, highly trivialised accounts of the Harding presidency. These rely upon anecdotes concerning Harding's private life and little else. Since the gap between stereotype and reality is so large in Harding's case, one of the purposes of this work will be to offer a more balanced, *political* perspective on this underrated president. It analyses and compares the presidencies of Harding and his successor and draws distinctions between the executive initiatives and responses of the two leaders. It suggests that the differences between Harding and Coolidge and between Coolidge and his successor, Herbert Hoover, were greater than previously believed.

Finally, this book attempts to explain both the nature and the origins of the 'normalcy' agenda, as promulgated by Harding and shaped by Calvin Coolidge. It contends that normalcy was less an angrily isolationist and anti-progressive impulse than a reaction against the more contentious or traumatic aspects of the Wilson era – particularly the League debacle, the anti-communist 'witch hunts' and the post-war economic recession.

Notes

1. Henry Bamford Parkes, *The American Experience* (New York: Vintage Books, 1959), p. 314.
2. Stevenson, Elizabeth, *Babbitts and Bohemians: The American 1920s* (New York: MacMillan, 1967), p. 8.
3. Henry F. May, 'Shifting Perspectives on the 1920s', *Mississippi Valley Historical Review*, 43: 3, December 1956, p. 412.

CHAPTER I

The Coming of Normalcy, 1920–1

We are as unprepared for peace as we were for war.
Will Hays, 1919.[1]

The 'Dry' Decade

On 16 January 1920, the Eighteenth Amendment to the Constitution of the United States came into effect, outlawing the 'manufacture, sale or transportation of intoxicating liquors'. A more inappropriate opening to the decade which historians would term the 'Roaring Twenties' could hardly be imagined. Prohibition was to have a profound impact upon American social, political and economic development, in ways which its supporters could not have foreseen. The 'noble experiment' infused the Twenties with a blend of bizarre and grotesque features which would become key elements of the decade's unique signature.

Prohibition was not the result of a sudden, national outburst of moral rectitude but the culmination of decades of planning and campaigning across the United States. The effort to restrict or ban alcohol consumption predated the Civil War but its origins as a major socio-political movement lay in the founding, in 1873, of the Womens' Christian Temperance Union, which believed that beer, bourbon and other alcoholic drinks led not only to intoxication and addiction but to the erosion of family bonds and the abandonment of Christian values. The movement gained added momentum in 1877 when the First Lady, Lucy Hayes, banned alcohol from White House functions, earning her the sobriquet 'Lemonade Lucy'.

In May 1893, a Congregationalist minister, Howard Hyde Russell, formed the Ohio Anti-Saloon League. With its motto – 'The Saloon Must Go' – and a carefully planned strategy of spreading its message through church services and town meetings, it quickly became a potent, non-partisan political force in the Buckeye State, targeting politicians of either party who refused to publicly commit themselves to the cause of temperance. Anti-Saloon Leagues soon sprang up in other states and a national movement, with its headquarters in Washington, was formally established in December 1895.

The League worked in concert with the WCTU. Crucially, it gained the support of many in the progressive movement who were concerned that beer and 'demon rum' were major contributory factors to the poverty and social degradation of the inner cities and of accidents and inefficiency at work. The swelling industrial centres of the North were the main targets for reformers. With their immigrant communities and often appalling living conditions, cities such as Chicago and New York were seen as breeding grounds for squalor, prostitution and drug trafficking. Reformers worried that impoverished workers, deprived of the supportive influences traditionally offered by religion and small-town life, were more likely to resort to criminal activities, alcohol-fuelled violence or, worst of all, Marxist doctrines as outlets for their frustration.

The success of the temperance crusade also arose from the desire of business leaders such as Henry Ford to squeeze greater productivity from their labour force and from the opportunism of many national and state politicians. William Allen White, the Kansan progressive politician and journalist, observed that 'the state leaders who were canny and probably never gave it much thought were for it.'[2] By 1917, twenty-six states had passed Prohibition legislation in some form.

The start of the national war effort in April 1917 gave the temperance crusade the final push it needed. Government propaganda spread the message that intoxication would reduce productivity in the munitions factories and slow the construction of vital tanks and ships. Further, it was claimed, drunkenness fuelled social disorders which could be exploited by the agents of Imperial Germany. Temperance was thus powerfully combined with patriotism and its momentum became unstoppable.

After the Eighteenth Amendment had been ratified in January 1919, a separate act was introduced into Congress to provide the administrative and legal muscle for enforcing Prohibition. The National Prohibition Enforcement Act (known as the Volstead Act, after its author, Republican Representative Andrew Volstead) was passed on 28 October 1919. President Wilson vetoed the act as unnecessarily authoritarian and unworkable but was overridden by the Republican sixty-sixth Congress. The Volstead Act forbade citizens to 'manufacture, sell, barter, transport import, export, deliver, furnish or possess any intoxicating liquor except as authorized in this Act.' 'Intoxicating liquor' was defined as any drink containing more than 0.5 per cent alcohol. The wording of the act was carefully designed to close as many potential loopholes as possible to those who already had plans to flout the new law. Sacramental and medicinal alcohol was specifically excluded from the terms of Volstead, whilst details on fines and prison terms to be handed down to law-breakers were included. Unfortunately, this attention to detail only served to highlight the overwhelming task confronting the Prohibition Bureau and its first commissioner, John F. Kramer. The consumption of alcohol was a habit which transcended class boundaries and was so deeply ingrained that the Bureau and its supporters would be forced to go to ever more extraordinary lengths to regulate the public and private conduct of American citizens.

Opposition to Prohibition came from many quarters. Immigrant communities, particularly Catholics and Hispanics, saw the new law, in Dumenil's words, as 'the ultimate nativist reform' – a method employed by the white Anglo-Saxon Protestant establishment to suppress any manifestation of non-WASP cultural heritage that failed to reflect Protestantism's strict moral and behavioural codes.[3] Labour leaders, too, resented the introduction of temperance, regarding it as a middle-class obsession which ignored the fact that, for the vast majority of factory workers in overcrowded inner cities, the relaxed environment of saloon bars and the soothing effects of alcohol were the only real sources of comfort available. Wealthier social groups also tended to deride, and, increasingly, to ignore, temperance laws as a misguided effort to impose morality through legislation.

All such groups, regardless of class or ethnicity, considered the most damning feature of the new moral order to be the highly authoritarian Volstead Act – which offended American democratic sensibilities by intruding upon the lives of ordinary citizens from its bureaucratic base in Washington D.C. Under the terms of Volstead, enforcement was the responsibility of the US Treasury, rather than the Justice Department. This created a dysfunctional bureaucratic system which undermined efforts at coordination. It was backed up by 1,600 enforcement agents and an unenthusiastic congressional appropriation of just over $5,000,000 a year. The long-term success of the Prohibition Bureau's crusade was, therefore, largely dependent upon cooperation from individual states. As the years passed, this dependency proved to be a weakness, rather than a strength. State politicians, religious groups and local civic leaders often gave in to temptation and harnessed the moral force of Prohibition for their own political gain or as a means to disempower opponents or isolate unpopular minority groups.

The *political* will for enforcement of the Volstead Act was also weak from the outset and disagreements cut across party lines. Pro-temperance progressives and some conservatives were happy to prod public morality along the 'right' path through federal legislation and hoped Volstead would yield significant improvements in social behaviour and industrial output. More traditional conservatives, suspicious of any extension of federal power and protective of the individual right of privacy, were quietly appalled at Volstead's dictatorial overtones. They found unlikely bedfellows amongst a number of progressives who saw Prohibition as an ill-advised effort to impose Anglo-Saxon, mid-western Puritanism upon the multi-ethnic urban centres of the Northeast. Clashes between these contending factions would dominate American political debate throughout the 1920s.

Overall, the 'noble experiment' served only to ratchet up social tensions in the United States at a time when most ordinary Americans sought to escape from the 'moral overstrain' of the recent past. Within two years of its introduction, Prohibition would be blamed by its critics for driving the average American to sex-driven Hollywood movies, gambling, smuggling and 'speakeasies' in their search for a high-octane substitute for alcohol. Temperance advocates, having badly underestimated the extent of popular resistance to Prohibition would eventually discover that Prohibition created more social and political problems than it solved.

Innovation and Unrest

Prohibition aside, the national mood in 1920 was a mixture of relief at the return of peace, frustration at the country's mounting economic problems and, for many, a growing sense of social disorientation. Patterns of everyday life, many of which had remained unchanged since the early years of the Republic, were now changing at a faster pace than that experienced by any previous generation. The horse and carriage, the main mode of transport at the turn of the century, were fast-disappearing from city streets. Over nine million Americans now owned cars such as the 'Oldsmobile', manufactured by Ransom Olds since the early 1900s, or Henry Ford's 'Model-T'. Nicknamed the 'Tin Lizzie', the Model-T was the twentieth car design produced by the Ford Motor Company, which had been established in Michigan in 1903. By the 1920s, it was America's most popular car, due to its fuel efficiency and fast speeds (maximum 40 m.p.h.) and it helped make Henry Ford one of America's wealthiest entrepreneurs and most respected cultural icons.

Ford's rags-to-riches story made him the modern personification of the 'American Dream'. He was raised in the small rural township of Dearborne, Michigan and took his first job as a repairman for the Westinghouse Electrical Company. Establishing his own car manufacturing enterprise through borrowed capital, he rapidly became a multimillionaire and an internationally revered figure, feted by politicians and featured in school text books as the outstanding example of American entrepreneurial genius. Although his plant was turning out 35,000 cars a year by the early 1900s, Ford constantly experimented with new methods of production, focusing particularly upon factory floor design and using ergonomic analyses of worker routines based upon the 'scientific management' theories propounded by Frederick W. Taylor. Innovations such as the moving assembly line slashed production costs and brought down the price of the Model-T to within the reach of millions of average American families. By 1920, a Ford car could be purchased for $350 and prices were still falling.

'Fordism' presaged the revolutionary changes in manufacturing techniques and in workforce management which helped stimulate industrial production to unprecedented levels during the Twenties. Both Ford and Samuel Insull, his equivalent in the power industry, believed that productivity and profit had been restricted, before the war, by bad housing conditions and by unhealthy, poorly educated and unmotivated employees. Ford and Insull pioneered new techniques to eliminate these problems by offering pensions, healthcare schemes and affordable, company-owned housing to his workers. By the mid-1920s, many corporations were involving themselves in employees' leisure time and private lives with company-run leagues for company-owned baseball and hockey teams, lunchtime music concerts and sponsorships for workers to attend night classes.

Manufacturing output and efficiency both improved, partly in response to these innovations, but some critics raised doubts about their social implications. Unions, in particular, worried that mass-output production lines were removing the need for more highly paid, skilled labour and reducing workers to the status of 'robots'. So reliant were these docile employees upon company housing and welfare that independent union activity, labour leaders feared, would become impossible. Moreover, the new, 'hands-on' management techniques frequently crossed the line between encouragement and coercion. Ford employed company 'spotters' to pick up factory-floor gossip and to document and report the activities of 'trouble-makers' and 'slackers'. Since Ford neither smoked nor drank, he clamped down on these habits amongst his workers, who faced the threat of eviction from their accommodation if they failed to mend their ways. Even the school set up by Ford was, according to Edmund Wilson, 'soon converted ... into a device for getting children to work in the shops – on the assumption ... that the mass production of radiators was the principal essential of a primary education.'[4]

The growing strength of organised labour was monitored carefully by company owners at the outset of the Twenties. Over the previous ten years, the size of the nation's unionised workforce had doubled to over 5,000,000 members and union leaders had begun flexing their muscles accordingly. In 1919, the US economy began slipping into a deep post-war recession. Falling orders and declining profits resulted in lay-offs. As the number of bankruptcies escalated, some companies relocated their operations to the South, where costs were lower, labour cheaper and the influence of radicalism less pronounced. Newly influential unions, meanwhile, maintained their demands for improved wages and working conditions and for legal recognition of the right to organise. Between late 1918 and early 1920, around 200 major industrial disputes occurred, with violence flaring frequently as managers retaliated by locking-out strikers and hiring 'replacement labour'. Twenty men died during confrontations in 1919 over the rights of steelworkers to form unions. These industrial disputes were an inevitable consequence of post-war economic conditions and the rapid removal of most federal wartime price and wage controls. Yet, they did not lead, as some conservatives had feared, to the formation of a powerful socialist movement. The unorganised majority of American workers, as well as existing union organisations themselves, generally accepted the nation's capitalist economic framework. More importantly, the class structures and social conditions under which socialism had flourished in war-torn Europe were not replicated in the United States. Despite the fact that industrialisation had begun more than half a century earlier, the Congress of Industrial Organisations (CIO), representing the interests of the factory workforce, did not come into being until 1935. Before then, the nation's most powerful union organisation, the American Federation of Labor (AFL), was chiefly concerned with the interests of skilled workers and crafts unions, amongst whom socialist activists made almost no headway.

High levels of social discontent also existed amongst black and immigrant workers, who were often discouraged from active union participation by racism amongst the white workforce. In desperation, many offered themselves as 'worker replacements' during strike actions and were subjected to violence and taunts from workers' pickets. In the South, the 'trek of the negro labourer' to the northern cities in search of work generated fears amongst white Americans of empty fields and imminent economic collapse. Those black agricultural workers who stayed behind, however, received no better treatment than before. A full-page advertisement in a New Orleans newspaper of the early 1920s claimed that thousands of members of the Industrial Workers of the World (IWW) or 'Wobblies', were preparing a takeover of Lousiana's agrarian economy by inciting resentful and easily led black labourers to revolution.

A mood of suspicion and resentment, coupled with sporadic outbreaks of intimidation and violence, spread across the United States in the period 1919–20. On 2 June 1919, Attorney General A. Mitchell Palmer narrowly escaped assassination when a bomb exploded outside his Washington home. More than thirty other bombs were discovered in packages addressed to politicians and business leaders during that year. In September 1919, the Boston Police strike threatened to bring about the collapse of law and order in the city. Political activism by groups such as the Wobblies increased during this period, prompting Palmer to lash out at the thousands of anarchists and Trotskyite 'infiltrators' who, he believed, were stoking the fires of discontent in preparation for the overthrow of American democracy. Over 6,000 foreign-born residents were picked up by the Justice Department in a coordinated series of arrests on 1 January 1920. Many were deported. The Palmer raids and resultant 'Red Scare' were fuelled mostly by fear, though political ambition was a secondary factor. Palmer aspired to the Democratic party nomination in 1920 and some members of Congress also believed that exploitation of nativist anxiety could improve their chances of re-election. Many Americans had been shocked by the November 1917 Bolshevik coup in Russia, which ended Alexander Kerensky's efforts to establish a democratically elected government. The new regime of Vladimir Illyich Lenin negotiated a separate peace with Germany in the

Treaty of Brest-Litovsk, repudiated all foreign debts and obligations, nationalised the land, repudiated religion and embarked on a ruthless war to exterminate the Russian aristocracy. The 'Red Terror' began, on 16 July 1918, with the murders of the former Tsar, Nicholas II, his wife and young children. The Bolshevik creed of atheism, class war and the abolition of private enterprise was anathema to American democratic ideals. Palmer's view that a new and terrible menace to freedom had arisen was widely shared across the political spectrum, providing support for US participation in the ill-fated Allied intervention in the Russian Civil War of 1919–21. The demands of Leon Trotsky for 'world revolution', uniting workers of all nations under the communist banner, were hardly conducive to calming American fears. Instead, they provided Palmer with the justification he needed to begin rooting out suspected 'subversives', primarily amongst immigrants and labour unions. The Justice Department's 'witch-hunt' had, at least initially, considerable popular support. It was, nonetheless, an excessive response to an exaggerated problem. Less than 150,000 politically active socialists, communists and anarchists existed in dozens of small groups, mostly concentrated in the cities of the Northeast. Although Lenin's Bolsheviks had achieved a lot more with substantially less, they possessed key advantages – weak and divided opposition, the collapse of the old social, economic and political order under the weight of its own contradictions and the almost complete breakdown of law and order. America's aspiring revolutionaries faced no such conditions, enjoyed negligible popular support and spent much of their time arguing the finer points of ideology amongst themselves. As a result, they failed to achieve broad organisational coherence. One observer commented, 'the whole lot were about as dangerous as a flea on an elephant – or not that dangerous, because they spent most of their time in biting each other.'[5]

Despite this, labour unrest and anticommunist paranoia heightened political and social tensions and handed the Republican party a useful weapon for the upcoming first presidential election of the new decade.

The Conservative Resurgence

From January 1919, the partisan political environment in which the election would be fought quickly took shape. Republican conservatives in Congress were determined that one of the campaign's major debates would focus upon the burgeoning size and power of the federal government. The war had permitted the Wilson administration to exert extensive control over almost all aspects of economic and social life to a degree unseen since the Civil War. Many Wilsonian liberals, whilst disturbed by the indiscriminate jailings of anti-war protestors, were also encouraged by the prospects for further post-war reform which they believed arose from the greater centralisation of political and economic control in Washington. The reformist shopping list included child labour and minimum wage laws, greater direct assistance for the unemployed, tougher regulations on industrial work and safety standards, reductions in the length of the working day, legal protection for the right of workers to join unions and bargain for pay increases without risking redundancy, legally enforceable national standards for housing and sanitation, progressive taxation, and reform of campaign financing and electoral practices.

Although the powerful progressive bloc within the Republican party had provided most of the motive force for reform before 1913, Democratic liberals had seized the reins after Wilson's first election. Numerous reforms were pushed through Congress covering housing, sanitation and working conditions, increasing government regulation of corporations and monopolies and overseeing passage of the Sixteenth and Seventeenth Amendments to the Constitution, which mandated a federal income tax and direct election of senators. The war, however, weakened liberal influence within the Democratic party and the more conservative states of the 'Solid South', the party's traditional power base, began to reassert their control after 1918.

The Republican congressional leadership was firmly in conservative hands by 1918 and had as little sympathy with its progressive wing as southern Democrats had with Democratic liberals. They vehemently opposed further federal government 'interference' in the nation's social and economic life and sought to curb what Idaho Senator William E. Borah termed, 'the remorseless urge of centralization, the insatiable maw of bureaucracy.' Conservatives of both parties had tolerated government expansion to meet the emergency of war. Once peace had returned, they united in demanding the immediate dismantling of wartime government controls, creating a conservative majority which liberals and progressives hoped would be overturned when the nation went to the polls in November 1918 for the mid-term elections.

The election results appeared to suggest, however, that the conservatives had accurately gauged voter sentiment. President Wilson committed a tactical error by openly calling upon voters to return a Democratic majority. This angered Republicans, who felt it was a poor reward for their bipartisan strategy since April 1917. The Republican party won control of both chambers in November 1918. In the Senate, a fifty-three to forty-two Democratic majority was replaced by a narrower forty-nine to forty-seven Republican margin. In the House of Representatives, the Democrats lost thirty seats, giving the Republicans a solid 240 to 190 edge. These results undermined the authority of the Wilson administration at a critical moment. Difficult times lay ahead for the economy as hundreds of thousands of returning 'doughboys' were about to be thrown onto the labour market. Businesses faced sharp falls in profits and orders as wartime demand subsided. The President needed the cooperation of the new sixty sixth Congress but Republicans were now determined to dictate the political agenda until they could recapture the White House in 1920.

The bitterly partisan, post-1918 atmosphere was partly a consequence of the high-handed manner with which Wilson's administration had often dealt with Congress. The final straw for Republicans was the President's insistence on Senate ratification, without amendments, of the Treaty of Versailles. This became the focus for one of the great confrontations of American political history, the outcome of which, more than any other single factor, paved the way for the 'Age of Normalcy'.

On 8 January 1918, Wilson outlined to Congress his 'Fourteen Points' for a secure world peace. These included freedom of the seas for all signatory nations, a peace settlement agreed through open negotiation, the removal of international trade barriers, deep cuts in military arsenals, the redrawing of national boundaries to permit as many peoples as possible to live under a government reflecting its racial and ethnic composition, the removal of occupying forces from Belgium, the return of Alsace-Lorraine to French control, an independent Polish state and self-determination for other peoples liberated by the collapse of the old Russian and Austro-Hungarian empires. The Fourteen Points programme was the most ambitious foreign policy design ever presented to Congress by an American president and its sheer scale alarmed isolationists, who began marshalling opposition to any treaty with similar ambitions. Although the President proclaimed that such issues transcended partisanship, he proceeded to needlessly offend Republicans by attending the Versailles peace conference in January 1919 with a handpicked delegation containing no senators and only one, minor, Republican diplomat. This attempt to prevent conservatives from diluting America's commitment to the final treaty was self-defeating. There was now no chance that a Republican Senate would pass, without amendment, any treaty upon which it had not been consulted.

Not all of the Fourteen Points found a place in the document which Wilson brought back from Versailles.[6] The President reassured disappointed supporters that the establishment of a 'League of Nations' would provide an international framework, through which all issues not covered by the treaty could eventually be settled. Meanwhile, the League would arbitrate international disputes and was empowered, by the collective will of member states, to use economic or military sanctions to prevent crises escalating into war.

To steer the treaty through the Senate, Wilson required a two-thirds majority in support. Most Democrats united behind the White House, but 'mild reservationist' Republicans, such as former President Taft, sought small changes to its provisions. 'Strong reservationists', including Senator Henry Cabot Lodge, chairman of the Senate Foreign Relations Committee, demanded stronger safeguards for US interests. The administration had no hope whatever of winning over the dozen or so 'irreconcilables'. These included Idaho's William Borah, Washington's senator Miles Poindexter and Hiram Johnson of California who regarded any form of international organisation as a threat to US sovereignty.

Lodge devised fourteen 'reservations' to be tagged on to the treaty before it could be passed by the Senate. Most were comparatively minor changes. The most important called for a new clause to be added to Article X. This article committed League members to respect each others' territorial and political independence. Lodge's reservation made this commitment dependent upon the will of Congress, on a case-by-case basis.

Wilson's political instincts again deserted him. He summarily rejected the 'Lodge reservations' and refused to authorise his congressional supporters to seek compromise. Instead, he embarked on a nationwide tour to raise support for the unamended treaty and lambasting Congress for its 'betrayal' of America's war dead. Public opinion was, in fact, cautiously favourable towards the League, but the furious Wilson-Lodge battle and the complex questions it raised, caused increasing disenchantment. Americans, many newspaper editorials concluded, were sickened by war, cynical of European intentions and disinclined to embark on an ideological crusade abroad. Hiram Johnson's appeal, 'Let us be Americans again!', struck a simpler and more responsive chord.

The strain of his speaking tour undermined Wilson's health. He collapsed on 25 September 1919 at Pueblo, Colorado. The doctor's official diagnosis was exhaustion but the President had suffered a stroke. A second, more severe attack, on 2 October, rendered him a semi-invalid for the remainder of his term of office. On 19 November, the treaty (with Lodge reservations added) failed to achieve a two-thirds majority in the Senate, with fifty-five votes in its favour and thirty-five against. The White House issued instructions that pro-Leaguers were to withhold their support and many did so. On 20 March 1920, a second vote (this time for a treaty *without* the reservations) produced the same outcome. A more flexible attitude could, perhaps, have produced a different outcome but the President believed himself bound by his commitment to the treaty's other signatories. An additional likely explanation was that Wilson's pride could not countenance Lodge's fingerprints on his handiwork.

Only ten months after his triumphant return from Paris, the federal government was effectively paralysed. The Republican opposition controlled Congress and set about demolishing wartime controls. Wilson remained secluded in the White House. Access to his sick-bed was denied, even to most cabinet members, by First Lady Edith Wilson. As the economy began to slip into deep recession, the business of government slowed to a crawl.

The Dark Horse Conventions

President Wilson's paralysis did not dim his political ambition or his hopes for the League of Nations. He refused to declare his intentions for 1920, however, leaving frustrated Democratic officials to guess whether or not he sought a third term in office. Consequently, presidential hopefuls, particularly former Treasury Secretary William Gibbes McAdoo and Attorney General Palmer, could not build campaign organisations or declare their candidacies without appearing disloyal.

On the Republican side, there was similar disarray. The sudden death of former President Theodore Roosevelt, aged only 62, on 5 January 1919 had dashed the general expectation that the great 'Rough Rider' would lead them to victory once again. Many Republicans regarded Roosevelt's return as essential to heal the party's deep divisions, which Roosevelt himself had helped create. As President, Roosevelt had pursued his own unique brand of limited, if noisy, progressivism – attacking the power of corporations and monopolies and pressing for social and environmental reforms. His activist interpretation of presidential power had delighted progressives such as William Allen White and Hiram Johnson but antagonised conservatives who favoured the less 'pro-active' style of Benjamin Harrison (1889–93) or William B. McKinley (1897–1901). Roosevelt outraged southern Democrats in 1901 by inviting black leader Booker T. Washington to dinner at the White House. His foreign policies were expansionist and supportive of the territorial acquisitions America had made after the Spanish-American war – a fact which alarmed isolationists. He involved the nation more deeply in Latin American affairs, negotiated peace between Russia and Japan in 1905, oversaw completion of the Panama Canal and built up US naval forces to a state of unrivalled power in the Pacific. Nevertheless, Roosevelt had been immensely popular with the public and his re-election for an unprecedented third term in 1908 would have been a certainty had he not categorically ruled it out.

His hand-picked successor, William Howard Taft, proved less dynamic and more conservative, causing a frustrated Roosevelt to challenge the President for the 1912 party nomination. The result was a schism in which Roosevelt and his supporters, after losing the nomination fight, bolted to form a new political organisation, the progressive 'Bull Moose' party. Many moderate and conservative party 'regulars' never forgave Roosevelt's 'treachery'. Their sentiments were pungently expressed by the editor of the Marion Ohio *Star*, Warren Gamaliel Harding, who wrote, 'The entire Roosevelt party campaign has been based solely upon selfishness, false pretense, envy and spite.' The ex-President, Harding declared, was 'the most dangerous agitator who has ever threatened the perpetuity of government.'[7]

The Republican schism opened the way to the White House for the Democratic Governor of New Jersey, Woodrow Wilson. Roosevelt immediately announced the dissolution of the Bull Moose party and worked patiently to restore his prestige with former Republican colleagues. The 1918 mid-term elections appeared to signal the imminent return of the Republican party to power and, in the expectation that President Wilson would run again, many Republicans believed only someone of Roosevelt's stature could take on and defeat an incumbent president.

TR's death, newspapers declared, now left the Republican nomination up for grabs. General Leonard Wood, one of Roosevelt's compatriots during the Spanish-American war, was considered a strong candidate since he had opposed League membership. Nonetheless, he possessed flaws which disturbed the conservative 'old guard'. Wood disliked partisan politics and his campaign was run by volunteer activists, operating largely outside the 'regular' party machine. This suggested the crusty General possessed more than a little of TR's independent streak, a fact unlikely to endear him to those with memories of 1912. The General was also unlikely to accept the conservative agenda of reducing presidential authority at home and US commitments abroad. The Wood campaign's refusal to consider 'deals' to secure the nomination appealed to grass-roots members but it was also debilitating. In 1920, nominations were often clinched by backroom bartering, where state party leaders traded their support for cabinet posts or other forms of patronage. Wood's high moral tone hampered his manager's efforts to build a delegate majority.

Wood's principal rival was Illinois governor Frank O. Lowden, whose pro-business stance appealed to conservatives. Lowden seemed more likely to unite the party since his support was evenly spread across the north and south of the country. The Governor was weakened, however, by rumours of financial impropriety in his campaign and by fears that Hiram Johnson would bolt the party if Lowden was nominated.

Other possible contenders included Johnson himself, who had a strong progressive following and had attracted as much preconvention primary support as Wood. His nomination, however, was unacceptable to conservatives. Philander Knox, formerly Theodore Roosevelt's Attorney General, was mooted as a possible choice, as was Herbert Clark Hoover, President Wilson's Food Relief Commissioner in post-war Europe. Hoover's reputation as an efficient administrator and humanitarian made him popular with progressives but regulars were unimpressed by his eleventh-hour conversion to the Republican party and his early sympathy for what isolationists referred to as 'Wilson's League'.

This left a scattering of long-shot, or 'dark horse' contenders, including Warren Gamaliel Harding, now an Ohio senator, Pennsylvania's governor, William C. Sproul, and Massachusetts' governor, Calvin Coolidge. Harding was, by general agreement, 'the best of the second-raters'. He had come to national prominence in 1912 when he had been chosen by Taft to present the President's name for nomination. As the keynote speaker at the 1916 convention, he had impressed delegates with his solemn demeanour and appeals for party unity. He remained, nevertheless, an outside chance. Governor Coolidge was an even longer shot, known outside the Bay State only for his memorable public utterance, during the 1919 Boston police strike, that 'There is no right to strike against the public safety by anybody, anywhere, any time.'

The Republican convention opened in Chicago on 8 June. By the seventh ballot, the Wood and Lowden forces were deadlocked. This scenario had been widely predicted and party leaders began casting around for a compromise choice. Claims later surfaced in the national press that a 'cabal' of leading conservative senators had manipulated the balloting in order to nominate a puppet candidate. This 'plot', allegedly orchestrated from Room 404 of Chicago's Blackstone Hotel, was designed to hand effective control of the White House and the nation to 'old guard' Republicans, including Henry Cabot Lodge, Pennsylvania's Boies Penrose, James Watson of Indiana, Reed Smoot of Utah and Frank Brandegee of Connecticut. The power behind the entire operation was, supposedly, the Standard Oil Corporation which sought control over all aspects of foreign and domestic policy affecting their profits. It was an entirely fanciful notion. The 'cabal' was, in fact, an ad hoc assemblage of sweating, frustrated officials who drifted in and out of Room 404 and had no particular aim in mind beyond finding *any* candidate acceptable to the public and strong enough to break the ballot deadlock. The rumour mill ground on, regardless.

Harry M. Daugherty, campaign manager for Senator Harding, pursued a careful strategy to promote his candidate. Harding had not performed impressively in the non-binding primaries but, as an Ohio senator, he could deliver the state's crucial twenty-four electoral college votes. In his favour, he had been a well-liked, if unremarkable, senator since 1915 – a conciliator with few political enemies. Even Roosevelt, whom Harding had once bitterly criticised, had considered him a potential vice-presidential choice for 1920. Although Harding 'looked like a President', he was also an affable and modest figure. Senior Republicans believed this would prove alluring to voters after eight years of the aloof, professorial Wilson. Harding was also the owner and editor of the Marion *Star*, a fact which gave him an advantage in dealing with the increasingly influential political press. Finally, the Senator was considered a staunch conservative and loyal party man who could be trusted not to deliberately alienate sections of his own party – unlike Johnson or Wood.[8] Harding was therefore ideally placed to bridge the dangerous divide between Republican pro- and anti-League factions. While the party's election platform was resolutely opposed to League membership, Harding himself was not an 'irreconcilable'. He rejected 'Wilson's League' on grounds of impracticality but was favourably disposed towards the concept of international cooperation. If he maintained this careful balance as the party's nominee, he would arouse suspicions from both camps but alienate neither.

Daugherty stressed these advantages continually as he cultivated contacts with each state delegation. His aim was to ensure that, in the event of a convention deadlock, Harding would be the natural *second* choice for a majority of delegates. The strategy paid off when party leaders at the Blackstone, despairing at the Wood-Lowden impasse, decided to 'run the table' of candidates, starting with Harding. State leaders would be encouraged to throw their support to the Ohioan beginning on the eighth ballot. If Harding failed to gain a majority within two or three ballots, the exercise would be repeated with Governor Sproul. In the event, Harding clinched victory on the tenth ballot, with 692.5 votes.

Commenting on the unexpected victory of the 'dark horse' Harding, the New York *World* lamented, 'What more pitiful choice could have been made?' whilst the Boston *Globe* noted: 'Once more, the Old Guard has got what it wanted. It now remains to be seen whether the voters will want what they have got.'[9] Harding's nomination was not achieved through conspiracy, but hostile press reaction would have damaging long-term consequences for his presidency.

In the 1920s, party conventions still selected vice-presidential candidates more or less independently – guided by, but not beholden to, the wishes of the presidential nominee. Here, again, Republican leaders in 1920 demonstrated a singular *lack* of control. Their favoured candidate, Irvine Lenroot of Wisconsin, was rejected by delegates, who promptly initiated a convention stampede for Calvin Coolidge.

A Harding-Coolidge ticket was not what most political pundits had expected and press reaction was generally negative.[10] The Republican choices were considered lacklustre and a clear demonstration that 'standpat' conservatives (those opposed to sudden change in an existing position) had kept their grip on the national party.

The Democratic National Convention took place in San Francisco between 28 June and 6 July. Like the Republicans, Democrats were divided on the issue of the League between those who believed, with President Wilson, that the entire election should be a 'solemn referendum' on the treaty and League and those who preferred to avoid a firm statement of intent for fear of playing into Republican hands. There was also bitter rivalry between southern and mid-western 'drys' and northern 'wets'. These divisions were exacerbated by the hostility expressed by southern conservatives towards Wilsonian liberals in the North, to the administration's agricultural and labour policies and to its fondness, as they saw it, for ignoring states' rights.

Demonstrations in support of a third term for Wilson took place early in proceedings, at one stage involving Assistant Secretary of the Navy, Franklin D. Roosevelt, in a fistfight over a state banner. There was no move, however, to place the President's name in nomination. Homer E. Cummings, the convention chairman, lashed out at Henry Cabot Lodge and Republican opponents of Wilson's foreign policy, but the party's statement on the League issue in its final platform deeply disappointed the White House. In an effort to straddle the gap between the two contending sides, it stated that the party 'would not oppose the acceptance of any reservations making clearer or more specific the obligations of the United States...' This was substantially less than Wilson himself had demanded in 1919. The White House considered the platform language to be both a snub to the President himself and a betrayal of administration principles.

When balloting commenced, the two main contenders, McAdoo and Palmer, were followed by the leading 'dark horse' candidate, James A. Cox, Governor of Ohio. To President Wilson, Cox was the most inconceivable choice of all. When told that the Ohioan's name was being strongly touted as a compromise choice, he protested, 'You know Cox's nomination would be a joke!'

Cox benefited, however, from the same convention stalemate which had favoured Harding in Chicago. McAdoo's candidacy was blocked by the New York delegation and by other northern states which disliked his strong support for Prohibition. Palmer was respected by conservatives for his anticommunist credentials, but his nomination was considered too controversial and a potential threat to the party's ability to attract moderate voters in November's election.

Cox was a pragmatist and, like Harding, a former newspaper editor concerned more with results and efficient administration than with ideological purity. As Governor of Ohio, he had remained largely independent of the Wilson administration, carving out a modest reputation for progressivism in areas such as education and taxation. Cox favoured League membership but accepted the need for compromise. His views on Prohibition and the Volstead Act were comparatively flexible, but the potential problems this raised with southern and midwestern delegates were offset by the advantage he held as the only man capable of mounting a serious challenge to Harding in Ohio. To northern delegates, Cox's damp inclinations also made him a more appealing prospect than the bone-dry McAdoo. Cox's supporters copied the Harding-Daugherty convention tactic of ensuring that their candidate was the *second* choice of as many delegates as possible. When Palmer's supporters realised their candidate could not win, many switched to Cox, who eventually defeated McAdoo on the forty-fourth ballot. Franklin Roosevelt received the vice-presidential nomination, largely due to his youthful 'star quality', his moderately dry views and his family name.

Democratic party leaders, having earlier expressed their contempt for the outcome of the Republican convention, ended by copying the Republicans move for move. Both parties, desperate to avoid deadlock, turned to former newspaper editors from Ohio, men with few enemies, a reputation for pragmatism and no clearly defined national reputation.

H. L. Mencken, bored by the Democrats' deliberations and depressed by the prospect of a Harding-Cox campaign, instead took a keen interest in efforts by some San Francisco government officials to circumvent Prohibition and provide alcoholic drinks for thirsty convention delegates. He later noted, approvingly,

> The municipality there ordered 60 barrels of excellent Bourbon ... and charged them to the local smallpox hospital. After the convention, the Methodist mullahs of the town exposed the transaction, and proved there had not been a patient in the hospital for four years. But the city officials who were responsible ... were reelected by immense majorities. Despite Prohibition, the people of San Francisco are still civilized ...[11]

The Harding-Cox Campaign

The 1920 elections were not the 'solemn referendum' the White House had hoped for. Harding and his campaign managers knew they held the advantage going into the fall phase of the elections and were determined to keep it. The candidate stayed in his home town of Marion, delivering speeches which reiterated the GOP's key platform themes – higher tariffs, aid to agriculture, tax cuts, streamlining of federal bureaucracy and immigration restrictions. His 'front-porch' campaign was to be the last of its kind in American political history. Reporters encamped in Marion looked on as marching bands, politicians, Rotarians, women's groups, Boy Scouts and movie stars gathered outside Harding's home to have their photograph taken with the nominee. Photographs of the

Senator holding court on his porch purposefully invoked nostalgia amongst older voters for the 1896 and 1900 campaigns of President McKinley, the most successful practitioner of front-porch campaigning. The Republican campaign strategy also served to emphasise the 'back to normalcy' theme which Harding had first raised in a speech in Boston in May 1920. His declaration that the country, after years of upheaval, needed 'not nostrums but normalcy', became the slogan of the Harding campaign. Cynics questioned not only the grammatical accuracy, of the word 'normalcy' but also its meaning. To some, it presaged a long-feared return to late-nineteenth-century conservatism, before Roosevelt challenged the power of J. P. Morgan and the trusts; before Lincoln Steffens, and Upton Sinclair pricked social consciences with 'muck-raking' revelations of inner city squalor; before the United States had been dragged into international conflict and before the federal income tax, the minimum wage campaign and progressive political reforms had cast their shadows over McKinley's capitalist 'golden age'. These fears seemed well-founded when Republican campaign manager Will Hays announced to reporters his intention to 'out-McKinley McKinley'.

For Harding himself, 'normalcy' was never intended to be a formal political programme. Rather, it was a vague collection of sentiments and aspirations. Its lines were broadly drawn and flexible. It implied the pursuit of the goal of greater freedom from government regulation for industry and commerce, but was not an emphatic denial of the federal government's role in the pursuit of a more 'just' society. Normalcy also meant lower taxes and government spending, but this pledge seemed a more radical change of direction than it actually was. The wartime emergency had increased taxation and expenditure to such high levels that even Wilson's Treasury officials considered them excessive. Substantial cuts would be needed simply to bring them down to pre-war rates. Normalcy also seemed to imply a return to pre-war social norms. Despite long speeches extolling the virtues of simplicity, faith and hard work, however, Harding did not seek the wholesale reversal of the recent social and political gains made by women and had every intention of speaking out *against* the political and economic segregation of black Americans. For some, normalcy implied the pursuit of '100 per cent Americanism' and a continuation of post-war nativist and political paranoia. Harding repeatedly stressed the virtues of patriotism but had no intention of presiding over more witch hunts. Finally, normalcy rejected 'Wilson's League', but left the door open for international cooperation in other forms.

If 'normalcy' could be defined at all, therefore, it was an effort to facilitate a breathing space for the nation, to calm partisan rancour, repair economic damage and make rational choices for the new decade. Harding was personally at ease with most of the social and technological changes taking place as the 1920s began. He believed, however, that private enterprise and individual initiative were better-equipped than government regulation and largesse to harness the energies of the new era.

The sole element of normalcy which could accurately be construed as 'backward-looking' was the candidate's views on presidential power and legislative-executive relations. At least initially, Harding sought the restoration of Congress as the leading political force in the nation and the curbing of the Rooseveltian-Wilsonian inclination to 'personal rule'. Although fully supportive of Wilson's centralisation of power during the war, he had wasted no time in calling for a greater degree of inter-branch cooperation after November 1918. Privately, he believed that the personal vanities of Roosevelt and Wilson had undermined stable, consensual government. Both men, he felt, had repeatedly ignored or browbeaten members of Congress and accrued degrees of personal authority which clearly ran against the intentions of the architects of the US Constitution.

Warren Harding lacked Wilson's formidable intellect but was the superior politician. He understood that League membership was not the issue closest to the hearts of 'Main Street' America. If he could match the Democrats' qualified endorsement of membership with qualifications of his own, presenting himself as neither internationalist nor isolationist, he would be free to press home attacks on other issues, exploiting Democratic divisions over Prohibition and reform. The strategy was therefore to saddle the Cox-Roosevelt ticket not only with the League dilemma but with responsibility, by association, for the post-war recession and for the actions of the Wilson administration.

The Republican campaign attacked 'Wilson's League', whilst hinting at broad sympathy for the principle of international cooperation 'without compromising national independence'. The most the Republican nominee would promise was that future proposals for international cooperation or association would be considered on their individual merits and with regard to prevailing domestic and international conditions. No new project would be promulgated without broad bipartisan support and public approval. 'It is fine to idealize,' he told an interviewer from the *Saturday Evening Post* in late July 1920, 'but it is very practical to make sure our own house is in perfect order before we attempt the miracle of Old World stabilization.'[11]

His straddling of the issue gave the Senator added clout within his own party, which relied upon him to avoid a disastrous schism. As November approached, Harding played one side off against the other. Hiram Johnson believed he had gained the nominee's agreement that membership of *any* international forum would be unacceptable. Johnson, delighted, carried the news to his supporters, causing Herbert Hoover and Bill Taft to press Harding for a qualification, which he duly gave. On 28 August, Harding came out in favour of the principle of an association of free nations. An angry Johnson was then pacified by private letters from Harding assuring him that the statement was simply a sop to the mild reservationists. It was hardly a courageous strategy, but it was politically necessary. Harding, Hoover later commented, 'carried water on both shoulders' during the 1920 campaign.

The Democrats were less divided over the League but, early in the campaign, they detected that public interest in the issue was waning. In contrast to Harding's front porch strategy, both Cox and Roosevelt undertook strenuous campaign tours. Cox covered over 22,000 miles by train, plane, boat and car, addressed around two million citizens and, at one point, was arrested for speeding. These tours revealed a discouraging trend – voters were most concerned with rising prices, taxes and unemployment – areas of vulnerability for the Democrats. Those groups most concerned with the League were key Democratic constituencies who *opposed* it. Irish-Americans, for example, feared that Britain would use its votes in any international council to exert influence over American foreign policy. Most disturbing was the anti-Wilson sentiment which seemed to pervade the nation and infected even Democratic loyalists. These problems presaged disaster for the party in November. The country, Samuel G. Blythe noted in the *Saturday Evening Post*, was determined to 'vote against Wilson and Wilsonism in all its political phases.'[12] Even H. L. Mencken, contemptuous of Harding, saw no other choice but a Republican vote. 'I conclude with melancholy,' he wrote as November approached, 'that God lays upon me the revolting duty of voting for the numskull Gamaliel ...'[13]

Main Street

On 2 November 1920, Warren Gamaliel Harding was overwhelmingly elected the twenty-ninth President of the United States. He won thirty-seven of the forty-eight states, gaining 404 of 531 electoral votes. His popular vote share of 16,133,314 (60.2%) was the highest yet recorded. Cox, predictably, carried most of the southern states, winning 96.1 per cent of the vote in South Carolina and 84 per cent in Mississippi. The Democrats lost Tennessee, however, for the first time since 1868. The Socialist candidate, Eugene Debs, languishing in an Atlanta jail on the orders of Attorney General Palmer, won 913,664 votes, the highest total for any Socialist presidential candidate before or since. Parley P. Christensen, candidate of the Farmer-Labour party, took 264,540 votes including a 15.4 per cent share of the popular vote in Texas.

The Republicans also consolidated their hold on Congress with a twenty-two-seat majority in the Senate and an unprecedented 168-seat margin in the House. Despite a relatively low turnout of just over 49 per cent, the Republican nominee had won the strongest possible mandate for his 'normalcy' agenda.[14] The election deeply disappointed reform factions in both parties. Democratic liberals regarded it as a lost opportunity to secure the Wilson legacy of reform. Progressive Republicans believed their party, as well as the country, would now be delivered into the hands of J. P. Morgan, the Rockefellers and the DuPonts by a slavishly pro-business administration.

Coincidentally, around the time of Harding's election, these misgivings were reflected in one of the defining literary works of the 1920s. Sinclair Lewis' *Main Street* was an instant best-seller and became one of the most famous satires on small-town American life. To many historians of the Harding-Coolidge years, this work (and Lewis' follow-up novel, *Babbitt*) were to become synonymous with the social and political values of the 'age of normalcy'.

Main Street told the story of Carol Milford, a culturally sophisticated young woman who abandons city life to settle down in her new husband's small mid-western home town – Gopher Prairie. She quickly becomes frustrated with the aridity of the town's cultural life and the narrow-mindedness of its inhabitants. Bored, she struggles to overcome the town's resistance to change and its entrenched views on gender and morality. Lewis highlighted the sterility of Gopher Prairie by paying exquisite attention to every detail of its daily life, its sexual repression and suspicious gossip, its dull social rituals and its antipathy for 'high-brow' art or literature. As the story progresses, Carol comes to realise that at least part of her problem with the town and its inhabitants lies with her own inner frustrations. After spending time in wartime Washington, she returns to continue raising a family, determined to chip away at Gopher Prairie's conservative carapace.

The novel's impact lay in its iconoclastic depiction of those negative aspects of American society most often identified with small-town life – conformity, philistinism, bigotry and smugness – which liberals, artists and intellectuals most despised and against which much of the nation's youth rebelled during the 1920s. The novel also had political resonance. To his detractors, Warren Harding was *Main Street* personified. His home town of Marion, Ohio, was eerily similar to Gopher Prairie. Harding was an inveterate 'joiner' of civic societies and social clubs, loved the status which editorship of the town's main newspaper had given him, had very few books in his house and enjoyed nothing more than alcohol-fuelled poker parties with close friends. His views on American history reflected the simplistic accounts provided by the standard school text books of his youth and his religious beliefs, whilst not fundamentalist, were simple and unquestioning. Lewis' follow-up to *Main Street* was published one year into Harding's presidency. *Babbitt* reinforced the association drawn by cynics between Harding and the narrow minds of Main Street America. The character of George F. Babbitt is a middle-aged businessman and 'solid citizen' of the mid-western town of Zenith, a Republican party 'booster' and proud member of the 'Brotherly and Protective Order of Elks'. Babbitt's world is materially full but devoid of spiritual meaning. He maintains a quasi-religious faith in business, but longs to escape the responsibilities of everyday life. Babbitt finds his own wife 'sexless' and secretly yearns to conduct an illicit romance with the 'fairy child'.[15] *Babbitt* again satirises middle-class morality but also lays bare its underlying insecurity. The fact that the character of George Babbitt shared many of Harding's characteristics has not been lost on historians of the period.[16] Commentators dismissive of the twenty-ninth President frequently made an explicit link between Harding and Babbitt and between Marion and Gopher Prairie. William Allen White's comment that Harding represented 'Main Street in perfect flower' regularly appeared in post-1923 histories.[17] H. L. Mencken's acidic attacks on Harding as the spokesman of America's middle-class 'booboisie' used the same cultural reference points as those Lewis deploys to dissect the character of George Babbitt. Harding, Mencken wrote, had 'the face of a moving-picture actor, the intelligence of a respectable agricultural implement dealer and the imagination of a lodge joiner …'[18] Samuel Hopkins Adams' 1939 dissection of Harding referred to the late President as a 'well-meaning, third-rate Mr Babbitt.'[19] Lewis later took aim at other 'pillars' of modern society, particularly in *Arrowsmith* (1925), in which a doctor is torn between idealism and the lure of commercialism, and in *Elmer Gantry* (1927), which satirised small-town religious values. *Main Street* and *Babbitt*, however, remain the most significant of Lewis' works for their impact upon political and historical debate. The word 'Babbitt' remains in use as an expression of contempt for individuals exhibiting 'small-town values'. Charlie Chaplin, according to Edmund Wilson, once derided his co-stars Mary Pickford and Douglas Fairbanks as 'babbitts'.[20] Lewis' novels are also notable for providing an early suggestion that doubt and insecurity lay behind much of the exterior confidence with which the 'Roaring Twenties' would come to be associated.

The 'Best Minds'

Between the election and his inauguration on 4 March 1921, Harding was preoccupied with the formation of his cabinet. His deliberations attracted heavy press coverage as reporters sought clues to the new President's governing style and policy priorities. Abraham Lincoln placed his strongest opponents in the cabinet to prevent them from fomenting party revolts. By tradition, incoming presidents also dispensed cabinet posts as rewards for loyal supporters or for those with whose loyalty had been bought at the nominating convention. The corrupt Simon Cameron, whose late switch at the 1860 Republican convention handed the nomination to Lincoln, was appointed Secretary of War.

In 1920, critical observers expected the President-elect's choices to be dictated by the Senate Republican 'cabal'. Instead, a number of his selections upset party leaders and created a series of stand-offs, all of which Harding won.

Harry Daugherty's appointment as Attorney General was highly controversial since he had little legal expertise and a well-deserved reputation as a political 'hatchet man'. He had, however, been Harding's closest political confidante for over twenty-five years and had managed his presidential campaign. The President-elect refused to back down in the face of criticism, telling a close friend, 'God! I can't be an ingrate.'

Henry Wallace, an agricultural expert respected by farmers' leaders, was appointed Agriculture Secretary over protests from north-eastern Republicans that he had led an 'anti-business' crusade against wartime profiteering in American industry. Senate irreconcilables lobbied hard for an isolationist Secretary of State, but when Philander Knox, their preferred choice, withdrew from contention, citing poor health, Harding turned to Charles Evans Hughes – a mild reservationist with internationalist sympathies. The old guard opposed the nomination of Herbert Hoover as Secretary of Commerce, despite his evident qualifications for the post. Harding called Hoover 'the smartest gink I know' but party regulars doubted his political loyalties and suspected him, not unreasonably, of harbouring progressive tendencies. A campaign to stop Hoover's confirmation by the Senate was reported to the President-elect in February 1921. At the time, he was contemplating candidates for the post of Secretary of the Treasury. When his first choice, Charles Gates Dawes, proved unavailable, Harding chose Andrew Mellon, the Pittsburgh multi-millionaire. Realising that Mellon's appointment would greatly please the same senators who threatened Hoover's confirmation by Congress, Harding indicated, via Daugherty, that, 'it's Mellon and Hoover, or no Mellon.' The Senate approved both appointments.

The President-elect explained to reporters his desire to build a cabinet of the 'best minds' in order to provide strong and coherent policies for the nation. He also freely admitted to reporters his hope that the weight of expertise in the cabinet would compensate for his own intellectual shortcomings. Whilst the President-elect's honesty was considered refreshing, it further undermined his credibility with those in Congress, particularly Lodge, Johnson and Borah, who considered themselves superior to their new leader in almost every respect.

The 'best minds' strategy led to the formation of what is still widely regarded as one of the strongest cabinets of the twentieth century. Harding favoured open discussion which would work gradually towards a consensus of opinion. Cabinet officials were given wide latitude for action and regular one-on-one consultations. All of Harding's appointees later attested to the strong collegial atmosphere which the President worked hard to foster. The institutional status of the cabinet was thus, at least temporarily, rescued from the state of relative impotence it had reached during the last Wilson years.

Despite Harding's refusal to back down over his appointments, the incoming sixty-seventh Congress remained confident that he would prove a malleable chief executive. During his farewell remarks to Senate colleagues in December 1920, Harding pointedly reminded them that, as custodian of the presidential office, he was duty-bound to protect its independent constitutional authority as fiercely as he had previously defended the rights of Congress. It was a warning, for those who cared to take it.

On Inauguration Day, 4 March 1921, signs of the quickening pace of change were everywhere apparent. A black Pierce-Arrow automobile conveyed Harding and Wilson to the ceremonies on Capitol Hill, replacing the traditional, horse-drawn carriage. The incoming and outgoing First Ladies also broke with tradition as they rode together in a second car, signifying the higher profile now accorded to the President's spouse and to women in general. For the first time, an electrical sound amplifier was to be used to carry the new President's address to the outer fringes of the crowd of thousands who gathered below. As Florence Harding appeared on the inaugural platform, the Marine band abandoned its solemn classical repertoire and broke into a modern jazz tune, prompting the new First Lady to dance a little jig.

The 'Age of Normalcy' had begun.

Notes

1. Quoted in Edward G. Lowry, 'Looking Ahead to 1920: A Birdseye View of the Political Situation', *The World's Work*, June 1919, XXXVIII: 2, p. 196.
2. William Allen White, *The Autobiography of William Allen White* (New York: Macmillan, 1956), p. 423.
3. Lynn Dumenil, *The Modern Temper: American Culture and Society in the 1920s* (New York: Hill and Wang, 1995), p. 30.
4. Edmund Wilson, 'Detroit Motors', in Edmund Wilson, *The American Earthquake: A Documentary of the Jazz Age, the Great Depression and the New Deal* (London: W. H. Allen Co., 1958), p. 238.
5. Isabel Leighton (ed.), *The Aspirin Age: 1919–1941* (New York: Simon and Schuster, 1949), p. 171.
6. The 'missing' elements included statements on freedom of the seas and general principles of disarmament.
7. Francis Russell, *President Harding: His Life and Times 1865–1923* (London: Eyre and Spottiswoode, 1969), p. 235.
8. Johnson snubbed Charles Evans Hughes during the latter's campaign visit to California in 1916, publicly exacerbating divisions within the party. Hughes subsequently lost California, and with it the election.
9. *World* and *Globe* quotes from 'How it Strikes the Country – A Poll of the Press.' *The Outlook*, 23 June 1920, 125: 8, p. 374.
10. It may have surprised press observers, but Harding's nomination had been forecast as early as 1916 by writer Brand Whitlock and a Harding-Coolidge ticket was predicted by former Vice-President Charles Fairbanks in February 1920, when Coolidge had already ruled himself out of the nomination race and Harding seemed to have no hope of success.
11. 'The Conscience of the Republic', *Saturday Evening Post*, 24 July 1920, 193: 4, p. 6.

12. Samuel G. Blythe, 'And Then On The Other Hand'. *Saturday Evening Post*, 30 October 1920, p. 4.
13. H. L. Mencken, *A Carnival of Buncombe*, *Writings on Politics* (Baltimore: Johns Hopkins University Press, 1956), p. 22.
14. Robert Murray suggests that turnout looked lower than it actually was. Voting lists increased in size because women were now permitted to vote. Many did not exercise that right in 1920, partly, Murray speculates, because the result seemed a foregone conclusion. Early results in September from Maine suggested those women who did vote were strongly pro-Harding. See Robert K. Murray, *The Harding Era: Warren G. Harding and His Administration* (Minneapolis: University of Minnesota Press, 1969), p. 66.
15. Though Lewis cannot have known at the time, Harding himself was reputedly involved in an illicit sexual liaison with Nan Britton, a young woman less than half his age. He was also said to be physically estranged from his wife. Accounts of their relationship continue to emphasise Florence Harding's 'lack of femininity', and to refer to the First Lady as 'formidable' or 'sexless'.
16. Mark Schorer (ed.), *Lewis at Zenith* (New York: Harcourt Brace and Ward Inc., 1961), p. x.
17. William Allen White, *Masks in a Pageant* (New York: Macmillan, 1928), p. 409.
18. Mencken, *A Carnival of Buncombe*, p. 15
19. Samuel Hopkins Adams, *Incredible Era: The Life and Times of Warren Gamaliel Harding* (Boston: Houghton-Mifflin, 1939), p. 190.
20. Edmund Wilson, *The Twenties* (London: Macmillan, 1975), p. 126.

CHAPTER 2

Normalcy in Practice, 1921–3

Mr Harding will face the most appalling mess.[1]

The New Administration

President Harding's inaugural address contained few specific policy details but offered, instead, an outline of the general themes and goals by which his administration would be guided. The nation, he declared, faced unpleasant choices in its struggle to overcome recession: 'The normal balances have been impaired, the channels of distribution have been clogged, the relations of labor and management have been strained.' Harding warned that all economic groups – farmers, businessmen and industrial workers – would endure a period of readjustment as the 'grim necessity' of falling prices and profits took their toll. For its part, the new government pledged to do all it could to assist recovery. This meant, primarily, tax reductions and significant cuts in federal regulation of trade and industry. The 'abnormal expenditures' of the federal government, necessary during wartime, would also be pared back.

Harding was a practical politician, not an ideologue. His inaugural address was finely balanced between encouragement for the free operation of market forces and appeals for a renewed spirit of altruism. As a conservative Republican, he believed that no government programme could prevent the unequal distribution of economic gains and losses. 'No statute enacted by man,' he stated, 'can repeal the inexorable laws of nature.' This Darwinian concept, however, had its limits. Harding attacked war profiteering as 'inherently wrong' and appealed to his audience to maintain, at all times, 'a mindfulness of the human side of all activities, so that social, industrial and economic justice will be squared with the purposes of a righteous people.'[2] Similarly, the President advocated a smaller, less costly, federal bureaucracy but hinted at a positive role for government in fostering social and economic progress. This role involved government aid to farmers and war veterans and protection of the interests of industry and commerce. The 'luring fallacy' of free trade was pointedly dismissed by Harding's pledge to maintain or raise existing tariffs on manufactured goods and foodstuffs imported from abroad.

Inevitably, the section of Harding's speech followed most closely by Congress and by international observers dealt with foreign affairs. Here, again, he sought balance. Irreconcilables were reassured by his flat declaration that 'a world super-government ... can have no sanction by our Republic. This is not selfishness, it is sanctity. It is not aloofness; it is security.' As a sop to internationalists, however, he rejected isolationism as a guiding principle of foreign policy. Long-term prosperity, he argued, relied upon expanded trade with other nations. 'We would not have an America living within and for herself alone,' the President declared. Further, since trade inevitably generated new economic and cultural ties to other nations, the United States should give at least qualified support to the notion of 'a world court for the disposition of such justiciable questions as nations are agreed to submit thereto ...' This announcement, pregnant with incendiary possibilities, attracted little comment at the time.

Harding's first presidential address was well-received. One bystander, in a comment which went a long way to explaining the size of the Harding election landslide, told a reporter, 'We have had Wilson eight years and I have not understood him. I understand Harding already.'[3]

It was widely expected that, once inaugurated, Harding would effectively surrender control of the government in Washington to the new Republican Congress, reserving to himself the 'dignified', ceremonial aspects of the presidential office. Congress members were therefore somewhat surprised to find themselves summoned into special session on 12 April 1921 and presented with a detailed agenda for action and reform. The President's message requested the abolition of the Excess Profits tax, in order to stimulate investment, and reiterated the need for an emergency tariff to aid farmers. Recognising the significance of recent technological advances, he also called for increased investment in military and civil aviation, the construction of a 'great merchant marine' and an increase in federal support for highway construction. Harding followed through on his campaign pledge by proposing the creation of a new Bureau of the Budget to modernise federal government finances and another new bureau to centralise aid for wounded war veterans. The creation of the budget bureau would give the executive important new

powers in controlling the spending and funding of government departments – a fact not lost on those who had expected a weakening, not a
strengthening, of the President's bureaucratic authority. A third proposed department would encourage improvements in public education,
health, sanitation and child welfare standards. Acknowledging the new
status of women as permanent members of the national workforce, the
administration's support for new maternity leave legislation was
indicated. Finally, the President courted controversy with southern
Democrats by requesting Congress to 'wipe the stain of barbaric lynching from the banners of free and orderly representative democracy', with
swift passage of an anti-lynching law.

The 12 April message was an important milestone and was favourably
received by moderate Republicans and the press. Conservatives,
however, were unsettled. The act of calling a special session of Congress
to present a detailed policy agenda had the inevitable effect of focusing
attention upon the White House and had been a tactic used by Roosevelt
and Wilson to push the legislature onto the back foot. This was not what
conservatives had imagined the term 'normalcy' to imply. The 12 April
address was also a useful method for disarming critics who had predicted
a 'do-nothing' presidency. Harding's intention, however, was not to
dictate but to *communicate* the administration's views. Aside from urging
immediate action on taxes and tariffs, he left the Republican leadership to
decide for itself the order of priority.

Given the prevailing mood on Capitol Hill, this was, perhaps, not the
wisest course of action. The sixty-seventh Congress was the most divided
and rebellious to confront any incoming president for fifty years. Released
from the behavioural constraints imposed by war and determined to
reassert their independence, members were disinclined to accept direction, either from the White House or from their own party leaders.
Harding's hopes for 'coordination and cooperation' at both ends of
Pennsylvania Avenue fell on stony ground. Rampant factionalism plagued
most legislative debates in 1921–3, with 'blocs' competing to manoeuvre
their own regional, political or constituency interests to the fore. Inter-
bloc rivalry was commonplace and eroded Republican party unity.
Discussions on revisions of tariff rates in 1922, for example, quickly
deteriorated into 'violent arguments ... over the proper duties for shelled
almonds, egg albumen, cocoa butter, soap, wallpaper, saddles and hides.'[4]

Bills laid before the House and Senate often suffered interminable
delays in committee, or were filibustered or torn apart on the floor. Blocs

often cooperated with each other, or with individual members, to stall or kill legislation, but since these ad hoc coalitions changed continually, it was difficult for the White House to develop a counter-strategy or maintain the coherence of its legislative timetable. Harding, to his chagrin, was often forced to back-pedal on election pledges or seek unsatisfactory compromises against his better judgement.

The largest of the congressional groupings, and the most unified, was the farm bloc, representing the interests of South and Midwest agrarian states. This group bissected party lines and its principal Republican leaders were Senators William S. Kenyon (R-Iowa) and Arthur Capper (R-Kansas). Southern Democrats such as John Nance 'Cactus Jack' Garner (D-Texas) often lent their support. Between them, they were easily able to mobilise 120–125 congressional votes – more than enough to block legislation perceived as harmful to farmers' needs. The bloc also received logistical and propaganda support outside Congress from the Farm Bureau Federation (FBF). One of a growing number of well-funded and professionally organised interest groups with headquarters in Washington, the FBF had over one million members by 1921 and operated an extremely efficient lobbying strategy. FBF representatives advised Congress, spoke at committee hearings and cultivated influential contacts inside the Department of Agriculture itself. By the early 1920s, the farm bloc-FBF coalition was one of the most potent organised forces in American politics and the single greatest obstacle to the administration's efforts to advance the interests of American industry and commerce. Agricultural leaders resented the growing influence of northern industrial and financial centres and frequently clashed with those who advocated lowering tariff barriers as a stimulus to trade. The farm bloc treated debates over such issues as a 'zero-sum game', in which legislation beneficial to business was regarded, by definition, as harmful to agriculture. The deliberate stalling of 'pro-business' legislation, a tactic which proved particularly successful in 1921, was justified by Kenyon and Capper as a means to ensure that the needs of farmers were addressed first. When this was achieved, however, the delaying tactics often continued for other reasons.

The faction most influential in shaping the policies of the Harding White House were the pro-business Republicans, whose leaders included most members of the old guard, such as Lodge, Smoot and Brandegee and others such as Joseph Fordney (R-Michigan) and Joseph S. Frelinghuysen (R-New Jersey). They regarded tax reductions and 'business-friendly' reforms as more important than farm subsidies to economic recovery and were locked in almost perpetual conflict with the farm bloc. Despite the rising strength of industry and commerce and the declining significance of America's agrarian economy, however, pro-business conservatives still could not match the voting power of the agrarian states. This produced an unhelpful disparity between congressional behaviour and national economic development.

Southern Democrats constituted a third, conservative faction which often formed part of, or cooperated with, the farm bloc. Their most prominent spokesmen included Byron P. Harrison (D-Mississippi) and Joseph T. Robinson (D-Arkansas) in the Senate and future congressional power brokers, Jack Garner and Sam Rayburn (D-Texas) in the House. The bloc focused upon a variety of regional and economic issues, paying particular attention to legislation which could be construed as detrimental to states' rights. Consequently, their support or opposition in legislative wrangles was not always predictable.

In foreign affairs, Senate irreconcilables played a key role in the sixty-seventh Congress, as they had in the sixty-sixth. Hiram Johnson, Wisconsin's Robert M. LaFollette Sr and William Borah, the 'Lion of Idaho', along with ten to twelve other senators, kept a watchful eye on foreign and trade policy for signs of incipient internationalism in the White House. Johnson, LaFollette and George Norris of Nebraska also acted as spokesmen for the diminished political force of progressivism. The elections of 1918 and 1920 had placed the nation, and the Republican party, firmly into conservative hands but LaFollette and Norris, by forming temporary alliances with other groups, would fight surprisingly successful rearguard actions against both the Harding and Coolidge administrations during the coming decade.

The disarray which characterised the sixty-seventh Congress increased the likelihood that the new administration would suffer defeats and reversals. The President's 12 April message attempted to mitigate this danger by offering early guidance but his failure to state *which* reforms were most important gave a green light to each faction to pursue its own narrow interests. Within three months of the inauguration, bloc warfare threatened to derail the 'Harding Programme'.

Agriculture

Congress first turned its attention to the crisis in agriculture with the passage, in May 1921, of an emergency tariff raising duties on imported corn, wheat, sugar, wool and meat. The White House and pro-business faction expressed their hope that swift action on the tariff would satisfy the farm bloc and permit the urgent consideration of tax cuts and assistance to manufacturing interests. Farm state representatives, however, saw the tariff as only the first step in a campaign for permanent protection and more government aid, *both* of which would have to be initiated before Congress was allowed to address the needs of business.

By the early 1920s, American farms had reached the end of a period of rising demand, production and profit. Wartime price supports had encouraged many farmers to invest heavily in crop experimentation, new machinery and the construction or renovation of farm buildings. When prices began to slide dramatically in 1920, with wheat falling from $2.50 to under a dollar per bushel by late 1921, thousands of small farmers had insufficient capital to meet their loan repayments. Although prices were still higher than they had been in the pre-war years, other factors hampered recovery. Small farm holdings, for example, were increasingly unable to compete with giant, corporation-owned farms which monopolised markets, bought up the best land and reaped the benefits of the latest farm technology and substantially lower operating costs.

The most important factor depressing agriculture was overproduction. Progress in the control or eradication of crop blights and livestock diseases had increased farm output throughout the early years of the twentieth century. By 1921, tractors and threshing machines were easing the burden of physical labour for farmers and pushed productivity still higher. Thousands of acres once reserved for growing feed for plough horses could now be sown with corn, wheat and cotton for sale on an already-glutted home market.

After enactment of the Emergency Tariff, the FBF lobbied hard for immediate government action to tackle the problem of overproduction and falling prices. When Harding and Treasury Secretary Andrew Mellon called for urgent consideration of tax cuts instead, the farm bloc, aided by southern Democrats and some progressive Republicans, moved a bill proposing payment of cash compensation to war veterans to the top of the congressional timetable in July 1921. This was a shrewd move, since the 'veterans' bonus' scheme was close to the hearts of many Congress members. The administration, finding its path to tax reform blocked, had little choice but to return to the issue of farm relief as the only question on which forward movement was possible. A fresh wave of legislation followed. The Packers and Stockyards Act of August 1921 reduced the power of interstate packing companies to control prices paid to farmers, whilst the Futures Trading Act restricted speculation and price manipulation by grain dealers.[5] The Emergency Agricultural Credits Act, signed into law by the President on 24 August 1921, permitted the extension of extra credit by the government's War Finance Corporation to farmers and additional cash loans for farms involved in the breeding and marketing of cattle.

These acts displayed the administration's willingness to aid farmers but they were little more than palliatives and failed to address the problem of continued overproduction. In later years, with the problem worsening, the FBF and farm bloc would mount a concerted effort to control government agricultural policy.

Harding, meanwhile, attempted to reassure farmers of his concern by convening a five-day National Agricultural Conference in Washington on 23 January 1922, bringing farmers and politicians together to discuss remedies for the overproduction crisis. The conference's remit – 'consideration of the immediate agricultural situation ... Examination of the agricultural future' – was somewhat vague and its recommendations were hardly radical. These included a permanent place on the Federal Reserve Board for a representative of the agrarian economy, cuts in the cost of rail freight for farm produce, reductions in crop acreage and a permanent protective tariff. Although most of these recommendations were, in time, enacted, the conference's main value for Harding was to boost public awareness of his efforts for farmers. This he achieved at the expense of farm bloc leaders, who were increasingly portrayed by political journalists as selfish and obstructive. Shortly after the conference ended, Harding offered William Kenyon a post on the federal judiciary, temporarily taking the wind out of the farm bloc's congressional sails.

In 1922, the administration cooperated with Senator Arthur Capper in passing the Capper-Volstead Act, designed to protect farm cooperatives by exempting them from antitrust laws. Capper-Volstead was hailed by the bloc as a significant victory, although it cost the administration little, since both Harding and Mellon favoured relaxing anti-trust laws as a matter of principle.

Immigration and the Nativist Impulse

Whereas the crisis in agriculture divided congressional Republicans, government action to restrict immigration provoked fewer splits in the party. Towards the end of his term, President Wilson had vetoed a bill which proposed limits on the number of foreigners allowed to settle in the United States but bipartisan support for the bill and the arrival of a Republican administration made its reappearance a certainty. In May 1921, President Harding signed the Emergency Quotas Act, setting a ceiling of 357,000 immigrants per year and a quota for each nationality equivalent to 3 per cent of its total representation in the US census of 1910. A limit of 20 per cent of the annual total was also imposed for any monthly intake. The impact was almost immediate. Harding had often expressed his view that immigration processes had not been handled carefully enough, remarking in 1920,

> I firmly believe that if our Government ... had taken as much pains to familiarize the incoming foreigner with American ideals ... as the radicals have taken to misrepresent and misinterpret our Constitution, there would be far less trouble in this country today.[6]

The Emergency Quotas Act was a landmark piece of legislation, finally bringing to an end the 'open door' policy towards immigration. Previous efforts at regulation had rarely been successful but the Quotas Act reflected the heightened tensions and suspicions prevailing amongst white, Anglo-Saxon, Protestant Americans in the early 1920s. The rise of socialism and communism in post-war Europe stirred a wave of anticommunist hostility across the US, which was directed primarily at East European immigrants. Advocates of tighter immigration controls, known as 'restrictionists', warned against the infiltration of the nation's democratic institutions by 'aliens who are members of the anarchistic and similar classes'. Despite the efforts of home-grown socialist agitators, organised labour was also unsympathetic to socialist doctrines and feared the impact of a flood of cheap labour onto the American job market. In 1920, immigrant arrivals were peaking at 5,000 a day and the American Federation of Labor (AFL), representing craft workers, and the American Legion, representing US war veterans, lost no time in demanding immigration restrictions to safeguard jobs and wages. These demands drowned out opposition from the National Association of Manufacturers (NAM) which argued that the domestic economy would derive long-term benefits from the cheap labour which immigrants supplied.

Aside from its political and economic justifications, the Quotas Act represented another expression of the nativist tendency which lay deeply embedded in American culture and sought to root out any perceived threat to 'Nordic superiority'. Nativism had found its most extreme expression in the anti-Catholic 'Know Nothing' party of the 1840s and 1850s and also in the Ku Klux Klan, which targeted blacks in the late 1860s but was also hostile to Catholics and Jews in its post-1915 incarnation. A less extreme form of hostility, in the form of arrogant condescension towards foreigners, pervaded all levels of American society in the early twentieth century. Joseph Levenson, a member of the Motion Picture Commission investigating the content of Hollywood movies in the early 1920s, believed the moral and social inferiority of newly arrived immigrants was crucial to understanding the problem of 'immorality' in films:

> The motion picture draws an enormous proportion to its trade from children of immature years, from a great many of mental defectives and a vast number of illiterates and the ignorant. The non-English speaking foreigners contribute great numbers to every one of those classes.[7]

The answer, restrictionists argued, was to slow immigration rates, at least for a few years, and speed the 'Americanisation' of those already settled in the USA. 'Americanisation', in this context, meant adoption of the language, social customs and religious and political values of WASP America. The belief that 'Americanisation' was proceeding too slowly, or not at all, led to claims that Catholic immigrants reserved their primary allegiance for the Vatican, that German-Americans could not help hoping for an Allied defeat during the war, that Italian immigrants had rejected the Protestant work ethic in favour of crime and that Jewish communities were engaged in conspiracies to control the nation's grain or money supplies. One prominent propagator of anti-Semitic views was Henry Ford, whose newspaper, *The Dearborn Independent*, often published allegations of Jewish 'plots' to seize control of an assortment of American markets and financial institutions. In the mid-1920s, the Dearborn Publishing Company considerably collected these into bound volumes and released them under the title *The International Jew: The World's Foremost Problem*.[8]

These accumulated resentments formed part of the motivation for the quota legislation. By setting the 1910 national census as a benchmark, the act's sponsors tried to ensure that northern and western European nations, containing high concentrations of white Protestants, would continue to take the lion's share of the new quota allocations, with fewer places open to immigrants from southern and eastern Europe, where

Jews and Catholics were more heavily concentrated. This strategy was viewed by restrictionists as a necessary 'correction' to what they perceived as an emerging ethnic imbalance in cities such as Detroit, Boston and New York. These were the urban areas in which the biggest wave of immigrants, originating mainly from southern and eastern Europe, settled during the 1880s and 1890s.

Much of this sentiment simply updated existing prejudices but its continuing prevalence, even amongst the elites of American industry and finance, fuelled resentment amongst 'hyphenated' Americans, who perceived the Quotas Act as further evidence of the government's disregard for their concerns and for their contribution to the social and economic life of the nation. The Harding administration preferred to portray it as a necessary pause for cultural readjustment and job protection. Whatever the primary motivation, the impact of the Quotas Act was almost immediately felt. From June 1920 to June 1921, 805,228 foreign nationals had been permitted to settle in the US. For the year to June 1922, the total fell sharply to 309,556.

In the longer term, the quota legislation backfired politically on the Republican party. The Democrats' hold on the electoral loyalties of immigrant communities strengthened, despite the strong nativist element within the Democratic party itself. Eleven of the nation's twelve largest cities, concentrated particularly in the Northeast, were voting solidly Democratic by 1928 and, in 1932, immigrant voters formed an important part of the New Deal coalition which put an end to Republican dominance of national politics.

The disenchantment of black Americans with the Republican party also grew steadily throughout the 1920s. By the time of Warren Harding's election, race relations in the United States had entered a new and potentially explosive phase. Since the late nineteenth century, black workers had been abandoning the rural South for the northern cities. Poverty, Jim Crow laws and lynch mobs had made life in the South untenable for black families. As agricultural conditions worsened due to crop failures resulting from bad weather and boll weevil infestations, the migration gathered pace.

America's entry into the war opened up new employment opportunities for those black Americans who did not go to the front to fight. The emergency restrictions placed upon immigration in 1917 and the departure of hundreds of thousands of white factory, shipbuilding and railroad workers for the European battlefront caused an acute labour shortage.

Northern companies began recruiting amongst the southern black population. From 1917 to November 1918, around 500,000 black Americans
relocated to Detroit, Chicago, New York, Philadelphia, Pittsburgh and
other major cities, in the expectation of steady, paid employment and
freedom from fear. Thousands arrived in Pennsylvania and Illinois to
work in the coal mines. By the beginning of the 1920s, the size of the
black population outside the South had virtually doubled. The black
population of New York alone doubled between 1920 and 1930.

The realities of life and labour in the North, however, disillusioned
many migrants. For the unskilled majority, work in the mines and
factories was menial and low-paid, whilst living conditions in the slum
tenements were overcrowded, crime-ridden and lacking basic sanitation.
Moreover, although the writ of Jim Crow did not run in northern cities,
de facto racism continued to deny blacks high-wage employment and
equal access to social amenities such as bars, restaurants and theatres.
After November 1918, their plight worsened as white soldiers returned
from Europe to reclaim their jobs and further competition arose from
newly arrived European immigrants.

Black discontent was further fuelled by the treatment many black
soldiers received upon returning home from the battlefront. Some
367,000 black men had been sent to Europe, with many individual
soldiers receiving decorations for valour. Some black regiments were
singled out for praise by General John J. Pershing. In the North, they
generally received an enthusiastic welcome home but in some southern
states, white residents feared the return of battle-hardened black veterans
who were trained in the use of weapons and who had been exposed to
alien notions of social equalitarianism. In the twelve months following
the Armistice, more than seventy black veterans were lynched and some
were burned alive. Resentment at white violence and social and working
conditions sparked an unprecedented wave of race riots across America.
Tennessee, Illinois, Washington, Texas and Nebraska all experienced
severe interracial violence between 1919 and 1921. One riot, in 1919, took
place only yards from the White House itself. What made these episodes
unusual and, from a nativist perspective, disturbing, was the extent to
which black rioters were now willing to retaliate – meeting white
violence with violence of their own.

Black political and civil rights organisations had grown in strength by
the outset of the 1920s. The National Association for the Advancement
of Coloured People (NAACP), founded in 1910, had an estimated

membership of 90,000 by 1920. Its principle tactic was to organise court actions against racial prejudice and it scored a notable victory in 1915 by persuading the US Supreme Court to outlaw 'grandfather clauses' – a ploy by which southern blacks unable to prove that their grandfathers had been able to vote were prevented from casting their ballots.

Magazines such as the *Messenger* (edited by the socialist radical, A. Philip Randolph) and *Crisis* (edited by W. E. B. DuBois), became more influential as their readerships were now heavily concentrated in the inner cities and thus easier to reach. The wider dissemination of stories of lynchings and burnings caused further radicalisation of black communities. DuBois experimented with black nationalism to battle 'the forces of hell in our own land' and tried to create an international black movement but eventually followed the NAACP's strategy of exerting pressure for change *within* the white political and legal framework. Marcus Garvey, founder of the Universal Negro Improvement Association (UNIA) refused to moderate his message. The UNIA advocated pride in the African heritage of black Americans, encouraged black citizens to consider leaving the US for Africa and called for the development of a separate black economy. This radical message had a strong resonance with working class blacks in particular. Garvey set up enterprises such as the Black Star Navigation Line and the Universal African Motor Corps, to duplicate white business models for the benefit of black citizens. Some UNIA supporters wore extravagant uniforms symbolising the black 'empire' which Garvey believed would arise from post-colonial cooperation between African nations. He derided DuBois and the largely middle-class NAACP for their integrationist ideals. Moderates' contempt for Garvey boiled over when he met privately with leaders of the Ku Klux Klan to discuss their mutual interest in racial separation and later praised their honesty. Randolph presided over a New York meeting on 6 August 1922 at which Garvey was denounced by Professor William Pickens, ex-dean of Morgan College, Baltimore, for plotting 'to get on the right side of the Ku Klux Klan so he could go and collect money from the southern negroes.' Pickens also attacked Garvey's scheme for encouraging black citizens to 'return' to Africa.

> There are not less than 12,000,000 negroes in the United States today, and there is not a possible way to get rid of them. The best thing is to see how best the whites and the blacks here can get along together. By being good citizens here we can help the African negro best.[9]

These developments – angry inner city black populations, defiant black war veterans, race riots and the radical messages of a new generation of black leaders – confronted Republican election officials with a dilemma in 1920. Since the Civil War, the party had been considered the 'natural home' for black voters, but successive Republican administrations, fearing the electoral consequences of antagonising the South, had given a wide berth to the problems of black social, economic and political inferiority. Now, however, the new electoral clout of northern black voters and newly enfranchised black women had to be considered.

The 1920 Republican platform, therefore, specifically denounced lynching and pledged a biracial commission to investigate abuses of electoral law such as 'literacy tests' and 'white primaries' which were being used by southern whites to disenfranchise black voters.[10] Blacks were more actively involved at the national campaign level than ever before. Black campaign officials were recruited to advise on election strategies within their own communities and a registration drive amongst black women voters was also conducted in several states, including Harding's home state of Ohio. The Republican nominee met several times with NAACP officials and promised a commission to investigate the practice of 'peonage' – a form of financial serfdom used in some southern states in which poor blacks were compelled to work for the person to whom they were indebted until the debt was cleared.

Despite attracting the support of a majority of black American voters, President Harding's major speeches of 4 March and 12 April 1921 gave no indication that civil rights were an administration priority. On 26 October, however, he delivered the most controversial address on race relations given by any American president since Reconstruction. Speaking in Birmingham, Alabama, before a segregated audience, the President called for equal educational opportunity, economic equality 'proportional to the honest capacities and deserts of the individual' and an end to the disenfranchisement of black voters. Newspaper reports of the occasion noted that the white section of the audience sat in stony-faced silence whilst the roped-off black sections cheered wildly. Harding's body-language appeared almost purposefully confrontational as he turned to face his white listeners, pointed a finger in their direction, and stated,

> I would say, let the black man vote when he is fit to vote; prohibit the white man voting when he is unfit to vote .... Whether you like it or not, unless our democracy is a lie you must stand for that equality.[11]

The Birmingham speech provoked a nationwide press frenzy. The El Paso *Times* commented that Harding 'faced the issue squarely, without quibbling or evasion.'[12] The New York *Age* declared, 'Few of our Presidents have exhibited such moral courage ...'[13] The Montgomery Alabama *Journal*, however, described the speech as a 'serious, if not fatal mistake', while the Birmingham *Post* described Harding's utterances as 'tactless' and a 'violation of the proprieties'.[14]

From one perspective, the President had thrown down a challenge to the South in a potentially explosive speech which he had been under no particular pressure to make. An alternative perspective interpreted the speech as a reassurance to southern whites that supporting full voting rights and economic equality for black citizens did *not* mean support for *social* equality. Indeed, the President had spoken of the 'fundamental, eternal and inescapable difference' between the races. Sections of the southern press preferred to interpret this aspect of the speech as an endorsement of the status quo. The Columbia *State* announced: 'Mr Harding's plain speaking was what the negroes ... needed to hear ... They can be Americans, but they cannot be white people ... and they will gain nothing by impatience and fretfulness.'[15] DuBois also detected this qualification. Whilst he praised Harding's outspokenness, he criticised his failure to endorse social equalitarianism. Numerous black magazine editorials complained that social stratification based upon race was the chief weapon employed to perpetuate black inferiority.

Despite Harding's good intentions, the administration's record on civil rights was disappointing to black leaders. No biracial commission to investigate peonage was created and the administration made no legislative moves to prevent the continued use of white primaries in the South. It did offer initial support when Missouri Republican Leonidas C. Dyer introduced legislation to outlaw lynching in Congress early in 1921. Dyer worked closely with the NAACP's James Weldon Johnson to lobby for the bill, which passed the House in January 1922 by a solid 230–119 margin. However, White House pleas, full-page newspaper advertisements and numerous petitions failed to overcome a Senate filibuster by southern Democrats, which was helped by general Republican indifference. By 1923, the President's diminished political capital in Congress precluded any serious effort to push Dyer through the Senate and White House support for the bill was dropped.

The Veterans' Bonus

The most persistent and angry lobbying encountered by the Harding administration in its first year came not from farmers, restrictionists or black Americans but from war veterans and their spokesmen in Congress. As noted earlier, the Soldiers' Adjusted Compensation Act (popularly known as the 'Veterans' Bonus') had been pushed to the top of the political agenda by a procedural tactic to stall congressional consideration of tax reform. It was, nonetheless, an important issue in its own right and Harding, whilst unsympathetic to the notion of paying cash compensation to ex-soldiers, had made improvements in their living conditions and job opportunities one of his major priorities. In his inaugural speech he had promised veterans, 'a generous country will never forget the services you rendered.'

A proposal to pay compensation to Civil War veterans had been vetoed, on grounds of cost, by President Ulysses Grant in 1875. In July 1921, the White House released a copy of Grant's announcement to add weight to its claims that the nation could not afford the financial drain of long-term bonus payments. The American Legion, representing wounded and able-bodied veterans, claimed that a precedent for bonus payments could still be found in the 1917–18 cash bonuses paid to government employees by the Wilson administration to help offset the effects of inflation. During the 1920 campaign, both major parties had promised help for soldiers but neither elaborated on what form the assistance would take or to whom – able-bodied or disabled veterans – it would be offered. Harding favoured extensive support for the latter group. In August 1921, the Federal Board for Vocational Education (which oversaw aspects of the rehabilitation of veterans) and the Bureau of War Risk Insurance (which handled compensation for injuries received in battle) were merged into one large department – the Veterans Bureau – under the leadership of Charles Forbes, with Charles F. Cramer appointed as legal counsel. The appointments would do untold damage to Harding's posthumous reputation but, at the time, the President had no particular reason to doubt his director's personal probity.

The Bureau's $450 million budget suggests that administration cost-cutting was only selectively applied. By late summer of 1921, 75,812 men held places on government-run rehabilitation and vocational training programmes at the cost of $160 each per month. The administration later sought to add a further 107,000 men to the rolls.

Although the President and Treasury Secretary Andrew Mellon remained firmly opposed to the idea of a federal cash bonus, thirty-eight states had already enacted some form of compensation law by mid-1921. The bonus also enjoyed cross-party support in Congress. In late June, the Senate Finance Committee approved a proposal for payments to all ex-soldiers of $1.25 for each day's service overseas. The scheme's estimated cost was $1,560,000,000, which, the committee argued, could easily be found if the United States pressed for prompt repayment of allied war debts. The committee's report also denounced the use of the word 'bonus' to describe such compensation. 'It is worse than erroneous. It stamps upon a just and unquestioned national moral obligation the designation "gratuity".'[16]

Harding, already considering requests from Britain and France for debt rescheduling, understood the futility of requesting full and immediate repayment. Instead, he offered to support a bonus funded by revenues from a new sales tax, calculating, correctly, that Congress would balk at passing an unpopular tax measure. Many Congress members, however, were more concerned at the influence of the American Legion on the votes of 5,000,000 ex-servicemen in the 1922 mid-term election than at the prospect of defying the White House and endorsed the bonus to protect their political careers. The bonus seemed certain of success until, on 12 July, the President unexpectedly appeared in person before Congress to demand its recommittal to the Senate Finance Committee. Warning of 'the threatened paralysis of our Treasury' he attacked the Senate's 'menacing effort to expend billions in gratuities'.[17] Not only economic recovery, he argued, but also existing efforts being made to help disabled veterans were endangered by the cost of the bonus.

This display of executive sabre-rattling provoked indignation in the legislature. Georgia Senator Tom Watson claimed the President's action breached the separation of powers by interfering with the legislative process. Others considered Harding's action reminiscent of Woodrow Wilson. Alabama's Pat Harrison suggested, 'if the President has changed his mind about the wickedness of executive encroachments, he ought to make a public apology for his past utterances.'[18] Harding's gamble paid off, nonetheless. The bonus bill was returned to committee on 15 July. The American Legion promised to resurrect it at the first opportunity.

Press reaction to the President's confrontational stance was almost wholly favourable. The *New York Times* considered that Harding had become 'President of the whole people, not an opportunist politician.'[19]

The *Seattle Times*, rather more bluntly, stated that 'there were people who believed he was a political jellyfish ... (but) he has astonished the skeptics.'[20] Many ex-servicemen, however, resented the President's action and a flood of angry letters descended upon the White House. From Brooklyn, an embittered veteran wrote:

> Am sending you my Victory Medal, I mean to say Victim Medal, for your fight for the war profiteers and slackers. Also would like to ask you a question. Do you think you would be President of the U.S. if you had expressed your views on the bonus previous to election? I doubt it. Thanks for your generosity.[21]

Continued pressure from the Legion ensured that the bonus issue remained on the political agenda. Within a year, Harding would be compelled to gamble his executive authority in a second confrontation with Congress and the Legion.

Taxation

After months of delay, by late summer 1921 Congress was ready to consider tax reform. The Revenue Act of 1921 proved controversial as it appeared to place more immediate stress on relieving corporate tax burdens than on assisting average- or low-income Americans. Andrew Mellon sought the repeal of the Excess Profits Tax, a wartime revenue-raising measure enacted by the Wilson Administration. The Treasury Secretary argued that taxation of corporation profits over 8 per cent at rates of between 20 per cent and 60 per cent undermined business incentives. Potential investors, he claimed, were diverting their funds into tax-exempt securities rather than investing in industry and creating new jobs, with the result that sources of government revenue from taxes were evaporating. 'Wealth', Mellon declared, 'is failing to carry its share of the tax burden.' He proposed to lower corporate tax rates and cut maximum surtax rates from 65 per cent to 32 per cent. To increase its impact, the repeal of the excess profits tax would be *backdated* to January 1921. Meanwhile, the existing general tax rates for average-income citizens (4% on the first $4000 of earned income and 8% thereafter) were to be retained for anyone earning under $66,000. Robert LaFollette denounced the plan for wilfully neglecting the economic needs of working-class Americans and demanded Mellon's resignation. Administration opponents within the House Ways and Means Committee also tried to sabotage the plan by increasing tax exemptions for low income-earners and by *raising*, rather than lowering, general corporate tax rates. The 32 per cent ceiling for the surtax and the repeal of the Excess Profits tax were approved, however, after President Harding privately offered to drop the back-dating of the latter and opt for a starting date of January *1922*, thus reducing the government's revenue loss. This was enough to secure victory in the House but the bill's passage through the Senate was more problematic. Senators insisted upon a 50 per cent maximum surtax rate, rather than the 32 per cent approved by the House. Harding proffered a compromise deal of 40 per cent, whereupon the House changed its mind, dropped its approval for Mellon's 32 per cent, ignored Harding's 40 per cent and adopted the Senate's 50 per cent rate instead. Amidst bitter recriminations and accusations of class prejudice, more than ninety House Republicans deserted the President and voted for the higher 50 per cent rate. Mellon and Harding were eventually compelled to settle for what they could get and return to the battle another year.

The debates were a further indication of the serious divisions between the legislature and the White House and of the weakening ability of the Senate old guard to exert its authority over progressive rebels. Nonetheless, the eventual passage of the tax-reduction measure was a landmark in 1920s fiscal legislation – the first of a series of tax cuts which laid the groundwork for the economic prosperity of the later Coolidge period and which eventually led Wall Street financiers to regard Mellon as the greatest Secretary of the Treasury since Alexander Hamilton.

'Metamorphosis'

The Harding administration had endured an unexpectedly bumpy ride during its first year. The recession had worsened, with 100,000 bankruptcies recorded during 1921 and unemployment reaching a peak of 12.5 per cent. Roughly one in ten farmers had lost their land since the end of the war and there was no sign of an abatement of the agricultural depression. The blame for these statistics could not realistically be laid at Harding's door. The administration had moved to aid farmers with tariffs and extended credit and to stimulate wealth and job creation through tax cuts but it was too early to judge the effects of these policies. Meanwhile, the administration showed some willingness, despite its conservatism and fiscal stringency, to deploy government funds and flex federal muscle wherever it seemed likely to stimulate industrial expansion or technological progress. At the President's request, Congress approved an annual appropriation of $75 million to construct highways linking all cities with populations in excess of 50,000. To the surprise of progressives, the Sheppard-Towner Maternity Aid Act, providing federal matching funds for any state hospitals running infant and maternity healthcare programmes, received Harding's support. The act was hailed as a major victory by its sponsor organisation, the League of Women Voters. Conservative complaints to the White House over the 'unhealthy' involvement of the government in family life and their appeals to block Sheppard-Towner, were ignored.

President Harding's popularity consistently outstripped that of his party in Congress and his displays of firmness won praise from those who had expected a lazier administration. The *Literary Digest* complimented, somewhat back-handedly, the President's 'gradual drift in the direction of aggressive leadership'.[22] Washington columnist Mark Sullivan noted, 'Harding was not merely underestimated. He was totally misapprehended.'[23]

The President, however, was disillusioned. He had already abandoned his rather naive hope that Congress could transcend partisan and factional divisions and cooperate with the White House for the wider national interest. In December 1921, he confessed to a close friend, 'I find I cannot carry my pre-election ideals of an Executive keeping himself aloof from Congress.'[24]

The President's diminishing respect for the legislature was discernible in his response to protests from some Congress members as he announced the release from prison of most of the 'political prisoners' jailed by the government for 'subversive activities'. The most significant detainee freed was the socialist activist, Eugene Debs. President Wilson had refused to release Debs, even though Atlanta Penitentiary's convict number 2253 had polled 900,000 votes in the 1920 elections. To Wilson's successor, a political amnesty was a psychologically important move which would help to dispel the legacy of paranoia and unease at the suppression of democratic freedoms left by the war. In early December, Debs, at Harding's request, travelled by train, unguarded, from Atlanta to Washington for a meeting with Attorney General Daugherty and the President. The formal release document specified New Year's Eve as the day in which Debs would leave jail but when the paper reached his desk, Harding scrawled across the bottom, 'Commuted to expire December 24 1921', in order, he explained, to allow Debs to spend Christmas with his family.[25] The American Legion, the Attorney General and the First Lady opposed the release of so prominent a socialist, but Harding was insistent. He explained to an aide, 'I thought the spirit of clemency was quite in harmony with the things we were trying to do here in Washington,' adding sourly, 'I could pick you out a half dozen members of House and Senate who deserved quite as much to be in the penitentiary as did Debs.'[26]

Media and Popular Culture

Despite its difficulties, the administration appeared to have made progress towards its goal of restoring 'normalcy' to the nation's affairs by the close of its first year. Newspaper editorials, whilst stressing that serious problems remained, claimed to detect a palpable change in the public mood since Harding's inauguration. 'The change is amazing ...,' one reporter enthused, 'distinctly, the sunny side is up.'[27]

Delayed relief at the ending of the war was primarily responsible for the lifting of the national mood, but rapid advances in technology were also influential. The impact of radio and moving pictures upon society had been muted by wartime austerity, but, as the 1920s opened, the American public enthusiastically embraced new forms of entertainment. Entrepreneurs in the field of radio and film possessed both the imagination and the capital, to meet the demand.

President Harding's election, on the night of 2 November 1920, was the subject of the first ever news broadcast over a licensed radio station – Radio KDKA in East Pittsburgh, run by the Westinghouse Electrical Company. As a former newspaper editor, Harding had no difficulty in understanding the new medium's political usages and its potential for commercial development.[28] His April 1921 address to Congress proposed federal government action to speed development of radio and cable services, 'so that the American reader may receive a wide range of news and the foreign reader receive full accounts of American activities.'[29]

New stations appeared in 1921, including Radio KLS, a Warner Brothers station operating from Oakland, California; Radio WGH, run by Alabama's Montgomery Light and Water Power Company; and Radio WDW, Washington D.C.'s own station, operated by the Radio Construction and Electric Company.

The trickle became a flood in 1922, with over 500 new stations applying for licences. It was clear that some form of regulatory framework was needed to forestall chaos, prompting Commerce Secretary Hoover to convene a conference of radio operators and government officials in February 1922. The conference recommended that distinct wavelength

bands, separate from those already designated for entertainment programmes, should be allocated for government, state and private broadcasting.

The first wireless set was installed in the White House on 8 February
1922, the same year that Mrs Harding ordered the first Hoover 'vacuum
cleaner' for the Oval Office carpets. The *New York Times* reported on
the arrival of radio at the White House,

> the President will be able to put the phones to his ears as he sits at his
> desk in his study, overlooking the lawn toward the Washington
> Monument, and hear the latest news or snatches of music.[30]

Another important milestone in 1922 was the airing of the nation's
first radio commercial – on Radio WEAF in New York, advertising the
virtues of the Queensboro Realty Company. During President Harding's
last tour of the western United States, in the summer of 1923, his speech
in St Louis, Missouri could be received by KSD in St Louis and
transmitted instantaneously to four different stations in New York,
Kansas, Pennsylvania and Illinois.

The growth of radio forced the pace of economic and cultural change
in the United States during the decade. Public opinion and behaviour
became increasingly 'nationalised' as Americans now had access to the
same information on almost every subject from politics, religion and
world affairs to fashion, cinema and sport. 'Syndicated' articles and
columns in newspapers contributed to this process, as thousands of
Americans read the same stories and cartoons over breakfast each day. A
WEAF-sponsored radio debate between pro- and anti-Prohibitionists,
attracted thousands of listeners and sack-loads of mail and audiences
were encouraged to write in with ideas for new programmes or to
express their views on the comparative merits of classical music and jazz.

Geographical distance was increasingly irrelevant. More isolated
communities could now gain instant access to breaking news stories – a
trend accelerated by improvements in newspaper distribution networks.
By 1923, a sizeable portion of the population from Boston and Philadelphia to Seattle and Tucson could experience for themselves 'live'
commentaries on sporting events, such as the World Series or the 1921
prize fight between Jack Dempsey and Georges Carpentier. Investors
could locate information on the progress of their stocks and shares,
whilst farmers altered their daily routines to catch weather bulletins.
Trains piped classical music concerts into carriages and national 'crazes',

such as those for crossword puzzles, 'flapper' fashion, and the game of Mah-Jong, spread more rapidly. The fad for Egyptian-style patterns and designs in women's clothing was generated by media interest in the 1922 discovery, by archaeologist Howard Carter, of the young pharoah Tutankhamen's tomb in Egypt. Even Florence Harding was seen wearing the black, gold and turquoise stripes of 'Tut' fashion.

The growth of Hollywood played a key role in reinforcing these trends. By 1920, the motion picture industry was already America's fifth-largest and the lives and loves of its stars were becoming national obsessions. Charles Spencer Chaplin's rise to fame embodied for American audiences the perennially popular 'rags-to-riches' story. After a poverty-stricken childhood in London, Chaplin became a music hall entertainer before signing a contract with the Keystone Film Company in 1913. By 1915, he was earning more than $1,250 a week and his fame was spreading across the nation as fast as the growing network of film distributors could carry it. Ironically, some of the bowler-hatted hobo's most popular films, particularly *The Gold Rush* (1925), and later works such as *Modern Times* (1931) and *City Lights* (1936), were morality tales which expressed the frustrations and nervous uncertainties of modern America, rather than its tub-thumping patriotism. They often explored the human dimension of poverty and exploitation and the threat to the freedom and dignity of the individual posed by rampant capitalism. Chaplin's creation, unlike Valentino's, was one with whom many cinemagoers could identify, consciously or unconsciously. He struggled against impossible odds, often losing his battles but rarely his sense of right and wrong.

Chaplin made his own contribution to the growth of corporatism by co-founding the United Artists studio in 1919 with co-star Mary Pick-ford, actor Douglas Fairbanks and director D. W. Griffith, producer of the high-grossing, white-supremacist hit of 1915, *Birth of a Nation*. Mergers and takeovers during the Twenties produced many of the company labels familiar to later generations, such as Paramount Studios (1927).[31] In 1924, a three-way merger between Mayer Pictures, the Goldwyn Pictures Corporation and the Metro Picture Corporation created the giant Metro-Goldwyn-Mayer.[32] By the late 1920s, capital investment in the film industry was more than $2 billion and the studios were turning out nearly 800 productions a year, a rate never equalled in later decades. Foreshadowing economic trends later in the decade, the largest studios, Paramount, MGM, the Fox Film Corporation and Warner Brothers, tightened their grip on the film industry through control of theatre

chains and distribution networks across the country.[33] Independent
theatres, unable to compete, dwindled in number whilst aspiring actors
became dependent upon studio contracts for survival.

Some early Hollywood stars paid an unpleasant price for media
interest in their private lives. In 1920, Mary Pickford was prosecuted by
California's Attorney General for bigamy. Rudolph Valentino (born
Rodolfo Guglielmi, son of an immigrant Italian vet), also faced bigamy
charges in 1922. Tabloid newspapers printed salacious, often inaccurate,
stories of wild parties, alcoholism, drug addiction, suicides and sexual
promiscuity in Hollywood. Far from alienating fans, these revelations
drove them to the theatres in increasing numbers and boosted circulation
figures for the papers which thrived upon the presentation of news as 'a
three-ring circus' of crime and gangsterism, sporting heroes and sexual
promiscuity. The most infamous press feeding-frenzy ended the career
of Roscoe 'Fatty' Arbuckle, who was accused of killing actress Virginia
Rappe at a party celebrating Arbuckle's new Paramount contract in
September 1921. Prosecutors claimed the inebriated, 120-kilogramme
Arbuckle had sat upon Rappe during a sexual assault, resulting in her
death from internal injuries. Arbuckle was not finally cleared of the
charges until April 1922, by which time his public image lay in tatters.
Church leaders and politicians concerned at the impact of such stories
upon the young, pressed Hollywood directors to 'clean up' their
products. Unfortunately for the guardians of public morals, films with
sexual themes, however subliminal, attracted larger audiences. Women
flocked to see *The Sheik* (1921) in which Valentino kidnapped and seduced
Agnes Ayres. The mob scenes which accompanied Valentino's public
appearances showed that thousands of Americans had become addicted
to the escapism of the decade's most popular film genres – swash-
buckling adventure, horror, westerns, slapstick comedies and bodice-
ripping romances. Although more serious films such as *Nanook of the
North* (1922) and Cecil B. DeMille's $1.5 million blockbuster *The Ten
Commandments* (1923) were also popular, the industry remained
vulnerable to criticism. Religious leaders and politicians, disgruntled to
find themselves competing for public attention with Rudolph Valentino
or cowboy hero, Tom Mix, accused film producers of debasing public
morals and corrupting the nation's youth.

The charges levelled against film-makers were, on occasion, con-
fusingly contradictory. Canon William Chase, campaigning in 1922 for
an investigation into the film industry in New York, claimed, on the one

hand, that Hollywood deliberately produced money-spinning films 'below the morality of the general public' and, on the other, that Hollywood 'immorality' in fact merely *reflected* the moral laxity 'into which the American people as a whole have fallen since the war.'[34]

The rash of Hollywood scandals lead to the formation of a new oversight body – the Motion Picture Producers and Distributors of America. Will Hays, President Harding's Postmaster-General, left the Cabinet to head the organisation and devised the 'Hays Code', which set detailed standards for on-screen portrayals of religious figures, criminals and scenes of sexual intimacy. Clauses requiring stars to meet strict standards in their *off*-screen behaviour were inserted into employment contracts. As time passed, motion picture producers found ways to circumvent the code but it continued to draw criticism from those who viewed censorship, like Prohibition, as a puritanical attempt to 'impose morality' through law.

The growing influence of radio and film upon the public made it inevitable that politicians would seek to manipulate the new forms of media and entertainment for their own purposes. The Harding administration was the first to properly explore the mutually manipulative relationship between politicians and the media. During the 1920 election, Republican campaign managers arranged for stars such as Al Jolson and Mary Pickford to be photographed with their candidate. Harding, unlike some of his colleagues, understood the importance of establishing cultural connections with ordinary Americans. Writing to Jolson in December 1921, he commented: 'There is wonderful influence in a song, and a very marked spread of that influence from the stage.'[35] The relationship, of course, worked both ways. Hollywood 'vamp', Mae West, took full advantage of her rising fame when she petitioned the White House for the release of Eugene Debs.

Harding's desire to establish a rapport with voters was not merely a political ploy but also a reflection of his personal nature. He was 'the antithesis of Wilson: modest mediocrity rather than arrogant genius.'[36] This distinction increased critics' doubts about the President's intellect, but his public relations skills created helped such comments. Harding's White House was the first to devise a rudimentary 'media strategy' and the first to recognise that the President could no longer remain aloof from reporters. Positive newspaper coverage was now an essential factor for a successful presidency. By 1921, the number of daily newspapers in the United States had been falling steadily for some years. The process accelerated in the first six years of the decade, with around 600 titles disappearing through merger, takeover or bankruptcy. Yet press influence over public opinion was *growing*, rather than declining. Newspapers and magazines could be printed faster and distributed further than ever before. Although many papers still maintained the nineteenth century tradition of loyalty to one political party, a growing number were opting for editorial independence to avoid being taking for granted by Republican or Democratic politicians. A new prestige surrounded the reporting of Washington politics and regular columnists such as Mark Sullivan and Walter Lippman built prestigious reputations as shapers of national political opinion.

Harding's press conferences were more informal, and more frequent, than those held by President Wilson. The former editor of the Marion *Star* enjoyed bantering with reporters but the traditional prohibition of direct quotation of the President without prior approval remained in force.

Unlike his predecessors, Harding's concept of the 'dignity' of his office did not preclude posing for photographers on the White House lawn with Boy Scout troops, baseball stars, industrial leaders, Nobel prize-winning scientists and visitors from every corner of the country. By June 1921, photographers' demands for access to the President had become unmanageable and a formal organisation – the White House News Photographers Association – was created to cope with it.[37]

The manipulation of image in politics had reached a watershed, one which gave another ironic twist to Harding's presidential career. As an Ohio politician, he had criticised Theodore Roosevelt's use of the presidency as 'a bully pulpit'. As President, his media manipulation techniques served only to *intensify* the press and public focus upon the occupant of the White House.

Trade and Industry

The emerging 'sunny side' of early 1920s America was not visible to all segments of the population. Heavy job losses in the coal, iron and steel industries and on the railroads had sparked industrial unrest in 1919 and 1920 as union leaders organised strikes against lay-offs, longer working hours and wage cuts or freezes. The Republican prescription for economic revival centred, inevitably, upon tax cuts, tariff hikes and other measures designed to protect American markets and workers from foreign competition. Mellon's tax cuts aside, the single most influential piece of legislation aimed at economic recovery was the Fordney-

McCumber Tariff Act of September 1922. Devised by the House Ways and Means Committee, under Representative Joseph W. Fordney (R-Michigan), and the Senate Finance Committee, under the chairmanship of Porter McCumber (R-North Dakota), it raised duties on goods imported from abroad to record levels. Agricultural products such as rye, wheat, beef and lamb were given further protection whilst duties were placed upon other products, including chemicals, dyes, textiles and jewellery. Harding approved the rises, ungrammatically announcing that his administration's intention was 'to prosper America first'. The President was also empowered by Fordney-McCumber to raise or lower rates by up to 50 per cent in line with rising or falling domestic production costs. Ridiculously protracted debates took place in both House and Senate, as regional factions and single-issue interest groups battled to ensure that *their* interests benefited from the tariff hikes.

Fordney-McCumber was to profoundly influence the development of both the domestic US and the international economies through the rest of the decade. It effectively reduced overseas competition, thus allowing industrial and corporate monopolies to increase their strength at home. However, it damaged US trading relations with other countries, who responded, unsurprisingly, with tariff hikes of their own. Unable to sell their goods in American markets, foreign producers were generating insufficient capital to maintain reasonable profit and employment levels. This worsened the social and economic dislocation in post-war Europe and thereby reduced foreign governments' ability to pay off their war debts. Although it generated a greater sense of economic security at home (and was popular with the American public), the Fordney-McCumber Act would eventually attract heavy criticism for its 'myopic' view of world trading patterns.

In industrial relations, the Harding administration was wedded to the principle of the 'open shop' as the essential underpinning for a successful capitalist economy. This commitment attracted open contempt from union officials and undermined administration efforts to pose as an 'impartial' arbiter of industrial disputes. Faith in the even-handedness of the White House was also undermined by Attorney General Harry Daugherty's publicly stated belief that organised labour was controlled by agents of the Kremlin bent on the overthrow of American democracy and capitalism.

Harding persisted, nevertheless, in efforts to calm industrial relations through peaceful dialogue. A conference of business and labour leaders, presided over by Commerce Secretary Hoover, was convened in Washington on 26 September 1921 to discuss possible solutions to the problems of job cuts and wage freezes. The scope of debate was restricted from the start by the President's insistence that federal relief and price fixing were not on the table for discussion. Agreement was reached, however, on the need to raise tariffs. Unusually, the conference also examined ways in which the *psychological* impact of unemployment might be lessened through voluntary, locally organised job clubs and retraining schemes.

Some labour leaders believed the administration might be prepared to modify its pro-business stance, but their hopes were dashed by the government's reaction to the wave of industrial unrest which erupted the following year. In April 1922, 650,000 miners struck in the face of deep wage cuts of up to 40 per cent and demands by mine operators for three- or four-day weeks to compensate for the falling demand for coal. Violence flared when strike-breakers were deployed by the southern Illinois Coal Company to work the mines near Herrin, Illinois. Clashes on 22 June between the battalions of replacement labour and pickets from United Mineworkers of America (UMW) resulted in eighteen deaths. The President reacted by calling upon state governors to use all means within their power to protect the strike-breakers and threatening to seize the mines with federal troops. After exacting promises for the retention of old wage rates and the establishment of a commission to examine miners' grievances, the UMW called off the strike.

The 'Herrin Massacre' hardened the administration's attitudes towards strike action. Harding would not countenance threats to the 'open shop' or to the rights of replacement labour to work. He also, however, held the mine companies themselves in contempt. 'The goddam operators are so stiff-necked', he complained, 'you can't do anything with them.'[38] Although it had won its case over wages, the UMW's agreement to cuts in the workforce weakened its claims of victory. UMW membership and bargaining power declined after 1922 and fell continuously until the advent of the New Deal.

Shortly after the mineworkers' dispute, in July 1922, 400,000 railroad workers were called out by the Railway Craft Workers union in protest at wage cuts and at the refusal of rail companies to abide by rulings handed down by the Railway Labour Board. The Board's rulings on wages and conditions were not, in fact, legally enforceable but the unions had previously accepted its recommendations on wage cuts in the belief that the operators would show a similar willingness to cooperate on job contracts and working conditions. The administration in Washington, already shaken by the UMW dispute, once again supported the use of strike-breakers on the railroads. In an effort to curtail the union's strike activities and fearing a repeat of the 'Herrin Massacre', Harding dispatched his Attorney General to Chicago to obtain an injunction from federal Judge James H. Wilkerson. Daugherty returned on 23 September with one of the harshest injunctions ever issued in the field of American labour relations. It banned strikers not only from picketing but from soliciting support by letter, phone or word-of-mouth. 'Hitler or Mussolini', wrote Samuel Hopkins Adams, 'might be proud to claim its authorship.'[39] The Wilkerson injunction provoked a storm in the 'best minds' cabinet. Hoover and Hughes attacked it as extreme and unnecessary since the strikers had already indicated their willingness to reach a compromise settlement. Harding, anxious not to appear uncompromisingly anti-labour, instructed Daugherty to soften the injunction's language. Nevertheless, confronting both the injunction and a lack of support from the four other main railroad workers' unions, the Craft Workers' Union eventually capitulated.

Overall, the administration handled the industrial unrest of 1922 just about as badly as it could have been done. Harding dithered between protecting the interests of the free market and fruitlessly prodding bosses towards a negotiated settlement which would meet at least some of the strikers' demands. The President's claims that the administration sympathised with the plight of the industrial labour force, however, were undermined by his reluctance to force the hands of industrial management and by Daugherty's treatment of striking workers as traitors. After the experiences of Herrin and Wilkerson, the Brotherhood of Locomotive Engineers publicly pronounced the Harding administration 'an enemy to organized labor'.

As if to compensate for the administration's bad reputation amongst the industrial workforce, Harding adopted a tougher attitude towards management after 1922 by pressing steel industry bosses to abolish the twelve-hour working day. This was achieved by threatening Elbridge H. Gary, head of US Steel, with eight-hour shifts imposed by government fiat if concessions over working hours were not forthcoming. The eight-hour day, hailed by organised labour as a significant move forward, came into effect on 2 August 1923.

A recovering, but still sluggish, economy, labour unrest and voter contempt for the performance of the sixty-seventh Congress combined to deal the Republican party a crushing blow in the 1922 mid-term elections. Seventy-five Republican representatives and eight senators went down to defeat. After the debacle, some editorial writers speculated that Harding's prospects for re-election were now in jeopardy. Mark Sullivan disagreed, pointing out that Harding's greatest asset – his personal popularity – was undamaged, according to opinion polls. 'The public thinks that President Harding has done rather well... (but) ... that the Senate and House have done rather badly.'[40] Harding privately concurred with Sullivan's view. Although he accepted his share of criticism for the setbacks of normalcy's second year, he became determined, after November 1922, to force congressional Republicans to tow the White House line. The stage was set for a final round of confrontations which would end only with the President's sudden death.

Normalcy Stalled

In late summer 1922, the veterans' bonus issue had made its long-expected reappearance at the top of the legislative agenda. Bonus proponents in Congress attempted to exert pressure on the US Treasury by threatening to withhold appropriations for the Army and Navy. Secretary Mellon maintained the now-familiar administration line that a new sales tax would be required to pay the $4 billion needed to sustain any compensation scheme. He reminded Republican rebels, that the $24 billion national debt, a rise of $22.8 billion since 1914, prohibited an unfunded bonus. This time, however, frantic White House lobbying proved futile. The Soldiers' Adjusted Compensation Act passed the House on 14 September 1922 and the Senate on 15 September. The President promptly vetoed the bill on 19 September. Efforts to override the presidential veto fell short by four votes. Harding's decisiveness won him further praise in the press but it was a pyrrhic victory – Republicans in the House and Senate were left embittered and somewhat surprised by Harding's aggressive stance. As Robert K. Murray noted, the President 'seemed prepared to crucify his party on the cross of fiscal integrity if necessary.'[41] Within eighteen months, Congress would resurrect the bill once more, but Harding would no longer be in the White House to face the bonus advocates down.

Further damage to executive-legislative relations arose from a dispute over the future of American shipping. During the war, the Wilson administration had bought up hundreds of naval vessels and the government's Shipping Board had also encouraged an ambitious shipbuilding programme. After 1918, the problem arose of how to get rid of over one thousand mostly unwanted and badly maintained ships. Harding's appointee to run the Shipping Board, Albert Lasker, failed in his efforts to sell off the government fleet at hugely discounted rates. Moreover, he uncovered extensive corruption in records of the negotiations between the Shipping Board and the private companies involved in building them. Lasker termed some of the contracts 'the most shameful ... looting of the Public Treasury that the human mind can devise.' In February 1922, with the Shipping Board's deficits running at over $15 million a month, Harding presented Congress with a plan for government subsidies of $30 million a year to encourage private contractors to buy up the fleet. Predictably, the farm bloc, despite having received millions in government aid itself, announced its opposition to federal largesse for eastern business interests. Republican floor leaders took quiet soundings of opinion on Capitol Hill and found that the administration did not have enough support to secure victory on a shipping bill. Harding backed off temporarily but refused to drop the issue. In November 1922, the President called Congress into special session to consider a fresh subsidies bill. Harding's tactics here were similar to those used in the fight over the veterans' bonus. He appeared before Congress in person to deliver his view that partisan interests were of secondary concern to economic recovery. 'Frankly,' he lectured scowling Congress members, 'I think it loftier statesmanship to support ... a policy designed to effect the larger good of the nation than merely to record the too-hasty expression of a constituency.'[42]

A carefully orchestrated campaign of pressures and inducements resulted in an administration victory in the House by 208 votes to 184. Unfortunately, the most powerful opponents of shipping subsidies lay in wait in the Senate, where southern and border state members were engaged in filibustering anti-lynching legislation. Senate Republican leaders shelved the Dyer bill in order to free up time for consideration of shipping subsidies, but a number of southern and farm bloc senators, including James Reed and Robert LaFollette, simply refocused their filibuster upon the shipping bill and spoke, in relays, for five days. An embittered Harding was compelled to give up the fight.

Scandal and Death

In March 1923, the President and First Lady travelled to Florida for a short vacation. Both were in a weakened physical condition. Mrs Harding had narrowly escaped death from nephritis in October 1922 and the President's health was causing concern to his doctors. Breathing difficulties made it impossible for him to lie flat in bed at night and he complained of chest pains and shortness of breath. Playing golf with his aide, Colonel Edmund Starling, Harding complained, 'Why, after playing eleven or twelve holes do I drag my feet and feel so tired?' To Starling's suggestion that he should play fewer holes in future, Harding retorted, 'Hell! If I can't play eighteen holes I won't play at all!'[43]

The President was suffering from hypertension from overwork. According to White House Chief Usher Ike Hoover, Harding worked harder, slept less and worried more than his predecessors in the presidency. Late night visitors to the Oval Office often found him still at his desk, penning personal replies to hundreds of letters from ordinary citizens. He now found only temporary relief in golf, poker parties and occasional secret visits by his lover, Nan Britton. Despite his continuing popularity with the press and public, the affable Ohioan had never fully come to terms with his position, once confessing to a friend, 'I don't think I'm big enough for the Presidency.'

Adding to the President's worries were the gradually surfacing rumours that corruption was endemic within his administration. Charles Forbes, head of the Veterans Bureau, had been selling government surpluses in provisions such as towels, soap and bed-sheets at enormous discounts and in enormous quantities to private buyers. The profits from the sales of goods intended for veterans were, it was alleged, finding their way into the pockets of Forbes and his friends. Harding initially refused to believe the rumours but, after reviewing evidence gathered by Daugherty, he demanded Forbes' resignation in February 1923. Forbes' sudden departure for Europe did not prevent a congressional investigation into the affairs of the Veterans Bureau, which began on 2 March. The Senate committee unearthed fresh evidence that land development and building contracts had been sold off by Forbes to an assortment of private companies. The bureau's legal advisor, Charles Cramer, was also implicated but committed suicide on 14 March before he could be called to testify. Harding then learned that Jess Smith, the close friend and personal assistant of Daugherty, had been using government contacts and facilities to arrange deals from which he received cash 'kickbacks'. Smith had been involved, it was claimed, in bootlegging operations and the illegal sale of government property. He allegedly used his connections to help a German family regain millions of dollars in frozen assets.

For this, Smith received a fee of over $200,000 which he deposited in a bank account bearing both his name and Daugherty's. Harding, according to some accounts, confronted Smith with the evidence and ordered him to return to his apartment at Washington's Wardman Park Hotel and await arrest. Like Cramer, however, Smith committed suicide before he could be interrogated.[44]

The scandal with the most devastating potential consequences for the administration, however, involved Interior Secretary Albert Fall Jr. In May 1921, Fall had arranged for the transfer of control of oil reserves from the Department of the Navy to the Interior Department. This action, which appeared to be a simple reallocation of administrative responsibilities was approved by Harding. Fall, however, intended to take advantage of certain pre-existing laws which permitted the leasing of oil lands to private developers. The leasing of Naval Reserve Number 3, in Wyoming, to Mammoth Oil and Reserve Number 1, in Elk Hills, California, to the Pan-American Petroleum and Transport Company, raised the suspicions of Democratic senator John B. Kendrick because the leasing procedures had not been advertised or subject to open, competitive bidding, as the law required. Fall resigned from the cabinet on 4 March 1923, citing his desire to return to private business. Another congressional investigating committee, chaired by Democratic senator Thomas J. Walsh, began probing the leasing deals in spring of 1923, with particular focus on the Wyoming oil reserve, which was nicknamed 'Teapot Dome' by local inhabitants after an oddly shaped rock formation located near the oil field. This rock was to lend its name to what was to become America's most notorious political scandal until the 1970s Watergate affair. The rash of rumours, resignations and suicides prompted congressional investigators to broaden the scope of their enquiries.

In June 1923, the President embarked upon a tour of the western United States, which he planned to use as the opening salvo of his re-election campaign and also as a platform for his campaign to secure US membership of the World Court. The schedule for the trip required the President to make speeches in seven cities between St Louis, Missouri and Portland, Oregon before joining the *USS Henderson* for a sea voyage to Alaska. The presidential party would return to Seattle, move by train through San Francisco and Los Angeles and make a stopover in Puerto Rico before returning to Washington. Herbert Hoover, who accompanied the President on the later part of the journey, described Harding as deeply depressed. At one point, the Commerce Secretary recalled, the President summoned him to his cabin and asked, 'If you knew of a great scandal in our administration, would you for the good of the country and the party expose it publicly or would you bury it?' Hoover advised honesty but Harding offered no further details on the matter. The Commerce Secretary was unable to determine precisely how much Harding had discovered about the corrupt activities of some of his associates but the President's behaviour alarmed him. Harding was gloomy and distracted, sometimes playing poker with members of the touring party in all-night marathons. His companions on the sea voyage nicknamed it 'the Death March'.

On 27 July, whilst speaking in Seattle, the President became confused and unsteady on his feet, dropping his papers on the floor. After completing the address, he was rushed through to San Francisco and put to bed at the Palace Hotel. Doctors released official bulletins attributing his condition to exhaustion complicated by ptomaine poisoning from eating tainted crabmeat whilst on board the *Henderson*. The crisis appeared to have passed when, at 7.30 p.m. on 2 August 1923, Harding suffered a sudden relapse and died.

Harding and History

Genuine mourning greeted the death of the President, with press obituaries focusing upon Harding's amiable personality, hard-working habits and consensual approach to politics. He was widely credited with having steered the country through the worst of the economic recession and with successfully restoring a sense of normalcy to the nation after the upheavals of the previous decade.

By the late 1920s, however, the Harding period had become a byword for sleaze and incompetence. *The President's Daughter*, a book published by Harding's young mistress, Nan Britton, in 1926, contained tales of sexual encounters in White House closets and the birth of the President's illegitimate daughter. Gaston B. Means' *The Strange Death of President Harding* (1930) was largely fiction but caused still more damage. Means, a former government agent, claimed to have been hired by Mrs Harding to spy on her husband's adulterous liaisons. The author's description of furious rows at the White House between Harding and his wife has been corroborated by other sources. His claim that Florence Harding 'confessed' to administering a fatal drug overdose to the President, in order to save him from impeachment, has never been corroborated and is unlikely to be true. Harding's health was extremely precarious by 1923 and cardiac arrest brought on by worry and overwork was almost certainly the cause of death. At least one physician, visiting the White House in March 1923, had predicted Harding would be dead within six months. Nevertheless, *Strange Death*'s melodramatic recounting of Mrs Harding administering the fatal dosage made it a best-seller:

His eyes were closed. He was resting ... then, suddenly, he opened his eyes wide ... and moved his head and looked straight into my face ... *You think he knew?*

Yes, I think he knew. Then he sighed and turned his head away – over – on the pillow .... After a few minutes, I called for help.[45]

The determination of Calvin Coolidge and the Republican party to disassociate themselves from the Teapot Dome scandals meant that Harding could be freely attacked as weak, unwise in his choice of friends, morally corrupt and unable to cope with the burdens of office. Interestingly, even his harshest critics did not suggest that Harding, himself, had taken part in the corrupt practices of the 'Ohio gang' which had followed him to Washington. As president, he had taken very seriously his responsibilities as a national leader and had, unfortunately, assumed his associates would do likewise.

The onset of the Great Depression and Second World War radically altered the American political consensus. New emphasis was placed on the virtues of an internationalist foreign policy, a strong, interventionist presidency and a large, high-spending government in Washington. The 'President of normalcy' was lazily dismissed by liberal historians as an irrelevance, a narrow-minded isolationist, a 'dunce' and a party 'hack'. Warren Harding was none of these things but, at least until the 1980s, it had become politically incorrect to say so.

In fact, Teapot Dome aside, the Harding presidency was largely a success. Its economic policies maintained their coherence, reduced the enormous public debt and helped foster the economic boom of the later 1920s, for which Harding's successor took the credit. It improved relations with Latin American countries, gained praise for its efforts on arms limitation and fought long-running battles with isolationists in Congress. Administration attitudes towards organised labour were hardly liberal, but they were also hardly out of step with majority opinion in both major political parties at the time. Its failure to pursue anti-lynching legislation resulted from congressional deadlock rather than any lack of sympathy on Harding's part. The administration's approval of the Sheppard-

Towner Act and its insatiable appetite for 'consultations' between government representatives and assorted delegations of farmers, union officials, black leaders and business entrepreneurs suggests that Harding's governing style was far more 'engaged', and more imaginative, than most historians allowed. His administration supported, often with government funds, the expansion of highway and radio networks, landmark reform of federal government budgeting, increased aid to agriculture, deep cuts in taxation, record tariffs, membership of the World Court, the overhaul of the shipping industry and expanded trade abroad. Assessments of the wisdom or desirability of these policies depend largely, of course, upon ideological perspective. Nevertheless, it was an oddly 'active' performance for such a reputedly 'lazy' administration.

One of the most interesting aspects of this short period was the change in the President himself, which was rapid and pronounced after 1920. He became a vigorous defender of presidential prerogative, a caustic critic of the Congress he had once held in high esteem and, most importantly, a disillusioned observer of partisan politics. Shortly before his death, Harding privately observed that the cause of the nation might be best served by the extinction of his own party. This 'metamorphosis' reflected his view of the presidency as a national office, not a party sinecure. It caused him to take decisions which alienated segments of his party, to ignore advice or demands from party leaders and to confront Congress rather than simply leaving the legislature to set the political agenda. His efforts did not always meet with success, nor were they always carried through, but, in the light of history's stereotypical portrait of Harding, it is a matter for considerable surprise that they were attempted at all.

With the reestablishment of conservative dominance in American politics since the 1980s has come a tentative reappraisal of Harding's tenure in office. The efforts of revisionists have so far failed to raise Warren Harding's name from the very bottom of the presidential rankings.

Notes

1. 'Tremendous Problems That Face Harding', *The Literary Digest*, New York, 5 March 1921, LXVIII: 10, p. 1.
2. This segment of his address reflected sentiments expressed in his July 1920 interview with the *Saturday Evening Post*, when Harding had criticised 'excessive wealth and its ofttimes insolent assumption of power.' *Saturday Evening Post*, 24 July 1920, p. 7.
3. 'Exit Wilson, Enter Harding', *The Outlook*, 16 March 1921, 127: 11, p. 415.
4. Murray, *The Harding Era*, p. 65.

5. Later invalidated by the Supreme Court for breaching constitutional guidelines on taxation powers.

6. Sherman Rogers, 'Senator Harding on Labor', *The Outlook*, 18 August 1920, p. 668.

7. 'Movie Morals Under Fire', *New York Times*, 12 February 1922, p. 80.

8. In 1927, an *Independent* article claiming the existence of a Jewish plot to monopolise wheat farming in the US led to court action by Aaron Sapiro, one of the named 'conspirators'. Both Ford and his newspaper editor denied the auto millionaire's involvement in, or even knowledge of, the *Independent*'s anti-Semitic rants and the action ended in a mistrial before Ford could be called to the stand. He then publicly apologised to Sapiro and to American Jews and closed the *Independent*.

9. 'Garvey Denounced at Negro Meeting', *New York Times*, 7 August 1922, p. 7.

10. 'Literacy tests' required black voters to read long, often complex texts to prove their competence to vote. Ill-educated whites were given easier tests or none at all. 'White primaries' treated parties as 'private' bodies when they engaged in internal nomination contests. This, some claimed, gave them the legal right to exclude any group from the process. Blacks thus lost their ability to choose between competing candidates for party nominations at the state level. Other exclusionary tactics included poll taxes, which poor blacks could not afford to pay.

11. Murray, *The Harding Era*, p. 399.

12. 'The Negro's Status Declared by the President', *The Literary Digest*, 19 November 1921, LXXI: 8, p. 9.

13. Ibid.

14. Ibid. p. 8.

15. 'The South and the President', *Florida Times-Union*, 5 November 1921. Warren G. Harding papers. Ohio State Historical Archive, Roll 230, #0964.

16. 'Report of the Senate Committee on Finance: Veterans' Adjusted Compensation Bill, 67th Congress, 1st session, Calendar 145, Report 133', *Senate Reports*, vol. 1, 20 June 1921, p. 1.

17. *Journal of the Senate of the United States*, 67th Congress, vol. 1, 12 July 1921 (Washington, DC: Government Printing Office, 1922), p. 193–4.

18. 'Why Harding Takes the Helm', *The Literary Digest*, 6 August 1921, LXX: 6.

19. Murray, *The Harding Era*, p. 127.

20. *The Literary Digest*, 6 August 1921, p. 12.

21. Letter: 'Arthur E. Colon to Warren G. Harding, 11 July 1921', Harding papers, Box 545, Folder 7.

22. *The Literary Digest*, 6 August 1921, p. 11.

23. Mark Sullivan, 'One Year of President Harding', *The World's Work*, November 1921, XLIII: 1, p. 29.

24. Letter: 'Warren G. Harding to Malcolm Jennings, 14 July 1921', Malcolm Jennings Collection, Harding Papers Roll 261, #0232.

25. Harry M. Daugherty, *The Inside Story of the Harding Tragedy* (Boston: Western Islands, 1975), p. 113.

26. Letter: 'Warren G. Harding to Malcolm Jennings, 6 January 1922', Folder J8.

27. Murray, *The Harding Era*, p. 113.

28. Oddly, given his broad 'laissez-faire' philosophy, Harding believed domestic and foreign broadcasting should be licensed by the federal government and his speech included a call for such regulation via the Department of Commerce. Federal licensing did not properly come into force, however, until 1927.

29. W. Richard Whitaker, 'Harding: First Radio President', *Northwest Ohio Quarterly*, 45: 3, pp. 75–6.
30. Whitaker, 'Harding: First Radio President', p. 78.
31. Paramount Studios became Paramount Pictures in 1935.
32. This particular merger gave a new twist to the 'rags-to-riches' story pleasing to East European immigrant communities. Louis B. Mayer was a Russian-Jewish immigrant who had started his working life as a scrap metal dealer.
33. Fox merged with Twentieth Century Pictures Company in 1935 to become Twentieth Century Fox. Warner Brothers was formed in 1923 by Jack, Sam, Harry and Albert Warner.
34. 'Movie Morals Under Fire', *New York Times*, 12 February 1922, p. 80.
35. Letter: 'Warren G. Harding to Al Jolson, 6 December 1921', Harding papers, Roll 229, #1092.
36. Wesley M. Bagby, *The Road to Normalcy: The Presidential Campaign and Election of 1920* (Baltimore: Johns Hopkins University Press, 1962), p. 101.
37. Stephen Ponder, *Managing the Press: Origins of the Media Presidency* (London: Macmillan Press, 1999), p. 114.
38. Karl Schriftgiesser, *This Was Normalcy* (New York: Oriole Editions, 1973), p. 121.
39. Samuel Hopkins Adams, *Incredible Era: The Life and Times of Warren Gamaliel Harding* (Boston: Houghton-Mifflin, 1939), p. 265.
40. Murray, *The Harding Era*, p. 316. At this point, Harding's attitude toward re-election seemed ambivalent. He expressed support for a proposed constitutional reform creating a single, six-year presidential term with no re-election option.
41. Murray, *The Harding Era*, p. 73.
42. Robert K. Murray, *The Politics of Normalcy: Governmental Theory and Practice in the Harding-Coolidge Era.* (New York: W. W. Norton and Company, 1973), p. 88.
43. Thomas Sugrue and Edmund W. Starling, *Starling of the White House* (New York: Simon and Schuster, 1946), p. 189.
44. Rumours persisted for many years after Smith's death that murder, rather than suicide, had taken place in the Wardman Park Hotel since there were numerous discrepancies in police descriptions of the death scene. Additionally, Smith was known to have had a pathological fear of guns and avoided contact with them.
45. May Dixon Thacker and Gaston B. Means, *The Strange Death of President Harding* (New York: Gold Label Books, 1930), p. 263. Means is an unreliable source who later served a prison sentence for fraud.

CHAPTER 3

Normalcy Abroad, 1921–3

The day of the Chinese wall, inclosing a hermit nation, has passed forever.[1]

Isolation and Engagement

In March 1921, President Harding and the new Secretary of State, Charles Evans Hughes, inherited probably the most complex set of foreign policy problems yet to confront an incoming administration. Most of the old European empires had disintegrated, international power balances were severely out of kilter and the economies of Europe were badly disrupted and, in some cases, on the point of collapse. Even after the signing of the Armistice, a typhus pandemic and the descent of Russia into civil war ensured that the mayhem and death of recent years would continue at least into the early part of the new decade. Amid the chaos, many European politicians looked to America for diplomatic reassurance and financial support. Some began to regard an alliance with the USA as a safeguard, backed by American military might, against future threats.

The war left its mark upon American society and affected the future development of both foreign and domestic policy. The spectacle of coffins of the nation's war dead being unloaded from transport ships strengthened the desire of many to reject further participation in international affairs. The impact of war upon the domestic economy was also severe, generating enormous profits in some sectors and hardship in others before 'readjustment' dragged the nation into a deep recession. For many ordinary citizens, peering through the gloom of 1920–1, involvement in the affairs of the wider world was associated with the fear of an immigrant flood and loss of employment as a result of cheaply bought foreign labour. It was also associated with the dark, brutal spectre of Soviet communism, which had set itself against virtually every totem of American society – representative democracy, freedom of speech, individual and states' rights, property rights and freedom of religious worship.

A less vocal strand of public and political opinion continued to argue that the United States had an active role to play in world affairs and that some form of 'association between nations' would play an essential role in preventing another worldwide armed conflict. Had the battle over Senate confirmation of the Treaty of Versailles not been reduced to a petty arm-wrestling contest between President Wilson and Henry Cabot Lodge, it is possible that US membership of the League of Nations, on amended terms, could have been achieved. Strong internationalist sentiments pervaded the business community in particular. American businessmen viewed the world in terms of market potential, not in terms of ideology or diplomacy. The expansion of the nation's international trade operations was considered not only essential to speed economic recovery but also desirable for the longer-term prospects of growth and investment. During the early 1920s, it was often, though not solely, pressure from American business concerns, the so-called 'dollar diplomacy', which stirred the Republican administrations of Warren Harding and Calvin Coolidge into diplomatic action. The activities of American oil companies, sugar refining manufacturers and other major enterprises operating in foreign countries inevitably influenced the domestic politics and economies of their hosts, which, in turn, affected diplomatic relations between the two countries.

Any incoming administration would therefore be caught between strong but countervailing forces which were active both in the political arena and amongst ordinary Americans. Isolationists and irreconcilables opposed any effort to involve the nation in 'foreign' law-making, mediating or enforcement institutions. Moderates were prepared to consider US involvement on certain, carefully specified, terms. Progressives opposed tightening immigration laws whilst conservatives and nativists favoured reducing the influx of foreign nationals to a trickle. Farmers and some sectors of industry supported high tariff barriers to prevent cheap foreign imports flooding the domestic market, whilst a vocal minority argued against this policy as damaging to American trade prospects abroad.

These divisions, and a host of more subtle differences, were difficult for Harding and Hughes to deal with effectively, since they were replicated inside *both* main political parties. Republicans tending towards isolationism stood with conservative Democrats and some progressive Republicans, whilst the party's moderate internationalists found occasional common cause with other Republican progressives and Wilsonian liberals. Complicating the picture still further was the intrusion of domestic political concerns into foreign policy debates, with ideological objections to international involvement sometimes traded off against the economic interests of Congress members' constituents. Harding was a moderate internationalist, not an isolationist. Perfectly capable of pandering to isolationist sentiment when partisan politics demanded, he was, nonetheless, sympathetic towards cooperative efforts aimed at peacefully reshaping the post-war world and believed America had a constructive role to play in such efforts. As President-elect, he had reassured Henry Cabot Lodge of his belief that the Wilson League was unworkable but added that he was 'equally convinced that the country does wish us ... to bring nations more closely together.' His motives were not entirely rooted in altruism. The President's sometimes rather simplistic political philosophy regarded the interests of business as congruent with those of American democracy and the spread of American economic influence as a positive development, both for the US and her trading partners. Isolationism, to the twenty-ninth President, was not only illogical it was not even good business sense.

This view was not universally accepted inside the Republican party. Progressives such as Hiram Johnson were deeply suspicious of big business, in particular the arms manufacturers who profited from war and the Standard Oil Company whose interests, Johnson contended, were a malign influence on American diplomacy and in the inner counsels of the Republican party itself. Johnson also remained convinced that any American involvement in international 'policing' bodies would lead inexorably towards the surrender of national sovereignty. Henry Cabot Lodge, like Johnson, had very little respect for either their new President or Secretary Hughes and suspected them of quietly plotting America's entry to the League of Nations 'by the backdoor'. Their fears were not entirely without foundation since, as noted in Chapter 1, neither Harding nor Hughes objected to close international cooperation, in principle, and Harding's main priority in any consideration of future involvement was to avoid a repetition of the 1919 debacle, *not* to avoid international involvement per se. The President understood that tentative steps towards internationalism could be made only with the support of Congress and the American public. There would be no repeat of Wilson's idealistic, one-man crusade. Secretary Hughes had similar convictions and was careful to avoid any impression of favouring extensive international cooperation. A pen-portrait of the new Secretary of State, published in 1921, noted: 'the thumbscrew and the rack could not wring from Mr Hughes the admission that we are after anything more lofty than our interests.'²

In early 1921, however, Harding knew that he had no alternative but to close the door upon Wilson's League. If one of the main aims of normalcy was to restore temperate and constructive dialogue to foreign policy debates, the running sore of the 1919–20 confrontation would have to be cauterised. Any effort to fudge the issue would have wrecked, from the start, any chance of forward movement. Lodge, Johnson and Borah were convinced that American voters had rendered an emphatically negative judgement on Wilsonian internationalism in the 1918 and 1920 elections and were perfectly prepared to immobilise the new administration's domestic and foreign policy agendas if necessary.

Harding's Special Message to Congress, on 12 April 1921, therefore contained the funeral oration for Woodrow Wilson's dream:

> In the existing League of Nations, world governing with its super-powers, this Republic will have no part. There can be no misinterpretation, and there will be no betrayal of the deliberate expression of the American people ... the League covenant can have no sanction by us.

The American government maintained contact with the League through its consulate in Geneva and unofficial observers were present at its opening session but these observers were 'powerless, helpless eagles without beaks or wings or talons.'³ A similar policy was adopted towards the Permanent Court of International Justice, operating under League auspices, which began sitting in January 1922.

Having finally rejected the League, the administration needed to close another chapter by bringing to a formal end the state of hostility which, technically, still existed between America and Germany. Although the Senate had passed the war resolution requested by President Wilson four years previously, Wilson himself had vetoed a resolution introduced by Senator Philander Knox in 1920 to have the war formally declared at an end. The White House viewed the Knox resolution as incompatible with the terms of the Versailles Treaty, which, it believed, could still be approved in the Senate and which would render the Knox resolution unnecessary. Negotiations between the House and Senate, with encouragement from Harding, produced a fresh resolution co-sponsored by Knox and Representative Stephen Porter, chairman of the House Foreign Affairs Committee, which was passed at the end of June.

After this was achieved, it would only remain for Secretary Hughes to handle the negotiation of individual peace agreements with each of America's erstwhile enemies – Germany, Hungary and Austria.

It only remained for the President of the United States to affix his signature to the document. This Harding did, in circumstances which were informal, even offhand, but peculiarly apt for the 'age of normalcy'. The joint resolution reached New Jersey on 2 July, where the President was on a two-day golfing holiday. White House aides lounged in chairs for some time before Harding ambled in, wearing his golfing attire and a red and green bow tie. He examined the papers, signed them, announced, 'That's all' and promptly returned to his game.

Peace and Disarmament

The administration had swiftly discharged its obligations to the irreconcilables, but the President was determined that the United States should, in some capacity, assume part of the responsibility for establishing a lasting peace. If this could not be achieved through the League, Harding and Hughes saw no practical reason why it could not be advanced in other ways. This view was shared, ironically enough, by the Senate's arch-irreconcilable, William Borah, who now proposed the calling of an international conference on disarmament and drastic reductions in American naval appropriations. The administration was anxious not to be out-manoeuvred by Borah, since success for the Senator's resolution would underline the view of Harding's detractors that the Senate, not the White House, dictated foreign policy. In fact, the President had broached the possibility of such a conference early in 1921 and, after a failed effort to have the wording of Borah's resolution watered down, he began using diplomatic 'back-channels' to sound out the opinions of the British and Japanese governments. When favourable responses returned, the White House announced to reporters on 10 July 1921 that invitations for a Washington Disarmament Conference had been issued. Press reaction to the news was overwhelmingly positive, although some newspapers speculated that it represented the first move in the campaign to create a new international association which had long been plotted by Harding and Hughes.

The President, whilst assuring reporters and nervous isolationists in Congress that it meant no such thing, had evidently learned the lessons of Woodrow Wilson's folly in playing partisan politics with conferences. Senators Lodge and Elihu Root were asked to join the official American delegation, along with Democratic senator Oscar Underwood, who had worked for Wilson during the campaign to endorse the Versailles treaty. Their presence would help reassure isolationists that American security and sovereignty would not be sacrificed. It may have occurred to Lodge at the time that, by accepting Harding's invitation, he was almost duty-bound to defend the administration against isolationist critics in Congress. Meanwhile, the President cobbled together a small coalition of twenty-one delegates to act as an 'advisory committee' and broaden public support for the conference and its aims. The committee members represented different regions of the country, different religious faiths and various sectors of the economy, including agriculture. Labour was represented in the form of Samuel L. Gompers, the long-serving president of the AFL. The scope of the conference was broader than Borah had wanted, since it included invitations to China, Italy and France to send representatives to Washington and also aimed to include *all* types of weaponry and military hardware in discussions, rather than just naval forces. This opened up the possibility of multiple treaties involving different combinations of nations, rather than a single, over-arching treaty – the favoured approach of US diplomacy throughout the 1920s.

Harding and Hughes were thoroughly prepared for the opening day of the conference. On 11 November, the President attended ceremonies to mark the burial of the Unknown Soldier in Arlington National Cemetery. His solemn speech, ending with the Lord's Prayer, served as an apt reminder of the reasons for calling the conference.

The next day, he entered the Pan-American Building in Washington to deliver a short speech, welcoming delegates to the conference and expressing, on behalf of the nation, his heartfelt desire for peace and disarmament: "I can speak officially only for our United States. Our hundred millions … want less of armament and none of war … we harbor no unworthy designs, we accredit the world with the same good intent."[4] As prearranged, the President then departed, as one reporter noted, 'still smiling and bowing bashfully' amidst a storm of applause. It was left to Secretary Hughes to drop the bombshell secretly agreed upon days earlier. Hughes' opening speech began with the predictable broad pronouncements on the desirability of peace. He continued,

> I am happy to say that I am at liberty to go beyond these general propositions and … acting under the instructions of the President of the United States, to submit to you a concrete proposition for an agreement for the limitation of naval armament.

The American plan consisted of proposals to scrap fifteen of its own existing battleships and fifteen currently scheduled for construction – a total of 845,740 tonnes of naval hardware. The Secretary called upon the startled British delegation to follow America's lead by scrapping twenty-three ships for a total of 583,000 tonnes. This included halting construction of the planned four new *Hoods* and the scrapping of the *King George V*. At this point, accounts of the conference recorded, Admiral Earl Beatty, seated with the British delegation, hunched forward in his chair and stared at Hughes in astonishment. The Japanese were requested to junk ten of their older vessels and seven new ones. The final naval tonnage after the cuts would be set at rations of 5:5:3 for Britain, America and Japan. French and Italian naval forces would stay within limits of 175,000 tonnes each. Production of replacement tonnage would be restricted to ensure that each country stayed within these limits, but replacements themselves would only be permitted after a ten-year moratorium on warship construction to be observed by all signatories. Tonnage restrictions were also to be placed upon aircraft carriers, with Britain and the United States permitted 135,000 tons each, and upon light cruisers. The Japanese delegation accepted the 5:5:3 ratio, though not enthusiastically, since it appeared to set in concrete the existing Anglo-American supremacy on the seas whilst dissolving pre-existing agreements between Japan and Britain. An attending Japanese official subsequently put his delegation's dissatisfaction into contemporary terms, deriding the 5:5:3 ratio as 'Rolls Royce: Rolls Royce: Ford.'

The scale of the American proposals startled foreign delegates, not least because no hint had been given in the weeks leading up to the conference that the administration had anything dramatic planned. Neither the domestic press, nor the foreign delegations had been warned in advance. Hughes and Harding sought, through this tactic, to generate an unstoppable momentum for disarmament. The tactic succeeded as a consequence of this, but also because the 'Five-Power Treaty' had widespread public support and because America, Britain and France in particular, were anxious to avoid placing extra pressure on their struggling economies by engaging in a costly naval arms race.

A separate 'Four-Power Treaty' was then negotiated, by which America, Britain, Japan and France agreed to respect each other's territorial rights and acquisitions in the Pacific and pledged to resolve differences through negotiation. The Americans arranged a separate deal with Japan to ensure continued US access to and use of international cable facilities on the Pacific island of Yap.

A 'Nine-Power Treaty' emerged from discussions over China. Under the agreement, signatory nations – China, the United States, Britain, France, Japan, Belgium, Holland, Italy and Portugal – pledged respect for Chinese sovereignty and fair, reciprocal trading arrangements in return for the Chinese government's pledge to respect the rights of foreign nationals to pursue commercial activities inside China.

The conference lasted for twelve weeks and, when it concluded on 6 February 1922, was universally regarded as a historic event in which, for the first time, the major powers had agreed to restrain armaments production, at least in naval terms, scale back existing arsenals and enact a framework of legally binding agreements to prevent future tensions leading to war. Some critics pointed out that the continued production of naval destroyers and submarines and the destructive capacity of air force and army weaponry had not been addressed. Hiram Johnson protested that the Four-Power Treaty had not been negotiated in open session, as had the others, but behind closed doors. These complaints failed to dent the consensus that the Washington conference had been a landmark achievement. Johnson, Borah and other Senate critics faced a dilemma. Lodge and Root, both powerful and respected within the Republican party and both cynical about any attempt to tie America into a formal international body like the League of Nations, had been part of the US delegation. Their imprimatur on the agreements reached at the conference made it difficult for Johnson to rally opposition. Further, as Borah had consistently argued that separate, interlocking agreements were more workable and infinitely preferable for the United States, they would find it hard to attack the Washington accords without inadvertently proving the claim of internationalists that only the League could be effective in securing world peace.

In the long term, the Washington conference failed to prevent the resumption of a competitive arms race or to reduce tensions in the Pacific. It was, nevertheless, an important development in post-war American foreign policy and the first of a series of efforts by the Harding and (to a lesser extent) Coolidge administrations designed to stabilise international affairs and reduce the risk of war. Though the Washington conference, and later initiatives such as the Kellogg-Briand Pact of 1928, were attacked by critics as 'naive' or 'unworkable', there were very few alternative strategies available to administrations of the 1920s.

Debts and Reparations

The question of the indebtedness of America's wartime allies was a complex one. It affected the direction of Harding administration foreign policy, particularly its attitudes to Europe. It also had vital ramifications for the shattered German economy and, to a lesser degree, for the Harding-Mellon domestic economic strategy. It impacted heavily upon US relations with other countries, particularly Great Britain, and upon her ability to engage in constructive negotiations at international conferences.

The US had contributed $10.3 billion to the war effort, money which both the Wilson and Harding administrations regarded as, in Andrew Mellon's words, 'loans, not contributions'. By the early 1920s, with their economic resources depleted, debtor nations such as Great Britain and France tried to argue that war financing had been a collective effort for the rescue of democracy and that they, too, had invested heavily, in terms of guns, ships, ammunition, tanks, and equipment. They pointed out, accurately enough, that much of the war materials they used had been purchased on the American market and that debt repayments should be reduced to account for the profits made by US manufacturers. The Wilson administration had refused to concede the point, even as economic chaos in Europe threatened to cause widespread debt defaulting and even as high American tariff barriers prevented Europe from raising the dollars needed to pay their debts through trade. Harding was powerless to lower tariff barriers, even if he had wanted to, since any such move would be blocked by farmers, manufacturers and isolationists.

Recognising that a clear structure needed to be imposed on the repayments process, Congress passed a Debt Funding Act on 9 February 1922, establishing a World War Foreign Debt Commission to oversee repayment agreements. The Act set a time limit for final repayments (15 June 1947) and a minimum interest rate ($4.25%). President Harding and Secretaries Mellon, Hughes and Hoover were disposed to greater flexibility, however, and when Stanley Baldwin, Britain's Chancellor of the Exchequer, arrived in the US for talks in January 1923, he found his American counterparts quietly prepared to ignore congressional guidelines. On 19 January, an agreement was reached for a sixty-two-year payment plan, with twice-yearly payments at 3.3 per cent interest for the first decade and 3.5 per cent for the following fifty-two years. Britain would thus discharge its debt in full by 1985. Harding could not be sure of Congress' response to this flouting of its authority, particularly as the British deal seemed so out of kilter with normalcy's agenda of spending cuts and national debt reduction. The President thus lobbied hard for Senate approval. 'Here,' he announced poetically, 'is the first clearing of the war-clouded skies in a debt-burdened world.'

Despite opposition from Hiram Johnson, who complained that America would be regarded as 'an international sucker', the Senate approved the British deal, thereby opening the way for separate negoti-ations with thirteen other debtor nations. European economic problems caused repayments to cease altogether after 1933, but the rescheduling undertaken by both the Harding and Coolidge administrations, softened, at least to some extent, the intractable, self-centred image America had been acquiring in Europe since Versailles.

The issue of allied repayments also impacted heavily on the economic condition of Germany. Initially, $33 billion in reparations had been demanded of the fragile Weimar Republic, with $375 million to be repaid in 1921–5 alone. Germany fell prey to a vicious circle of financial demands in which the Allies, desperate for funds to repay their own debts, pres-sured Germany for faster reparations payments, further crippling the German economy. The defeated nation's inability to meet the demands caused it to default on payments, leading France and Belgium to occupy the Ruhr in January 1923. The increasing economic chaos in Europe now threatened to upset not only the American economy, by devastating potential markets for American goods, but also her diplomatic efforts to secure disarmament agreements. The priority was clear, as Mellon declared in December 1922, 'there can be no economic recuperation in Europe unless Germany recuperates.'

The result was the August 1924 'Dawes plan' to rescue the German economy. Under the plan, a twelve-month moratorium on reparations was allowed, to be followed by reparations payments of $250 million a year. The German currency was stabilised using the gold standard, after a period of wild inflation which had seen German workers trundling their wages home in wheelbarrows full of virtually worthless banknotes. A new Reichsbank was set up and a loan of $200 million in gold was jointly furnished by the US, UK and France. The plan had its drawbacks, chief amongst them being the absence of any flexibility in the $250 million annual reparations payment to account for future fluctuations in the health of the German economy.[5] Further, Germany was now simply paying reparations to the Allies using the loan monies it had just received from them. However, the immediate meltdown of the German economy, with its attendant consequences for European stability and world trade, had been averted.

America and Russia

The era of normalcy in the United States coincided with the consolidation of communism's grip upon Russia. Although the Bolshevik coup had taken place in November 1917, it was almost four years before Lenin and Trotsky succeeded in ending the civil war by beating back the White counter-revolutionary forces, led first by Kolchak and, later, by Deniken, and by repelling the American, French and British forces which supported them. Upon taking office in March 1921, Harding was the first American president to face a fully fledged Soviet government in Moscow – a government fundamentally hostile to Western capitalism and democracy not simply on ideological grounds but also as a consequence of President Wilson's military intervention in Siberia. The question of opening formal diplomatic relations with the new Russian Soviet Federated Socialist Republic (RSFSR) was a difficult one for the American State Department. Hostility to the new regime and to the doctrines of communism was so intense in Congress, and across the nation, that Harding and Hughes were compelled to move slowly and cautiously. The nation had neither forgotten, nor forgiven the 1918 Brest-Litovsk agreement, through which the Bolsheviks had bought peace for Russia and breathing space for the revolution in a treaty with Kaiser Wilhelm II's government which could have fatally undermined the Allied war effort.

President Wilson had refused any suggestion of formal recognition of the Soviet government until a pledge was received to honour the treaty obligations, trade agreements and debts of the former Tsarist and Provisional governments. To do otherwise, Wilson and his Secretary of State, Bainbridge Colby, had argued, would be to legitimise arbitrary land and property seizures, condone murder and persecution and, effectively, to support the overthrow of traditional diplomatic conventions, creating anarchy in international relations.

From 1921, with the revolution a *fait accompli* and Lenin firmly ensconced in the Kremlin, President Harding was willing at least to reconsider the pros and cons of recognition. His cautious, conservative approach was, ironically, countered by the loud demands for immediate recognition made in Congress by Senator Borah. The 'Lion of Idaho' maintained that the Russian people had the right to establish whatever governing system they chose inside their own country.

The 'best minds' cabinet opposed the idea, however, unless certain clear guiding principles were endorsed by the Soviet government – 'the safety of life, the recognition ... of private property, the sanctity of contract and the rights of free labor.'

The American government considered its position on this issue separately from the response it knew it must give to the growing humanitarian disaster of the Volga famine. In August 1921, with more than 30,000,000 facing death from starvation in the Volga region, the administration authorised Commerce Secretary Hoover to set up a 'relief administration', operating over 18,000 stations across Russia to organise the distribution of food and medical aid to more than 10,000,000 people. The move pleased American farmers, who were able to send a sizeable amount of their grain surplus overseas. Although a large amount of aid was generated by private capital, the federal government contributed $28 million, thus putting a sizeable dent in the government's budget plans. Hoover considered the expense worth the effort, not only to forestall catastrophe but also because the central governing body in Russia, the *Sovnarkom*, was beginning to experiment with modified capitalism through its 'New Economic Policy' (NEP). Hoover conjectured that the success of the famine relief operation might persuade Moscow to modify its more extreme left-wing policies.[6] This prospect appealed to the Commerce Secretary, who believed that much of foreign policy was dictated not by diplomats but by business entrepreneurs and the movements of capital. Hughes, however, believed firmly in the importance of observing diplomatic conventions. Throughout the 1921–3 period, he was dealing simultaneously with the question of recognition of the government of Mexico, his objections to which were almost exactly the same. Since it was not politically justifiable to adopt two diametrically opposed policies to the same problem, Lenin's flirtation with capitalism failed to impress the State Department.

Harding would not go against his Secretary of State over this matter and refused to send a delegation to an international conference in Genoa to discuss aid to Eastern Europe in case pressure was exerted on the US to recognise the RSFSR.[7] The President continued to maintain a close interest in Russian-American relations and, in 1923, gave his personal assent to private visits to Russia by Interior Secretary Albert Fall and Raymond Robbins, a progressive Republican from Wisconsin. Harding died before Fall or Robbins could report but it was unlikely their report would have altered the administration's 'wait-and-see' policy. Domestic politics and the conventions of diplomacy made recognition an impossible move for Harding, even if he had favoured it.

Latin American and Caribbean Relations

Normalcy's policies toward Latin America and the Caribbean were an interesting mixture of reform and retrenchment, idealistic proclamations of good neighbourliness and 'dollar diplomacy'. At the outset of the Twenties, relations between the United States and the governments of Haiti, Cuba, the Dominican Republic, Puerto Rico, Nicaragua, Colombia and Mexico were at low ebb. US foreign policy since the late nineteenth century was regarded across Latin America as exploitative and imperialistic, a view with which Harding, as a member of the Senate Foreign Relations Committee, had not been entirely unsympathetic. As a presidential candidate, he had questioned the wisdom of President Wilson's military interventions in the region and scathingly criticised the young Democratic vice-presidential candidate, Franklin D. Roosevelt, for his cheery boast, in 1920, that he had had 'something to do with the running of a couple of little republics ... I wrote Haiti's constitution myself.' Such arrogance, Harding proclaimed, 'made enemies of those who should be our friends.'

The new President had a particular interest in Latin American affairs. This was partly based upon the natural calculations of a pro-business conservative that stable, cooperative relations between the US and her neighbours were necessary for American businesses to profit from their investments. It also stemmed from a deep-seated uneasiness, shared by many Americans, at the trend towards armed intervention, on a short or long-term basis, which had characterised American policy in Latin America and the Caribbean since the Spanish-American war broke out in 1898. These interventions were viewed by the President as potentially dangerous, no matter how much sabre-rattling 'expansionists' dressed them up as 'civilising' crusades. Harding did not necessarily disagree with the widely held view that the 'little brown brother' would benefit from the adoption of American cultural, political and economic values but, at the same time, he believed that imperialistic designs subverted the purposes of America's 'Founding Fathers' by pushing the nation towards a policy of colonialism for its own sake.[8] His principle objective in developing policy approaches to the region with Secretary Hughes was to terminate existing American military commitments as soon as conditions inside the country concerned permitted whilst avoiding future armed intervention unless it was considered absolutely necessary. In achieving this, the administration was pledged, as its predecessors had been, to ensuring that the basic tenets of the Monroe Doctrine, forbidding foreign intervention in America's backyard, were not threatened.

In Cuba, therefore, troops ordered into Camaguey Province during the Wilson administration were withdrawn by Harding and negotiations were opened to allow Cuba to press her territorial claim to the Isle of Pines. The State Department also arbitrated boundary quarrels between Costa Rica and Panama, in 1921, and between Peru and Chile in 1922, securing peaceful settlements which generated a modest improvement in the reputation of US diplomacy. This improvement was sealed by the signing of the Colombian Treaty, on 20 April 1921, which mandated payment of $25 million to Colombia as an 'apology' (though the word was not used) for US involvement in the 1903 Panamanian Revolution which had deprived Colombia of its former territory. The idea for the goodwill gesture did not originate with Harding but, typically, he pushed for it in the knowledge that it would facilitate easier access to the Colombian oilfields for American developers.

In the Dominican Republic, the administration prepared for the removal of the occupation force sent in by Wilson in 1916. Secretary Hughes, together with Special Envoy Sumner Welles, laid out plans for the stabilisation of the Republic's social and political structures, opening the way for a final withdrawal in September 1924. Haiti proved a tougher proposition. Diplomats stationed in Port-au-Prince warned the State Department that chaos would be the consequence of withdrawal unless the operation was phased in over a long period and remained contingent upon fiscal and social stability. Nevertheless, the White House continued to prod the State Department and officials in Haiti to prepare the ground as rapidly as possible.

In other areas, the administration engaged in gesture politics to demonstrate its friendly intentions. Harding made his first post-inauguration trip outside Washington to New York on 19 April 1921 to dedicate a statue of Simon Bolivar, sent as a gift to the city by the Venezuelan government. The move was intended to underline Harding's commitment to fostering good relations between the two countries. The United States played an active role in the 1922 Central American Conference, from which emerged treaties aimed at fostering closer cultural ties, improving economic relations and reducing the likelihood of armed conflict. Although it was never prepared to go as far as to renounce completely the right to armed intervention in defence of American lives or business interests, the administration's efforts to reduce the likelihood of such action met with a positive response.

Speaking in Rio de Janeiro, on 8 September 1922, Hughes laid out the basis of what was, to all intents and purposes, the 'Good Neighbour' policy of the future Roosevelt administration of the 1930s. 'We covet no territory; we seek no conquest; the liberty we cherish for ourselves we desire for others and we assert no rights for ourselves that we do not accord to others.'[9] These sentiments, applauded throughout Latin America, were particularly welcomed by Mexico. Throughout the Wilson years, relations between the United States and successive Mexican regimes had been marked by sporadic violence and the threat of full-scale military conflict. The American government, hoping for the installation of a democratic regime friendly to the United States, had refused diplomatic recognition to the usurping government of Victoriano Huerta, which had overthrown and killed the reformist president Fransisco Madero in 1913. Tensions between the US and Mexico escalated further in 1914, after the arrest of American sailors at Tampico, prompting Wilson quickly, though reluctantly, to ratchet up the pressure on Huerta by ordering American marines to occupy the port of Vera Cruz in April 1914. The President tacitly encouraged rebellions against Huerta by Venustiano Carranza and Fransisco ('Pancho') Villa, as a result of which, Huerta eventually fled the country. The forces of Carranza and Villa proceeded to fight amongst themselves for control of the government. Wilson initially withheld recognition from Carranza until it became evident that the victory of Villa would not be in America's interests. After the murder of thirty-three Americans by Villa's forces, early in 1916, Wilson dispatched General John J. Pershing on an ultimately fruitless mission to capture or kill the rebel leader.[10] Carranza provided more diplomatic headaches for the American government by instituting economic and agrarian reforms which threatened the rights of American property-holders in Mexico. Congress established a committee, under New Mexico Senator Albert Fall, to examine the problem.

America's entry into World War One put the 'Mexican problem' temporarily on ice until, in May 1920, Carranza was overthrown by General Alvaro Obregon. In the same month, the Fall Committee announced its findings that Mexico was no longer a safe place for

American investment or citizens and that a warning should be issued to the Mexican government implying possible US military action if conditions did not improve.

Although Obregon was democratically elected to the presidency in December 1920, the American government refused to grant diplomatic recognition unless the new regime guaranteed, *by formal treaty*, the security of American property and business investments, together with restoration of lost property or compensation for damages incurred by American citizens and businesses during years of political and military conflict.

This hard-line policy was picked up by the new Republican administration. Secretary Hughes was particularly concerned by the sweeping confiscatory powers deriving from Article 27 of the Mexican constitution (adopted by Carranza in 1917). The article stated that 'subsoil rights' belonged entirely to the Mexican people. If applied retroactively, this law would strip American oil and mining companies of their land and assets at the whim of the Mexican government.

In May 1921, Hughes pressed for a formal Treaty of Amity and Commerce between the United States and Mexico, guaranteeing that land titles and subsoil rights granted to American citizens *before* 1917 would not be retroactively revoked and that the numerous social and economic reforms promised to the people of Mexico by its government would not harm American property or investments in any way. Additionally, all American losses sustained since 1910 should be either returned or financially compensated and to increase the pressure on the Obregon government, heavy investors in the Mexican economy, such as J. P. Morgan, were encouraged by the State Department to withhold investment and refuse loans until treaty negotiations began.

Hughes was not alone in his view that the ability of any regime to (1) meet its international financial obligations and (2) guarantee the safety of foreign nationals living and working inside their borders, as well as the inviolability of their property rights, were the fundamental prerequisites for diplomatic recognition of one nation by another. Obregon, however, regarded the State Department edicts as an affront to Mexico's dignity, a threat to its sovereignty and an attempt to undermine his government's ability to control its own domestic economy or natural resources.

The Mexican leader wrote to Harding in June 1921, assuring him that all claims by American citizens could be settled in good faith *without* resort to a formal treaty. He also gave an assurance that Article 27 would not be applied retroactively and that the rights of US citizens would be protected. Harding, satisfied with this 'good faith' declaration, wanted to recognise the Obregon government immediately and stabilise diplomatic and economic relations but he faced strong opposition from conservatives in Congress who did not trust Obregon's word. Albert Fall was now Secretary of the Interior and thus able to bring pressure to bear upon Harding from inside the cabinet. This did not help improve Mexican faith in American intentions, since Fall had once publicly advocated the overthrow of Huerta and the occupation of Mexico by 500,000 US troops.

Business leaders, however, were becoming increasingly concerned at the damage which anti-American sentiment in Mexico could inflict on their existing commercial operations and capital investments. These concerns were transmitted to Harding by his own private business contacts, persuading him to suggest to Hughes that a more flexible attitude from the State Department on the issue of recognition might well give Obregon the opportunity he needed to 'avoid the appearance of submission to our dictation' thus 'closing the Mexican business' once and for all. The President was reacting, in part, to intelligence from inside Mexico which suggested that the regime's opponents were planning to use the humiliation of Obregon at the hands of the United States to destabilise his government and replace it with a more radical and openly hostile one.

Despite this possibility, the impasse continued. Diplomatic letters and cables, exchanged between the State Department and the Mexican government during 1921–2 produced only the monotonous restatement of already established positions. Frustrated, Harding dispatched one of his own private business contacts, General James A. Ryan, an official of the Texas Oil Company, to sound out Obregon informally. Ryan reported back to the White House his impression that the Mexican leader genuinely desired an amicable settlement and shared Harding's frustration at the deadlock.

Fortuitously, the Mexican Supreme Court ruled, in 1922, that oil leases could not be retroactively revoked under Article 27. Mexico subsequently reached an agreement on a timetable for the settlement of her foreign debts with international banks. Reassured, Hughes fell into line behind the President and supported the de-coupling of the issue of recognition from the conclusion of a formal treaty. Ryan proceeded to arrange a conference on the question of claims settlements, which opened in Mexico City in May 1923. Delegates to the meeting agreed to arrange conventions for *separate* arbitration of 'special' claims, for losses incurred by US citizens during upheavals of 1910–20, and of 'general' claims made by both countries dating back to 1868. Consequently, the green light was given for formal diplomatic recognition of Obregon's government on 31 August 1923 – twenty-nine days after President Harding's death. It was to be eighteen years, however, before all the claims presented for arbitration were settled.

The Mexican recognition issue provided an interesting insight into the operation of US foreign policy under Harding and Hughes. Harding instinctively opted for a pragmatic approach, preferring to circumvent obstacles rather than charge head down at them. Whilst accepting his Secretary of State's insistence on a formal treaty, Harding reached out in other directions. His decision to send a private envoy from *outside* the State Department proved crucial in resolving the problem, by helping to convince Obregon that the settlement of debts and a judicial ruling on non-retroactive application of Article 27 would remove any need for a treaty declaring the submission of the Mexican government to Washington's dictates.

Administration policies in the Latin American and Caribbean regions displayed coherence and a certain degree of imagination. They reflected, particularly, Harding's views that 'normalcy' did not mean sullen isolation. He preferred cooperation over dictation, negotiation rather than conflict and was not inclined to browbeat other regimes for their failure to adopt American morals and values. A prime objective of this approach was, of course, to stabilise regimes in the region, thus permitting American trade and oil exploration to flourish. Nevertheless, it was widely regarded as a more 'enlightened' approach than that used in previous years. In the 1920s, Hughes stated, America would aim to be 'co-workers with our sister Republics and not masters.'

The World Court

The issue of US membership of the Permanent Court of International Justice came to dominate the last stages of the Harding administration, embroiling the increasingly exhausted and ailing President in a dispute which threatened to divide the Republican party and revive the controversies which had attended the League of Nations debate of 1919–20. Like Wilson, Harding appealed over the heads of congressional leaders to the American public. Like Wilson, he embarked on a tour of the country to publicise the issue. Finally, Harding's health, like Wilson's buckled under the strain – this time with fatal consequences.

The President had, since the 1920 elections, consistently maintained that American participation in efforts to construct new forums for the mediation and peaceful resolution of international disputes was highly desirable. In his 12 April 1921 address to Congress, the President had declared, 'we pledged our efforts in the direction of world political cooperation and the pledge will be faithfully kept.'

The 'law not war' principle was also supported by Secretary Hughes. Both men, however, faced a highly vocal minority of isolationists. Hiram Johnson's self-appointed role as 'guardian of the back door' was, to Hughes and Harding, simple 'obstructionism' of a radical, indiscriminate and dangerous nature. Johnson's differences with Harding had emerged during the time when both men had served on the Senate Foreign Relations Committee. Harding had favoured 'unofficial' US participation in, or observation of, international negotiations and agreements and had strongly supported the expansion of US trade links abroad. Johnson opposed both, viewing informal participation as one step removed from official involvement and held American armaments manufacturers, amongst other business interests, responsible for pushing the US into the European war. As a result of these differences, Johnson became convinced that Harding was an incipient 'internationalist' – a judgement which was, to an extent, correct. The California senator's distrust was increased by the appointments to the cabinet of Hughes and Hoover. Both men, he considered, were deliberately downplaying their internationalist leanings until a more favourable political climate gave them the confidence of their convictions.

As if to confirm Johnson's suspicions, the President, in 1921, authorised Charles Evans Hughes and Chief Justice Taft to take quiet soundings of European political and diplomatic officials on the possibility of US membership of the World Court. These consultations were aimed at establishing under what *conditions* American membership would be acceptable to the World Court's other member states. Since the State Department could effortlessly predict the list of objections and concerns which would be raised by Johnson, Borah, Brandegee and other irreconcilables, it was determined to pre-empt them by suggesting its own special conditions for membership, agreed a priori with existing Court members.

First, it would be categorically stated by the administration that US membership of the Court would *not*, under *any* circumstances, imply League membership, the likelihood or possibility of League membership or any formal or informal obligation of the United States to the League. Second, Court membership would bring with it the right of American members to participate in the election of Court judges, *despite* the fact that, technically, only participating League members who were also members of the Court currently held this power. Third, congressional appropriations resolutions, *not* Court requirements, would decide the extent of America's financial commitment to the Court. Finally, the original statutes upon which the Court was founded could only be amended with US approval.

With these conditions, Harding and Hughes hoped to circumvent or neutralise much of the opposition to Court membership expected from isolationists in Congress. It was also calculated that such conditions would strengthen public support for the scheme.

Harding caught Senate leaders on the hop by submitting a formal proposal for Court membership on 24 February 1923, without prior warning and only a week before Congress was due to adjourn. This tactic may have reflected Harding's desire to increase the pressure on his rebellious party, in the aftermath of their 1922 mid-term election losses, to fall in line behind the White House. It may also been designed to deprive Court opponents of a chance to marshal their forces in the national legislature before the formal recess – a tactic used by several of Harding's predecessors.

Despite this, battle-lines were quickly drawn. Lodge, Borah, Johnson, Brandegee and LaFollette, aided by other isolationists, including Medill McCormick and New Hampshire Republican George Moses claimed the administration was opting for League membership via the back door. Harding countered, with substantial press support, that the conditions outlined by the administration rendered such an argument nonsensical. America would not, the President insisted, enter the League, 'by the back door, or the side door or the cellar door.' It was, nevertheless, 'a God-given duty to give of our influence to establish the ways of peace throughout the world.' Beyond Congress, organisations such as the US Chamber of Commerce and the Federal Council of Churches supported the White House, as did the larger part of the nation's press (although William Randolph Hearst's influential chain remained implacably opposed). William Jennings Bryan added his voice to calls to join the Court, as did the presidents of Harvard and Stanford universities, former Supreme Court Justice Clarke and assorted peace organisations. The statements of support from many of these individuals and groups often clumsily undermined Harding's carefully planned strategy by expressing the additional hope that American entry into the League of Nations might eventually result from success with the Court. Since the League was, by 1923, considered a 'dead' issue and generally produced either disinterest or cynicism amongst voters, such sentiments merely provided ammunition to Harding's delighted opponents.

The most interesting aspect of the Court battle and, for Harding, the most dangerous, lay in its effect upon relations between the President and his Republican colleagues. The White House knew that, some mischief-makers aside, most Democrats could be counted on to support Court membership, either as a substitute for or as a preliminary step towards adherence to the League. Pro-League Nebraska senator, Gilbert Hitchcock, chortled, 'It looks as if we may get in on the instalment plan.'

Congressional Republicans were, predictably, less united. In the last months of his life, Harding became grimly determined to whip his party into line, whatever the political cost. He reminded party leaders that the Republican platform of 1920 and most of the President's pronounce-ments on international involvement since then, had reiterated their willingness to engage with other nations in considering new forums for cooperation. If they now chose to abandon this commitment it was the *party*, rather than the presidency, which needed to re-examine its attitudes. Harding stated, 'In simple truth, I get discouraged about the stability of popular government when I come in contact with the abject surrender of public men to what appears to be one half of one percent of the voters ...'[11]

This may partly explain why the President invested more time and effort in the World Court campaign than in any other single foreign policy issue. Available evidence suggests that he regarded the World Court as the 'make-or-break' issue for America's diplomatic influence, for the future of the Republican party and for his own presidency. Having endured more than two years of frustration and delay at the hands of congressional Republicans, his patience was finally worn out. He confided to Secretary of War John W. Weeks, 'I should be quite without respect for myself ... if I turned tail and ran away ... because of threatened political embarrassments.'[12]

On 20 June 1923, the President, the First Lady and several cabinet members including Hubert Work, Albert Fall's replacement as Interior Secretary, left Washington D.C. aboard the presidential train, the *Superb*, for a 15,000-mile speaking tour of the Mid-west and western

United States and Alaska. Although not specifically described as such by the White House, the tour was widely regarded as Harding's attempt to stir public opinion in favour of the World Court. The 'Voyage of Understanding' was also, effectively, the first round of the 1924 presidential election campaign and some of the states selected for presidential visits were important farm belt bulwarks of the Republican party such as Kansas. The tour prioritised these in order to forestall a possible revolt by farmers against Republican agricultural policies. Other states encompassed by the trip included Missouri, Colorado, Utah, Ohio, Indiana, Idaho, Oregon and California. The President was scheduled to deliver eighty-five speeches in six weeks and the first of these, on the subject of the World Court, was given in Missouri, where a resolutely unimpressed audience, sat mostly in silence, heard the President condemn those who wished to see the United States become a 'hermit nation'. Harding appealed to his audience's sense of humanity and Christian spirit, in a speaking style which was emotionally charged and, for Harding, unusually focused. He stressed his detestation of war and his wish that the United States should join with other nations in an effort to create a lasting peace. He closed,

> I could not do otherwise. My soul yearns for peace. My heart is anguished by the sufferings of war. My spirit is eager to serve. My passion is for justice over force. My hope is in the great Court. My mind is made up.[13]

Harding's rhetoric on the matter of the Court was reminiscent of Wilson's anguished pleading during his 1919 speaking tour. What is particularly interesting, however, is that Wilson had no room for manoeuvre in terms of the *timing* of the debate over the League, an issue which arose from the Paris peace talks and which, inevitably, dominated national and international political discourse, Harding *chose* to provoke a firestorm over the World Court. Although internationalists continually pressured the White House for positive action on the Court in 1921 and 1922, the President could have continued, had he so wished, to sidestep or fudge the issue in 1923. There was no surging public demand for Court membership and even less voter interest in it than that displayed towards the League in 1920. Nothing, aside from Harding's own convictions, required the President to place his own authority and his future in office on the line by poking the dozing lions of isolationism with a sharp presidential stick.

Hiram Johnson, once roused, was determined to force the President onto the defensive. On 25 July, speaking on the other side of the country at New York's Waldorf-Astoria, the 'great irreconcilable' argued that Europe should be left to attend to its own affairs, particularly as their interest in American participation was, in reality, an interest in employing American money and arms for their own political and territorial purposes. The World Court, he claimed, was 'part of the League machinery' and an 'utterly futile agency for peace.' Johnson knew that he and the President, his one-time colleague on the Senate Foreign Relations Committee, differed sharply in their perspectives on foreign affairs. Surprised and alarmed by the White House's assault, he lashed out at Harding himself, hinting that the President was being controlled by the internationalists Hughes and Hoover. Referring, ominously, to 'the administration for the moment in power', he declared,

> Some of us will neither be cajoled nor driven nor browbeaten into advocacy of a foreign policy at variance with what we deem our country's weal. What we condemned under a Democratic administration we will not accept under a Republican administration.[14]

During the 'Voyage of Understanding', the President indicated that he was still open to negotiation over the *terms* upon which America would enter the Court. He was, for example, prepared to press the Court's current membership to detach the process of electing judges from League of Nations supervision. 'The big thing is the formal establishment of the court ...' Harding said, in a speech to have been delivered in San Francisco, 'All else is mere detail.' By the beginning of August 1923, however, there was no indication that the Senate's irreconcilables were prepared to negotiate under any conditions whatsoever. A head-on collision, with either the presidency or the congressional Republican leadership humiliated and effectively disempowered, was prevented only by Harding's sudden death on 2 August.

American foreign policy in the 1921-3 period operated in, and was strongly influenced by, harsh social and economic conditions abroad and highly charged partisanship and ideological division in domestic politics. Under these conditions, it is to their credit that Harding and Hughes managed to attain any of their objectives. In the cases of both the League of Nations and the World Court, the administration worked under exceedingly difficult conditions to end the bitter divisions generated by the former whilst making incremental steps towards the latter. Considered alongside its willingness to engage the irreconcilables in Congress over the Court and the 1922 naval treaties and its encouragement of the expansion of trading links, it becomes clear that traditional views of the 1921–3 administration as 'isolationist' are somewhat misguided. High tariff barriers were certainly in operation throughout the period but these were raised in reaction to the deep recession of 1920–1. Though some of the supporters of protectionism were undoubtedly motivated by hostility towards international involvement, it is likely that the administration was wedded to high tariffs only as long as they were considered economically necessary and only as long as their removal by Congress was politically unfeasible. Also erroneous is the assumption, widely held by historians, that Harding generally left foreign policy to the State Department and showed no interest in, nor understanding of, foreign policy problems. The twenty-ninth President was far more engaged with international issues than his successor as, again, the memoirs of his Secretary of State suggest.

The Harding-Hughes-Hoover nexus was the key organising and motivational influence of administration foreign policy in the early 1920s. To this fascinating relationship, each man brought their own particular skills. Harding contributed political shrewdness, an instinctive ability to define areas in which compromise between contending factions was possible, skill in communicating administration policies to the American public and a willingness, where necessary, to delegate authority and share credit or blame. Neither Hughes nor Hoover, despite their other undoubted talents, possessed any of these strengths, which possibly explains why both, later in their careers, expressed high regard for Harding's management skills and role as 'team leader'. Hughes contributed diplomatic skill, legal expertise and a reputation for integrity which made him well-respected by foreign leaders. Hoover brought to the relationship his unmatched organisational talent, his conviction that America's future lay in commercial expansion and his ability to consider innovations or solutions *outside* of the domestic political context. Harding was also capable of this but, as President, was forced to anticipate and deal with partisan demands from Congress.

As a consequence, American foreign policy under Harding was more stable and coherent and less subject to the whims and caprices of the Chief Executive than had been the case under Theodore Roosevelt or Woodrow Wilson. It consistently recognised political realities, as its approach to tariffs and the League problem demonstrated, but did not shirk from engaging in, or even provoking, heated debates when the situation demanded them, as the naval treaties and World Court campaign indicate. It operated, at all times, with an emphasis upon dialogue, flexibility, cooperation and incrementalism. For liberals who favoured Wilsonian internationalism, this was simply not enough. For conservative believers in the policy of 'America first' it was far too much.

Notes

1. Warren G. Harding speech on Canadian-American relations, July 1923.
2. Anonymous, *The Mirrors of Washington* (New York: G. P. Putnam's Sons, 1921), p. 82.
3. Andrew Sinclair, *The Available Man: The Life Behind the Masks of Warren Gamaliel Harding* (New York: Macmillan Company, 1965), p. 207.
4. Mark Sullivan, 'The Conference, First and Last', *The World's Work*, March 1922, XLIII: 5, p. 552.
5. This flaw was addressed after Germany again defaulted on payments in 1928. The 'Young Plan' (devised by industrialist Owen D. Young), set annual payments at $153 million between 1929 and 1989.
6. These hopes proved unfounded. After NEP, with Lenin dead, Soviet economic policy moved even further along the road of state control and eliminated the last vestiges of private enterprise.
7. The RSFSR succeeded in securing recognition from Germany in the 1922 Treaty of Rapallo.
8. Harding is credited by some historians with the first public usage of the term 'Founding Fathers'.
9. Eugene P. Trani and David L. Wilson, *The Presidency of Warren G. Harding* (Lawrence: University Press of Kansas, 1977), p. 137.
10. Home-grown Mexican blood feuds eventually accomplished what Pershing could not. Villa was ambushed and killed near his ranch in Guadalupe, by a band of assassins lead by a former Mexican congressman, on 20 July 1923.
11. David W. Jennings, 'President Harding and International Organisation', *Ohio History*, 1966, 1, p. 164.
12. Robert D. Accinelli, 'Was There a "New" Harding? Warren G. Harding and the World Court Issue, 1920–1923', *Ohio History*, 1975, 84: 2, p. 176.
13. Russell, *President Harding*, pp. 575–6.
14. 'Johnson Launches World Court Fight Warns Harding', *New York Times*, 26 July 1923, p. 1.

CHAPTER 4

Coolidgean Normalcy, 1923–5

The heavenly hierarchy seemed to be in a conspiracy to protect him and help him along.[1]

The Accession of Coolidge

Calvin Coolidge's first priority, on succeeding to the presidency, was to calm the nerves of the American public and Wall Street. Harding's cabinet was retained intact and at its first meeting, on 14 August 1923, the new President confirmed that the 'Harding programme' would be continued. Coolidge's first message to Congress, in December 1923, covered much the same ground as Harding's in 1921 – tariff protection for industry, help for agriculture, further tax cuts, restrictions on immigration, federal assistance to the highway-building programme, support for US involvement in the World Court and rejection of a cash bonus for veterans. It was widely assumed that Coolidge would seek the Republican nomination in 1924. Having been Harding's Vice-President, he could not reject, even if he had wanted to, the late President's policies without damaging his own credibility. Further, the state of legislative-executive relations had deteriorated under Harding to such an extent that Coolidge was unlikely to enjoy the 'honeymoon period' traditionally granted a new occupant of the Oval Office. Introducing new policies in this environment would unnecessarily risk fresh clashes with Congress.

Of the five vice-presidents who had entered the White House through their predecessors' deaths only one, Theodore Roosevelt, had subsequently won a full term in his own right. Whereas Roosevelt had first served three-and-a-half years of McKinley's unexpired second term, however, Calvin Coolidge would face the electorate after only fifteen months. With the worst of the Teapot Dome scandals still ahead, the Republicans' prospects in 1924 did not look promising.

The Scandals

The threat to the President's re-election came not only from Democrats but from Republican progressives who had not forgiven the administration's ham-fisted handling of the 1922 labour disputes and what they regarded as its 'knee-jerk' subservience to the priorities of special interests and large corporations. Through Teapot Dome, LaFollette, Johnson, George Norris, Peter Norbeck (R-South Dakota), Smith Brookhart (R-Iowa) and other progressives saw an opportunity to weaken the conservative grip on the Republican party.

From autumn 1923 through to the late spring of 1924, congressional investigations consumed the attention of the press and the nation. Former Secretary Albert Fall denied taking 'kickbacks' from Harry Sinclair of Consolidated Oil or Edward L. Doheny, president of Pan-American Oil, but evidence soon arose that Fall's 'Three Rivers' ranch in New Mexico had undergone significant and costly improvements after the Elk Hills and Teapot Dome leases had been allocated. During the same period, Sinclair had been Fall's guest at the ranch. Fall's contention that he had borrowed the money from *Washington Post* owner Edward 'Ned' McLean (a close friend of President Harding), fell apart when McLean flatly denied it. In January 1924, Doheny confessed to 'lending' Fall $100,000 but insisted it came from his own private funds and had not been a quid pro quo for obtaining the oil lease. At one point, Doheny's testimony before the investigating committee of Senator Walsh threatened to bring disaster to Democrats as well as Republicans when he claimed to have funnelled money to President Wilson's Attorney General, A. Mitchell Palmer, and $50,000 to his Treasury Secretary, William G. McAdoo.[2]

Fall appeared before the Walsh committee on 2 February 1924, invoking his Fifth Amendment rights against self-incrimination. He was found to have financially benefited to the tune of $400,000 from his dealings with Doheny and Sinclair and was sentenced to one year in prison and a $100,000 fine. Sinclair served six months for attempting to tamper with the jury at his own trial but Doheny escaped punishment.

The Veterans Bureau scandal, also under investigation, threatened to tarnish the new administration. Harry Daugherty appeared to have multiple links to the series of emerging scandals. He had been, from the outset, a controversial Attorney General. Critics considered him ill-qualified for the post and distrusted his background in the corrupt world of Ohio politics. Harding had loyally supported his old campaign manager but Coolidge felt no such obligation and was privately keen to be rid of Daugherty as soon as possible. The Attorney General was a close friend of the late Jess Smith and also of Doheny and Sinclair. His Justice Department had proclaimed the Elk Hills and Teapot Dome oil leases legal. Rumours of graft and corruption swirled around Daugherty and Smith and the 'little green house on K-Street' in which they and their associates allegedly met to plot the defrauding of the federal government and arrange bootlegging operations. On 1 March 1924, the Senate set up a separate committee, chaired by Smith Brookhart, to investigate the allegations.

Daugherty's reputation made him a soft target for Brookhart and his fellow-committeeman, Democratic senator Burton K. Wheeler. Although they found no conclusive proof of collusion between Daugherty and Jess Smith, the Attorney General undermined his own cause by directing the Justice Department to withhold official documents demanded by the Brookhart committee. Coolidge used this unwise action to force Daugherty to resign. The former Attorney General was subsequently tried twice and found not guilty by narrow majorities on both occasions. He retired from public life a discredited and embittered man.

By not interfering with the Teapot Dome and Veterans Bureau investigations, Coolidge protected the reputation for incorruptibility which he had gained as Governor of Massachusetts. He also strengthened claim to the leadership of his party. Progressives gained little of the political leverage they had been expecting from the scandals, whilst moderate Republicans saw little to be gained by humiliating their own President in an election year.

The Sixty-Eighth Congress

Political tempers were sufficiently frayed in 1923–4 to ensure Coolidge got little of substance from the sixty-eighth Congress. The sharp reduction of Republican House and Senate majorities after the 1922 mid-terms meant that party rebellions in this Congress were far more dangerous than those which had regularly occurred in the sixty-seventh. The presence of seventeen GOP progressives in the House, acting in concert with wavering Republican moderates and mischievous Democrats, ensured that a Republican majority over the Democrats of 225-205 could be reduced to a wafer-thin majority for *either* side on any issue dividing the progressive and conservative wings of the Republican party.

An early demonstration of the continuing clout of the progressives arose from the decision of Congress, in March 1924, to approve the sale of the Muscle Shoals power plant complex in Alabama. Built during the war, on the banks of the Tennessee River, Muscle Shoals consisted of two nitrogen plants, originally intended to produce explosives, and several large dams. The Harding administration, as part of its campaign to cut government costs, had proposed selling them off soon after taking office. Henry Ford promptly submitted a $5 million bid, with pledges to continue supplying cheap explosives to the armed forces and to produce cheap nitrates for Tennessee farmers. A formidable coalition – the White House, conservative Republicans and conservative Democrats, the AFB and the AFL – favoured the Ford plan but George Norris, deriding it as 'the most wonderful real estate speculation since Adam and Eve lost title to the Garden of Eden', ensured the offer was rejected in committee by a two-vote margin.[3]

The controversy resurfaced in December 1924, when Norris introduced his own bill for *government* funds to be used to develop the Muscle Shoals facilities. The Coolidge administration took the unusual step of supporting a bill sponsored by the conservative Alabama Democrat, Oscar Underwood, which permitted leasing of the plants and dams to private companies. Although the Underwood bill passed both House and Senate, Norris and his supporters again out-manoeuvred the White House by exploiting a loophole in the congressional timetable to block consideration of any other business until Republican and Democratic party leaders agreed to abandon attempts to bring the bill to the floor for a final vote.[4] Although Coolidge continued to show interest in leasing or selling Muscle Shoals' facilities, Norris' agriculture committee blocked each attempt. In 1927, the Senator successfully sponsored a bill providing government funds for completion of the unfinished Wilson Dam, forcing a veto from the White House.

Progressive antipathy towards Coolidge did not appear to strengthen the loyalty of conservative Republicans to the White House in 1923–4. Cabot Lodge and other pro-business conservatives generally acknowledged Coolidge's right to the party's 1924 nomination but were bruised and defensive after their confrontations with the Harding White House. Their immediate priority, therefore, was to flex congressional muscles in order to intimidate, without completely undermining, the new administration. This lead to a series of embarrassing rebuffs for the administration. Two such rebuffs were calculated slaps at the memory of the late

President Harding. Coolidge's request for consideration of US membership of the World Court was summarily rejected and a reformulated veterans' bonus bill was passed over the President's veto in February 1924.

Elsewhere, the administration's stance tended to be *reactive*, rather than *proactive*. In May, Congress followed up the 1921 Emergency Quotas Act, placing restrictions on immigration, with the 1924 National Origins Act. Sponsored by Representative Albert Johnson (R-Indiana), it reduced the overall limit to 165,000, with the aim of a further reduction to 157,000 by 1927. The 3 per cent quota imposed at the start of the Harding period was cut to 2 per cent and the benchmark against which calculations would be made became the 1890 census rather than that of 1910. This permitted a further curtailment of southern and eastern European immigration since the quotas were, as in 1921, based on numbers of each nationality resident in the US at the time of the census in question. The Johnson Act pragmatically exempted Mexico and the Philippines, since American industry thrived on the cheap labour from these countries. The White House did not object to the principles laid down in the act, which had widespread popular support and which echoed Coolidge's own statement in his 6 December 1923 message to Congress that 'America must be kept American.'

The administration was embarrassed, however, by the Johnson Act's exclusion clause barring Japanese immigrants, who were classed as 'aliens ineligible for citizenship'.[5] This clause significantly damaged US-Japanese relations, which had appeared to be improving after Japan had supported the Allies during the war and since the J. P. Morgan Company had organised a $150 million loan to aid reconstruction after the massive 1923 Tokyo earthquake. The Japanese government denounced the exclusion clause as racist and an obstacle to the improvement of relations between the two countries. It is unlikely that President Coolidge held strong views one way or the other on the 'threat' posed to the US economy by hardworking Japanese immigrants, but industrial and labour leaders were lobbying strenuously for the ban. Herbert Hoover cabled the White House from California, advising that exclusion, though controversial, was probably unavoidable. The Commerce Secretary may have been influenced by his location at the time his cable was sent to Harding. California state law banned marriages between Asians and whites, many schools were effectively segregated and many public swimming pools and movie theatres were declared off-limits to Asians both in California and other states in the West. Further, widespread protests against the exclusion clause from the public or the press were unlikely, since derogatory remarks about Japanese immigrants were commonplace. The *Saturday Evening Post*, in an October 1920 article, announced, 'Politicians are like the Japanese. They initiate nothing and imitate everything.'[6] The President's hands were finally tied when the Japanese government overplayed its hand and issued an official statement warning of unspecified 'grave consequences' resulting from a ban. Coolidge had no alternative but to approve the bill or risk accusations of weakness in the face of intimidation.

The most serious setback suffered by the administration in its first year centred upon Treasury Secretary Mellon's plans for a further round of tax cuts. Having reluctantly settled for a 50 per cent surtax rate in the 1921 Revenue Act, Mellon now requested a further reduction to 25 per cent, with a minimum starting level of $10,000 rather than the existing $6,000 which had come into effect under President Wilson. Coolidge, along with most of the American business community, shared Mellon's jaundiced views of taxation. He informed the National Republican Club in February 1924 that 'an expanding prosperity requires the largest possible amount of surplus income should be invested in productive enterprise under the direction of the best personal ability.' This would be impossible, he warned, if taxes continued to devour that surplus.

Republican progressives had not changed their view, expressed during the 1921 debates, that the reductions were unfairly skewed towards the wealthiest Americans. Supported by Democrats, they permitted only a 10 per cent reduction from the 50 per cent rate. The Estate Tax, which Mellon wanted abolished altogether, was, instead, *raised* from 25 per cent to 40 per cent to compensate for the surtax revenue loss. Responding to critics, Mellon argued that 70 per cent of his requested reductions would significantly benefit those earning $10,000 a year or less. For those earning over $100,000, the pick-up would be a mere 2.5 per cent. Even an annual income of $10,000, however, was well beyond the reach of most Americans. Coal miners in the mid-1920s earned, on average, around $1,600. The average teaching salary was around $1,200. Neither would have benefited greatly from the 1924 adjustments. Opponents were also concerned at the prospective drop in government revenues resulting from the surtax reduction. The tax had been progressive, rising in proportion to income levels, and was bringing around one billion dollars into government coffers in the first years of the decade. It was argued, therefore, that the administration's stated goal of slashing the national debt could best be served by maintaining, not reducing, revenues. Liberals and progressives feared that further deep spending cuts would be introduced to make up the revenue loss.

Critics who attacked the 'pro-wealth bias' of Mellon's plans tended, however, to downplay the fact that a growing number of citizens were being removed from the income tax rolls altogether through the application of special exemptions. This process had started under the Wilson administration, shortly after passage of the 1913 federal income tax amendment to the Constitution. Under Mellon's plans, couples earning less than $3,500 would be paying no income tax at all by the fiscal year 1926–7. Conversely, the share of taxation paid by higher-income Americans was rising. Those earning, on average, $50,000 and over were contributing 78 per cent of the nation's taxes by 1928. At the start of the decade, the figure had been around 45 per cent. The prospect of removing lower-income Americans from the tax rolls helped sway some Republican moderates from the progressive campaign against Mellon, though not enough to ensure easy passage for most of the Treasury Secretary's tax cut proposals.

Coolidge in the Ascendant

In the first twelve months of the Coolidge presidency, the sixty-eighth Congress failed to pass a single White House-sponsored bill. Despite this, a powerful tide of popularity was swelling behind the thirtieth President, making his nomination for a full term in his own right a foregone conclusion. The electorate appeared as comfortable with the taciturn farmer's son as they had been with the jovial newspaper editor from Ohio. The personality of Calvin Coolidge, however, differed in almost every respect from that of his predecessor. Where Harding had been expansive in manner and appearance, Coolidge was thin, quiet and peevish. He had few close friends and no equivalent to the 'Ohio gang' which had followed Harding to Washington. The political philosophies of the two men were also more at variance than had, at first, been supposed. Harding's conservatism had been forged in the hard-headed and corrupt arena of Ohio state politics, an arena in which pragmatism and deal-making were prerequisites for political success. Consequently, Harding's political philosophy mixed an emotional attachment to conservative principles with a practical willingness to consider policies which smacked to some of progressivism and to pursue an interventionist path when necessary. Coolidge's beliefs, on the other hand, were rooted in the values of rural New England and its small towns and hamlets, where thrift, honesty, temperance and hard work were regarded as cardinal virtues and government activism was deeply distrusted. Coolidgean conservatism, rooted in this solid, Puritan environment, was far more resilient than Harding's. It also appealed to many Americans who, in the restless decade of the 1920s, wallowed in nostalgia for a vanishing and over-romanticised past, even as they excitedly welcomed accelerating socioeconomic and cultural change.

The circumstances of Coolidge's accession to the presidency were perfectly pitched to appeal to this sentiment. The Vice-President had been asleep at his father's farm in Plymouth Notch, Vermont, having spent the previous day trimming a maple tree and attending to farm chores. The Coolidge homestead had neither electricity nor a telephone, so a car from the nearby town of Bridgewater was forced to rattle along dark, country lanes to deliver news of Harding's death in the early hours of 3 August 1923. John Coolidge, a notary public, became the first father to administer the oath of office to his own son by the light of a small kerosene lamp. This humble scene was reproduced by artists in newspapers and magazines across the country, reassuring a grieving nation.

The new President, in stark contrast to the verbose Harding, was renowned for his economy with words. Anecdotes on this theme quickly established him as something of a national icon. During a White House reception, one story went, a guest attempted to establish some common conversational ground by saying, 'Mr President, I'm from Boston.' Coolidge allegedly retorted, 'You'll never get over it,' and moved on. Some of these stories may have been apocryphal, but they underlined the fact that Coolidge did not conform to the stereotype of the conventional 1920s politician. He appeared outwardly lacking in ambition and energy, was inclined to take naps during the day and finish work early. 'If a man can't finish a job in the daytime he's not smart,' the President once informed his aide, Colonel Starling. He displayed little of the egotism which propelled men like Lodge, Wilson, LaFollette and Johnson to political prominence and once confessed that his first thought on hearing that he had become President had been a modest, 'I believe I can swing it.' The American electorate in 1923 still warmed to the concept of a low-key presidency, partly to provide reassurance that all was essentially right with America. Coolidge was temperamentally more inclined to oblige them than the restless Harding had been.

The President's popularity secured his nomination on the first ballot at the Republican National Convention in Cleveland, Ohio, with 1,165 delegate votes from a possible 1,209. The high point of an otherwise dull assembly was Illinois Governor Frank Lowden's rejection of the vice-presidential nomination. Delegates chose as his replacement Charles Gates Dawes, Harding's first budget director and author of the 'Dawes Plan' to rescue the German economy. The convention platform called for World Court membership, despite isolationist objections, and arms limitation initiatives. It also called for more aid to farmers, continued high tariffs, more restrictions on immigration, more tax cuts and further debt reduction through governmental economies. Though the name of Warren Harding, already becoming an embarrassment to the party, was barely mentioned, the 1924 platform signalled the continuation, for another four years at least, of the normalcy programme he had initiated.

The Democrats Divided

On 24 June, Democrats assembled in New York's Madison Square Garden for what proved to be one of the most divisive conventions in the party's history. Although both major parties were influenced by the cultural, ethnic, religious and economic differences dividing the electorate in the early twentieth century, the Democrats were more prone than Republicans to serious schisms, arising from the geographic distribution of their supporters. Moderates and liberals tended to dominate the powerful Democratic machines of the northern and eastern industrial centres. Here, immigration and the concentration of ever-larger numbers of poor workers in overcrowded tenements demanded a very different set of social and political values to those practiced in the South and Mid-west, where everyday lives had changed little from the rural, white, Anglo-Saxon Protestant norms of the previous century. The Democratic party, like the nation itself, was increasingly torn between this older America and the emerging urban, multi-ethnic, capitalist power of the twentieth century.

In the 1924 convention, delegates were evenly split between the supporters of Alfred E. Smith, the Catholic Governor of New York, and those of former Treasury Secretary, William G. McAdoo of California, whose support came mainly from southern and western states. Prohibition and the growing influence of the Ku Klux Klan were the main areas of contention. Smith, an unrepentant wet, detested both in almost equal measure. McAdoo relied heavily upon dry support, whilst holding that action for or against the Klan was a matter for individual states, not the federal government. It was, as William Allen White observed, a recipe for chaos,

> to the Klansmen it seemed that Smith, the Roman Catholic, was the candidate of the big cities and to Smith's supporters, McAdoo represented the bigotry of the anti-Catholic, anti-Jewish and prohibition forces ... People were feeling, not thinking.[7]

Whilst northern liberals believed the Klan's existence was antithetical to modern democratic and moral values, southern conservative opinion ranged from indifference to active support. Few politicians, however, could afford to be openly hostile.

The Klan's twentieth-century revival had begun in November 1915, with the ritual burning of a cross on Stone Mountain, Georgia. Colonel William Joseph Simmons planned this symbolic act as a first step towards resurrecting the old Ku Klux Klan of the post-Civil War era.[8] For five years, the project made slow progress until two new assistants hired by Simmons in 1920 – Edward Young Clarke and Elizabeth Tyler – set about the efficient restructuring of the new Klan and the clearer distillation of its message.

They divided the Klan into eight regional 'domains', each headed by a 'Kleagle'. These were subdivided into administrative 'realms', each to be controlled by a 'Grand Goblin'. Its book of rules and regulations – the 'Kloran' – contained a list of questions which, if answered in the affirmative, denoted a loyal Klansman. Two key questions – 'Are you a native born, white, gentile American?' and 'Do you believe in and will you faithfully strive for the eternal maintenance of white supremacy?' left initiates in no doubt as to the purpose of the Klan's reinvention.[9]

In the South, the Klan of the 1920s, like its nineteenth-century precursor, played upon white prejudice against blacks. The tactic was particularly effective after 1918, when returning black veterans requested full citizenship rights as their just reward for defending the nation. Klan propaganda argued that full equality was impossible, given the inferior biological status of the black race. Permitting blacks and whites to freely intermingle, it warned, could result only in the 'mongrelisation' of the white American race. Lynching, beating, tarring and feathering, flogging and threats were deployed to intimidate black citizens. The Klan's obsession with secrecy, its talent for intimidation and the tendency of law enforcement bodies in many areas to ignore, or collude with, Klan activities, made it hard to assess the depth and breadth of its operations.

However, this was, the editor of one South Carolina newspaper for black Americans wrote, somewhat beside the point, since,

> with a white judge, a white jury, white public sentiment, white officers of the law, it is just as impossible for a Negro ... even suspected of a crime, to escape the white man's vengeance ... as it would be for a fawn ... that wanders accidentally into a den of hungry lions.[10]

Beyond the states of the old Confederacy, new branches of the Klan fed upon nativist hostility to Catholic, Asian and Jewish immigrants. Propaganda identified non-WASP communities as sinks of 'moral degeneration', laying at their door the blame for bootlegging, prostitution, political corruption, atheism, 'papism', gambling, jazz and other 'social evils' of the modern age. Diversifying targets and messages in this way made the revived Klan a dangerous force, since it could not simply be tagged as a narrowly based, anti-black militia. The issue of Prohibition, for example, provided fertile recruiting ground for the Klan. Its operations in areas lacking large minority ethnic communities focused, instead, on excoriating local white civic and religious leaders for failing to enforce the Volstead Act and thus encouraging 'un-Christian' vices, such as alcoholism and wife-beating. In Indiana, where both the Klan and the Anti-Saloon League were politically powerful, Klan members exploited an old state law in order to have themselves sworn in by the governor as temporary 'horse thief detectives', before riding out to enforce Nordic supremacy. Journalist Louis Francis Budenz recalled, 'Rum, anti-catholicism, anti-semitism, "nigger-hating", and radical baiting are lumped in the mind of the man on the street as one.'[11]

Klan members held elaborate initiation rites for new members, usually at night in secluded rural areas. The robes, hoods, crosses and loyalty oaths which accompanied these ceremonies were designed to strike fear into the hearts of non-white, non-Anglo-Saxon communities. They also added 'mystical' and 'fraternal' layers to the Klan image which heightened its recruiting strength particularly amongst alienated, poverty-stricken whites.[12] Recruitment methods also reflected changes which had taken place since the 1860s, including the creation of special groups for women and children, the fostering of links with other fraternal organisations such as the Freemasons and recruitment at local barbeques and charity events. These tactics helped ensure that Klan membership cut across not only age and gender lines but also across class boundaries.

The Klan's influence was approaching its peak by 1924 under Simmons' successor, Dr Hiram Wesley Evans. Membership totalled nearly 5,000,000 and the forces of the 'Invisible Empire' paraded openly along main streets in many cities and towns. During the 1924 campaign, its political clout was a malignant fact of life affecting (in some cases, *involving*) both Republican and Democrat officeholders in twenty-seven states, including Texas, Louisiana, Michigan, Colorado and Indiana. Oregon voters elected a Klansman as governor in 1922. Klan influence was strongest in rural areas and small communities but it was also felt in cities such as Denver, Los Angeles and Chicago.

Alabama senator Oscar K. Underwood, a long-shot contender for the 1924 Democratic nomination, was privately convinced that racism had retarded the economic development of the South.[13] Outright attacks on the Klan were, nonetheless, politically unwise. The Democratic party platform committee debated for many hours behind closed doors but could not agree whether to include a flat condemnation of the Klan in the final platform draft. Failing to achieve this, Smith's supporters took the fight to the convention floor but were narrowly beaten by the McAdoo forces. To liberal disgust, a generic denunciation of bigotry was inserted in the platform which omitted any specific reference to the Klan.

These altercations might not have affected the party's electoral prospects so badly but for the unfortunate convergence of two other, unrelated factors – new technology and antiquated nomination rules. Party laws governing presidential nominations, largely unchanged since the 1830s, imposed a 'two-thirds rule', which required the winning candidate to secure two-thirds of convention delegates rather than a simple numerical majority. Smith and McAdoo were deadlocked in the balloting, with neither able to reach a two-thirds majority and neither, initially, willing to back down.[14] Multi-ballot conventions were not unusual, but the 103 ballots taken in 1924 frayed delegates' tempers so badly that fighting broke out on the convention floor and police reinforcements were called in to restore order. The nomination was given, in desperation, to John W. Davis, a rather colourless Wall Street lawyer and former ambassador to Great Britain. The campaign against Coolidge was lost before it had properly begun.

Unfortunately for the Democrats, the New York convention was the first to be broadcast live on radio. Audiences across the country listened, amused or appalled, as the party tore itself apart on air. The advent of radio in the 1920s had brought important changes to both the physical nature of politics and to the rules of political communication. In physical

terms, speeches were increasingly delivered from behind large micro-
phone banks, a fact many politicians found off-putting. The exaggerated
style of the nineteenth-century 'stump speech', with its shouting, arm-
waving, fist-shaking and finger-wagging, was invisible to radio listeners
and unnecessary in any event. Radio audiences were not large crowds
gathered in one place but families and individuals gathered around
wireless sets in countless living rooms and workplaces across the United
States. A potential audience of 12,000,000 could tune in to Calvin
Coolidge's inauguration on 4 March 1925 – considerably more than could
fit on the lawn in front of the Capitol. This mandated a new 'intimacy' in
the relationship between politicians and their audience. The old theatrics
seemed anachronistic. Such changes worked to Coolidge's advantage.
His voice carried a nasal 'twang' which did not project well from the
speaker's platform but gained gravitas when broadcast on radio.
Recognising the public relations value of the new medium, Coolidge
made a total of sixteen radio addresses during his five-year presidency.

If radio helped politicians reach wider audiences and adopt more
relaxed speaking styles, it also created new pitfalls. The presence of
microphones and newsreel cameras meant that delegates could no longer
speak or behave without restraint. In future, politicians would have to
consider not only their policies but also the *image*s the party projected to
voters.[15] The Democrats began learning this painful lesson in 1924.

In the best of times, the Democratic party was hard to unite and still
harder to control. In 1924, however, it faced an impossible task unseating
a popular White House incumbent presiding over an economy which
was, at last, emerging from recession. The country seemed in no mood
for change. The Republicans circulated folksy tales of Coolidge's home-
spun lifestyle and produced what was, in marketing terms, the inspired
slogan of 'Keep Cool with Coolidge'. Against such tactics, the opposition could make little headway.

Conservative Republicanism appeared to dominate the politics of the
mid-Twenties, but whilst the Democrats could not prevent a second
electoral triumph for normalcy, the progressive movement remained
surprisingly strong and mounted its own challenge in 1924. LaFollette
had helped to initiate the investigations which lead to Teapot Dome by
demanding an enquiry into the naval oil reserve leases in April 1922. The
subsequent revelations of the influence of 'oil money' in politics
prompted 'Fighting Bob' to launch his own bid for the presidency,
backed by the Conference for Progressive Political Action, which he had

helped found in 1922.[16] He was nominated at a convention of Progressives held in Cleveland in July 1924 and selected Burton K. Wheeler as his running-mate. The third party's platform was almost entirely LaFollette's handiwork. It called for Congress to be empowered to overrule Supreme Court judgements, direct election of the President, Vice-President and federal judiciary and government action to rein in the power of the monopolies and restore public control over the nation's natural resources. With an eye to the 1922 railroad strikes, it also demanded an end to the use of injunctions in labour disputes. Harding-Coolidge foreign policies were denounced as representing only 'the interests of financial imperialists, oil monopolists and international bankers'. Progressives also called for an end to conscription and a public referendum before American troops were sent out to fight abroad.

Regular Republicans viewed LaFollette as a demagogue and, potentially, a more serious threat to the Coolidge-Dawes campaign than John Davis and the Democrats. A strong progressive vote could, conceivably, result in an electoral college deadlock and throw the election into the House of Representatives. More worryingly, anti-conservative forces were displaying a new unity in 1924. LaFollette received support from liberal-leaning Republicans, some northern and eastern Democrats, the American Federation of Labor, the Socialist Party and the Famer-Labour Party. Republican campaign managers worried that voter apathy, arising from improved economic conditions, might benefit LaFollette by depressing Republican voter turnout. Coolidge's campaign team decided, therefore, to ignore Davis and focus upon LaFollette and his progressive battalions. Republican speeches and campaign literature attempted to link the Wisconsin senator to Bolshevik Russia, alleging that his campaign funds came direct from the Kremlin. Charles Dawes demanded of his audiences, 'Where do you stand? With President Coolidge on the Constitution with the flag, or on the sinking sands of socialism?'[17] Coolidge, typically, remained more or less aloof, causing Davis to complain that the Republican campaign was 'a vast, pervading and mysterious silence, broken only by Dawes warning the American people that under every bedstead lurks a Bolshevik ready to destroy them.'[18]

Coolidge's silence was partly characteristic but also the result of personal tragedy. In July 1924, his eldest son, Calvin Jr, had developed a blister on his toe whilst playing tennis. Blood poisoning set in and he died shortly afterwards. 'When he went,' the President told a close friend, 'the power and the glory of the presidency went with him.'

In November 1924, the Coolidge-Dawes ticket won 382 electoral votes to 136 for Davis and Bryan with a popular vote of 54.6 per cent to the Democrats' 28.8 per cent. The Democrats were beaten back to their strongholds in the South, regaining Tennessee and Oklahoma, which were lost to Harding in 1920, but losing Kentucky. LaFollette polled 4,814,050 votes (a 16% share of the total) and took only the thirteen electoral votes of his home state of Wisconsin. Progressives were encouraged by LaFollette's impressive showing in the western states – Washington, California, Wyoming, Minnesota, Idaho, Nevada and the Dakotas. Their support in these states seemed a clear indication that the flame of reform, though burning less brightly than in the pre-war years, had not been extinguished. Nonetheless, the regional concentration of progressive support dashed hopes that a nationwide groundswell of reform sentiment would bring an end to the era of normalcy.

The House of Representatives in the new sixty-ninth Congress had 232 Republicans and 183 Democrats, with twenty others associated with LaFollette's progressive bloc. The margin in the Senate was narrower, with fifty Republicans, facing forty Democrats and six progressives.

It was not quite the landslide of 1920, but, in the aftermath of Teapot Dome, it was a better result than Republicans could reasonably have expected only a few months before. Inasmuch as a turnout of barely more than 50 per cent of qualified voters could be seen as an accurate gauge of public sentiment, the 1924 election was an affirmation of voter satisfaction with the general direction of the country and with the programme of normalcy. Although congressional investigations of former Harding officials went on late into the decade, the electorate had already lost interest. Ahead lay the boom years of 'Coolidge Prosperity' and a fresh mandate for tax cuts, smaller government and unrestrained corporate growth.

Culture and Society

The low voter turnout in 1924 was interpreted in the press and by Republican leaders across the country as a sign of general public satisfaction with the direction the nation had been taking since 1921. It was certainly true that the 1924 campaign failed to ignite the public's imagination and no single issue, such as League of Nations membership or participation in war, dominated the election. Some commentators accused the newly elected Vice-President Dawes of using the Bolshevik bogeyman simply to keep his audiences awake.

Public disinterest was partially attributable to the recovery of the American economy which had begun around late 1923. Unemployment had fallen to 5 per cent and average earnings had started to rise slowly, as did the prices of some farm commodities such as wheat, which attained its highest market value since 1921. America's gross national product rose by $8 billion in 1923–4, whilst the budget surplus, swollen by Harding-Mellon frugality, had jumped by $672 million from its March 1921 level of $291 million.

Public attention was now increasingly diverted away from Washington politics. In the new age of film, radio, motor cars and consumer capitalism, many Americans had never had so much with which to occupy their leisure time. Technological advances spurred the production of labour-saving devices. In the mid-1920s, an estimated 80 per cent of homes with electricity also had electric irons and 37 per cent had vacuum cleaners. Refrigerator sales leapt 150 per cent between 1924 and 1929. Radio and magazine advertising promoted these goods as essential to any 'modern' lifestyle, generating a feeling of anxiety amongst those who did not yet own them. The phenomenon itself was not unique to the 1920s, but its sheer scale was unprecedented. No previous decade had provided such an enormous range of available goods – electric ovens, washing machines, electric toothbrushes, portable record-players, toasters – and none had possessed such a formidable array of tools for marketing them.

Marketing became a major growth sector of the economy. The amount invested in magazine advertising in 1914 had been $250 million. By 1929 it would total $3 billion. Its colourfully intrusive impact was felt everywhere, from highway billboards and radio broadcasts to 'product placement' in newspaper and magazine articles on other topics. This latter practice helped sales but devalued and, sometimes, distorted factual reporting. Accounts of the dramatic rescue of the crew of the SS *Florida*, in late February 1929, were printed in newspapers alongside an advertisement for Lucky Strike cigarettes. George Fried, the captain of the rescuing ship, the SS *America*, gave his own account of the drama, which contained puzzlingly frequent mentions of the vital role played by 'Luckies' in the operation. Lucky Strikes, Fried explained, helped calm down the rescued crewmen, soothed the nerves of the rescuers. He smoked them often himself, he added, as part of his health regimen. Sinclair Lewis complained, in *The Nation*, 'The hand is the hand of Fried but the text is the text of the American Tobacco Company.'[9]

Advertisers developed ingenious new ways to stimulate the public's appetite, not merely by describing the quality and usages of their products but by hinting darkly at the consequences of *not* purchasing them. One series of adverts, promoting a cure for halitosis, zeroed-in mercilessly upon the misery and embarrassment of the sufferer, proclaiming, 'Edna's case was really a pathetic one,' or '*That's* why you're a failure!'[20] The 1920s consumer generation was the first to exist in a state of almost perpetual anxiety over breath and body odour, lack of fashion sense, inability to use long words in conversation, mistaken smoking of the 'wrong' tobacco brand, or callous neglect of their children's health by buying the 'wrong' brand of breakfast cereal. This aggressive style was effective in driving up consumer spending but also increased the sense of unease and dissatisfaction which pervaded much of American society during the Twenties.

Strands of this unease were strongly apparent in the work of contemporary novelists and poets. The literature most closely associated with the early mid-Twenties reflected the disillusionment of a 'lost generation' of authors who wrote of their disillusionment with the 'emptiness' and 'futility' of human existence and of the moral and spiritual scars left by the world war. This lost generation did not exhibit conservative yearnings for a bygone social order – it despised the old as much as the new – but the relentless pursuit of material goods, the crushing anonymity of city life and the central importance of commercialism and new technology to 1920s American society aroused as much despair amongst poets such as Edna St Vincent Millay and Ezra Pound as the nocturnal cavortings of hooded Klansmen. In the new 'machine age' they detected the crushing of the individual and the increasing irrelevance of 'spectators of a soulful temper.'[21] These frustrations emerged in the works of writers such as John Dos Passos, who railed at the shrinking status of the 'ant-like' individual before the might of giant factories and corporations. F. Scott Fitzgerald's novels, *The Beautiful and Damned* (1922) and *The Great Gatsby* (1925), depicted the spiritual rootlessness afflicting the upper echelons of society, where the absence of behavioural restraints and easy access to money and leisure created confusion and emptiness rather than personal fulfilment. If their self-expression carried any partisan sentiment at all, it reflected progressive disgust at the apparent supremacy of the Babbitts in American politics and society. Some, like Ernest Hemingway, became so disenchanted with their homeland that they left America for Europe. Many never returned, giving rise to the historical image of the Twenties as a culturally barren period, a reputation which it did not really deserve.

American culture was in a state of flux throughout the decade. The concentration of millions of black Americans in New York gave rise not merely to influential new black political movements but to a flowering of black culture of such intensity that it spilled over into white society, cross-fertilising with strands of white literature and music and tempting the races into closer social interaction. This was the period of the 'Harlem Renaissance', which began shortly after the war in the 'overcrowded, vulgar and wicked' atmosphere of Harlem, a district of New York city lying roughly between Seventh and Lennox avenues.[22] White and black writers, artists and musicians met frequently to discuss their work and personal motivations in one of Harlem's many clubs, such as the Cotton Club and the Savoy. Black writers flocked to the district, drawing strength and inspiration from its crowded streets and vibrant cultural life. In this fertile atmosphere, Claude McKay, a Jamaican immigrant, produced *Harlem Shadows* (1922) and *Home to Harlem* (1928), Langston Hughes published *Weary Blues* (1925). Also in 1925, Countee Cullen published his most famous collection of poems, *Color*. In Harlem, they found magazines such as *The New Negro* and *Crisis* which were eager to publish their writings as well as a readership which closely empathised with the mixture of anger, pride, frustration and hope which infused their work.

Towards the end of the nineteenth century, the relaxed, improvised musical style of jazz began to spread outwards from its birthplace in New Orleans, following the path of the black migrants into New York, Chicago and other northern cities. Although it first came to cultural prominence through the pre-Twenties compositions of Ferdinand 'Jelly Roll' Morton, it was in the 1920s that it became widely popularised through Joseph 'King' Oliver, through Fletcher Henderson's jazz band – the first black American band to be covered live on radio – and through Louis Armstrong's band at Chicago's Dreamland Cafe. The rise of jazz was greeted with consternation by some whites, who blamed its free-flowing rhythms and 'ungraceful wiggling' for the declining popularity of more 'dignified' dance styles amongst the young. Some complaints, though by no means all, were racially motivated, in response to the increased intermingling of young white and black Americans in jazz cafes. An Episcopalian minister observed, 'Jazz is retrogression. It is going to the African jungle for our music. It is a savage crash and bang.' To traditionalists, the rhythmic physicality and looseness of jazz presaged nothing less than the breakdown of civilised society. One professional dance instructor sniffily observed,

The public has prostituted modern dancing and the present-day music is at the root of it all. Music can lift us to great heights or make barbarians of us and at the present time we have barbarian jazz or, as I say, the explosion of insanity in music.[23]

The United States was literally, as well as metaphorically, on the move. Henry Ford's Model T was now easily within the reach of those on average or slightly below average incomes. Almost 4,300,000 cars rolled off the production lines of Ford and its major competitors such as General Motors and Chrysler in 1926. They came in new vibrant colours and with luxury extras such as ash trays and automatic windscreen wipers. Americans travelled faster and further than ever before, weekend getaways became popular, spreading the benefits of prosperity by encouraging tourism wherever the new roads and highways reached. The roadside 'motel' made its debut in 1925 and, by the end of the decade, highways were plastered with billboards advertising Gillette razors, Wrigleys chewing gum or Kodak cameras. The car made it easier for ordinary Americans to stretch the geographical parameters of their lives and to relocate to other towns or states. Inevitably, family and community bonds were further disrupted as a result.

Cars also liberated the young, who often used them to escape the disapproving eyes of parents and chaperones and drive to secluded areas for sexual encounters. Women took to the road with enthusiasm, their new, independent mobility having significant effects upon their work and family lives. There were, inevitably, negative aspects to the motoring phenomenon. 'Commuting' and 'traffic jams', not to mention road fatalities, became features of daily life. Traffic lights made their unwelcome appearance in 1923, with licence fees and gasoline taxes following close behind.

The Twenties brought other changes to the social lives of ordinary Americans. Through radio and the press, audiences avidly followed their sporting heroes, including the legendary boxer Jack Dempsey and his rival, Gene Tunney, who ended Dempsey's reign in spectacular fashion in 1926. Devoted fans followed the fortunes of tennis star William 'Big Bill' Tilden and golfing legend, Bobby Jones. Coverage of Jones stimulated interest in the sport and new golfing clubs sprang up across America. In California alone, devoted middle-class golfers were spending half a billion dollars a year on their addiction by 1929. George Herman 'Babe' Ruth, pitcher and outfielder for the New York Yankees baseball team became the iconic figure of the sporting Twenties, hitting sixty home runs in 1927, a record not surpassed for nearly forty years. The 'Sultan of Swat' garnered as much publicity, and substantially more money, than the President of the United States himself and his exploits, both on and off the field, helped convert sport into a national obsession and boosted radio sales as the nation sought a 'ringside seat' at the great sporting occasions.

The same urge for a ringside seat drove the public's appetite for media coverage of 'celebrity' scandals and criminal trials. The press, naturally inclined toward sensationalism, responded to this demand with saturation coverage of private and courtroom dramas.

The most controversial trial of the decade, and the one generating the longest-running 'media circus', involved Nicola Sacco and Bartolomeo Vanzetti who were charged with the murder of a shoe factory paymaster during a $15,700 robbery in Braintree, Massachusetts on 15 April 1920. The fact that the two men were Italian immigrants, as well as anarchists, did not help the defence in its efforts to clear them. Judge Webster Thayer flaunted his deep personal prejudice against the men outside the courtroom and permitted it to affect his conduct inside, to such an extent that a failed attempt was made to remove him from the case. Sacco and Vanzetti were found guilty on 14 July 1921, but numerous appeals delayed the actual sentencing for another six years. During this period, socialist activists, liberals, progressive groups and public figures such as journalist Walter Lippman, Harvard law professor Felix Frankfurther and authors H. G. Wells and John Dos Passos, pleaded for clemency or, at the very least, for a second trial under a different judge. A committee set up by Massachusetts governor Alvin Fuller and chaired by Harvard University president A. Lawrence Lowell, rejected clemency and Sacco and Vanzetti finally went to the electric chair on 23 August 1927. Demonstrations were held against the trial, the verdict and the execution itself not only in the United States but in cities across Europe and South America. The Sacco and Vanzetti case remains, arguably, the most controversial in American legal history – viewed by many on the American left as a miscarriage of justice in which bigotry and paranoia undermined constitutional rights to a fair trial.[24] The impact on liberal and radical political groups and the liberal intelligentsia was profound, deepening their cynicism about the condition of democracy in Calvin Coolidge's America. One year after the executions, Edmund Wilson wrote,

As (John) Dos Passos said, it was ... as if, by some fairy-tale spell, all the different kinds of Americans, eminent and obscure, had suddenly, in a short burst of intensified life, been compelled to reveal their true characters ...[25]

During the summer of 1924, those bored by the Coolidge-Davies election also avidly followed the trial of Nathan F. Leopold Jr and Richard A. Loeb. The two well-to-do young men had confessed to the stabbing and suffocation of fourteen-year-old Bobby Franks in Chicago on 21 May. Franks was killed in a car driven by Loeb and his body drenched in acid before being dumped, naked, in a ditch. At their trial, their attorney, Clarence Darrow, changed the defence plea from innocent to guilty at the last minute in order to avoid a jury trial. Leopold and Loeb escaped the electric chair but were sentenced on 10 September 1924 to two life sentences each. The press frenzy over the trial was heightened not just by the brutal nature of this motiveless murder or by the fact that the victim, selected at random, was Loeb's cousin. Disturbingly, both murderers were teenage boys of wealthy and respectable parentage. Well-spoken and well-educated, they had killed purely for the 'thrill' of killing and expressed no remorse for their crime. The Loeb case caused particular disquiet amongst conservative civic and religious groups, who attributed the killers' cold disregard for human life to the younger generation's growing penchant for moral relativism. This problem, they feared, was now beginning to infect the uppermost echelons of American society. Although criticism of youth behaviour and misgivings about the future were hardly new phenomena, there was a new urgency in the warnings of religious opinion leaders of the 1920s that the country had entered a period of deep moral and spiritual crisis. Some blamed the 'overstrain' brought on by years of war and reform. Others saw the dissemination of communist and anarchist literature, and its discussion on university campuses, behind what appeared to be a steep decline in religiosity and a simultaneous rise in motiveless criminal activity. To some extent, these fears were exaggerated and can be attributed to the bouts of national introspection which often follow periods of conflict or upheaval. They also tended to be exaggerated for political advantage in the propaganda of the Ku Klux Klan and other extremist organisations. What was new in the angst which bubbled below the surface of society in the 1920s was its breadth and complexity. The pace of economic and cultural change by the decade's mid-point was almost dizzying. The revolution in communications inevitably speeded up the process by which controversial ideas and opinions spread to the smallest towns and villages, often challenging existing moral and behavioural norms. The excited chatter of advertising spread information of 'alternative' lifestyles along the nation's new highways and across the airwaves. The sheer *quantity* of this information, and the multiple channels now available for its transmission, weakened the ability of churches, social clubs, parents and political leaders to filter out its more 'harmful' elements. As the decade progressed, conservative social opinion struggled grimly with trends which, it believed, subverted youthful innocence and degraded women. Attacks were directed particularly at 'sensual' dance styles, 'petting parties', 'lewd' films and immodest modes of dress. The first 'Miss America' pageant, held in New Jersey on 8 September 1921, was condemned for parading 'bathing beauties' in revealing swimming costumes before photographers and a largely male audience. Jazz was banned from the Executive Mansion in Kentucky in December 1923, as incoming governor, William J. Fields, announced that dancing would be replaced by prayer meetings.

The dichotomy between the political and cultural spheres of American society, always present to a greater or lesser extent, was sharpening noticeably. Conservatism may have held sway in the nation's legislatures and town halls, but, on the issues of manners and morals, it often appeared to be fighting a futile rearguard action.

Faith and Modernity

In one area, at least, the leaders of liberal and conservative opinion appeared united. The quickening pace of mergers and takeovers in the corporate sector of the economy disturbed progressives, who saw unrestricted monopoly capitalism as a threat to individual self-determination and political democracy. Their conservative counterparts, on the other hand, criticised the 'greedy' and 'amoral' lifestyles which, they believed, were promoted by consumer capitalism. Religious leaders, in particular, worried that the veneration of business and the iconic status accorded to individual entrepreneurs such as Ford and Insull were reaching 'devotional' levels that not only obscured the traditional Christian message but also bordered on blasphemy. These fears were not without foundation. In 1925 and 1926, the top-selling, non-fiction book in the United States was Bruce Barton's *The Man Nobody Knows*. Barton characterised Jesus as the 'founder of modern business' – a man who had established a powerful, pyramidal organisation (the Christian church) run by a hand-picked board (the twelve disciples) in the best traditions of American capitalism. Reformist elements within some mainstream churches did not see anything particularly threatening in this attempt to 'make faith relevant' to twentieth century worshippers. Traditionalists, however, viewed Barton's work as breathtakingly presumptuous. It seemed that the President of the United States himself had taken Barton's message to heart when Coolidge declared, in 1925: 'The man who builds a factory builds a temple. The man who works there, worships there.' Frederick Lewis Allen observed,

> So frequent was the use of the Bible to point the lessons of business and of business to point the lessons of the Bible that it was sometimes difficult to determine which was supposed to gain the most from the association.[26]

Despite this controversy, fears of declining religious faith were exaggerated. The movement of millions from the South and Mid-west to the urban industrial centres of the Northeast inevitably led to the closure of some churches in small, rural communities, but simultaneous *increases* were being recorded in the number of places of worship and the size of congregations in Chicago, Detroit, Boston and New York, as migrants continued to practice their religions in new locations.

In the 'Age of Anxiety', nevertheless, many Americans were encountering unfamiliar cultural and social forces which caused them either to question their own beliefs or to seek new sources of moral and ethical guidance. Sociological studies, increasingly in vogue, attributed this phenomenon to the impact of 'alienation' on modern society. The flight to the cities, social scientists speculated, had caused millions to lose their family and cultural moorings as they jostled for living space and employment, often in dehumanising conditions. The robotic toil of factory production lines intensified their frustration, which often erupted in violence or psychosis and which could not find compensation in religious worship or community activity. A vague sense of *ennui* also affected many in the more prosperous middle classes, as the writings of the 'lost generation' (themselves mainly from the American middle class) had demonstrated. In an effort to understand their restlessness and dissatisfaction, many Americans turned to psychology. The theories of Hans Jung and Sigmund Freud were popularised through the national press, cheap paperback books and radio in the Twenties. To some, confronting childhood traumas and phobias was a reassuringly scientific and rational approach, more likely to yield results than the rather more literal 'casting out of demons' prescribed by religion. The growing fascination with the 'self' also increased interest in IQ tests and in 'Pelmanism' – one of the many 'mind-improvement' courses offered to those who believed they possessed extraordinary mental capabilities but had not yet been able to fully exploit them. An application form for a $35 cash-down course in Pelmanism promised: 'Pelmanism teaches you how to develop ORIGINALITY – how to develop PERSONALITY – how to build CHARACTER – how to strengthen INDIVIDUALITY. How to SUCCEED!'[27]

In a similar vein, factory owners updated Henry Ford's pre-war tinkering with factory layout and processes by hiring 'industrial psychologists' to assess ways in which employee motivation and productivity could be improved. In these and other ways, ordinary Americans sought a greater degree of control over the direction and meaning of their lives, placing their faith in rational scientific enquiry. Few were inclined to leave their fate in the hands of 'divine providence'.

Secularism was also evident in the increasing tendency of the state-sponsored, social welfare groups operating in north-eastern cities to exclude religious instruction from their programmes. One Methodist minister complained, in 1928, of a prominent social service organisation 'doing wide-reaching work in New York, with a budget of $150,000 a year (in which) ... the name of God was never allowed to be mentioned.'[28] Although the Constitution forbade the 'establishment' of religion through government sponsorship, the dominance of Protestant Christianity in America had always ensured that the borders separating religious activity from the structures of temporal power were somewhat porous. In the racially and ethnically diverse cities of the North, as more Catholics, Jews and other non-Protestant citizens sought political office, this status quo was becoming hard to sustain.

America's churches reacted to these changes in different ways. 'Modernists', particularly strong in the Episcopalian and Presbyterian churches, tended to adapt concepts such as the 'virgin birth' and the 'resurrection' to modern audiences by presenting them as allegories, rather than literal events. This theological flexibility was condemned by conservatives, who argued that dilution of core tenets of faith harmed Christianity far more than the writings of Freud or Charles Darwin. Fundamentalists, meanwhile stepped up their crusade against the evils of

communism, materialism and alcohol, undeterred by the pronounce-
ments of liberal intellectuals that religious belief was irrelevant in
modern life.

Inevitably, frequent clashes took place between modernism and
fundamentalism. The most famous of these was the 'Monkey trial' of
1925. Early in 1925, the Tennessee legislature passed a bill introduced by
Representative John Butler which forbade the teaching of 'any theory
that denies the story of the Divine Creation of man as taught in the
Bible.' Alarmed supporters of Charles Darwin's theory of evolution
contended that the teaching of biological science would become almost
impossible under this law. Before the 1920s, Christian activists had
successfully restricted the teaching of evolutionary theories. Anti-
evolution laws were passed in Florida and Oklahoma in 1923 and the
1924 school text, *Biology and Human Welfare*, was one of several which
omitted any discussion of Darwin's theories on the origins of mankind.

Fundamentalists nationwide supported the Baptist evangelicals in
Tennessee, hoping other states would follow suit. Liberals and academics
opposed the Butler Act as a violation of First Amendment freedoms. The
American Civil Liberties Union offered its support to anyone prosecuted
under the new law and a young biology teacher, John T. Scopes of
Dayton, volunteered for the dubious honour of being the first man
arrested for teaching evolutionary theory from a class text entitled, *A
Civic Biology*.

The Scopes trial was the first to be broadcast live by radio and the last
battle in the long public career of William Jennings Bryan. A three-time
Democratic nominee for the presidency, Bryan had been President
Wilson's first Secretary of State.[29] Though his *political* views were usually
to the left of Christian evangelicals, Bryan shared their religious convictions and readily agreed to appear for the prosecution. Scopes' defenders
hired Clarence Darrow who, the year before, had saved Leopold and
Loeb from the electric chair. National public interest was intense. When
the trial opened on 10 July 1925, so many people had packed the
courtroom that its walls buckled under the pressure. Thousands more
waited outside, sweltering in the summer heat and consuming lemonade
and hot dogs while evangelical speakers berated Scopes and Darrow.

Scopes' acquittal was never likely. Presiding judge, John T. Raulston,
was a committed Christian, as were eleven of the twelve jury members.
Raulston ruled as inadmissible a large body of testimony from academics
and scientists submitted by Darrow and co-counsel, Dudley Field Malone,

which stressed the centrality of Darwin's research to the teaching of biology and pleaded for a spirit of open, rational enquiry in the nation's classrooms. Darrow appealed to jurors to 'prevent bigots and ignoramuses from controlling the educational system of the United States', but his most memorable accomplishment in the trial was to subject Bryan to a humiliating public grilling about his belief in the literal truth of the Bible. The 'Great Commoner' revealed a simplistic faith in the literal truth of the Bible's parables which appeared out of touch with modern America. William Allen White observed:

> He had read little and understood nothing technically about the doctrine of evolution, about modern ideas of social progress, about the higher critics who had been studying the Bible text for a hundred years. The whole literature of the subject ... was a vast, unexplored waste to him.[30]

The trial was abruptly ended by Judge Raulston on 22 July. John Scopes was found guilty of violating the provisions of the Butler Act and fined $100, although his conviction was later overturned on a procedural technicality by the Tennessee Supreme Court. Amendments were made to *A Civic Biology* by its author, George W. Hunter and drawings depicting man's progression from ape to *Homo sapiens* were removed. The Butler Act remained in force in Tennessee until the late 1960s. Although the numbers of schools teaching Darwinian theory actually declined for many years after the great 1925 courtroom clash, the victory of the creationist forces attracted much negative publicity and derision and, in the long term, did the anti-evolutionary movement as much harm as good. Religious opinion itself was divided over Scopes, with moderates denouncing the Butler Act as narrow-minded and damaging to the cause of religion, particularly with the younger generation. New York Unitarian minister Charles F. Potter lambasted the fundamentalists' anti-evolution stance, arguing, 'it is the very genius of religion itself to evolve from primary forms to higher ones ... It is not only the Tennessee people who should be ashamed, we are all to blame.'[31]

The Scopes trial did not, of course, end the rivalry between science and religion and, although it degenerated into a media circus, its significance in the ongoing debate on the origins and purpose of humanity is still acknowledged. It reflected, moreover, the unusually high degree of interest shown in such debates by Americans in the 1920s. This interest was still evident in December 1928, when New York's

Cardinal Hayes devoted his entire sermon, before 4,000 worshippers at St Patrick's Cathedral, to the declaration by the American Association for the Advancement of Science that the concept of a 'god' should be subjected to objective, scientific research. 'It is the fashion of the day,' Hayes declared, 'to see conflict and contradiction between religion and science.' Rejecting the Tennessee fundamentalist line, however, he argued that scientific discovery should be embraced by Christians for confirming the existence of intelligent design behind the forces of nature.

It is merely human knowledge to reveal the material, the mechanical and the organic forces of the universe ... it is the perfection of human reason to use this knowledge as a stepping-stone to higher things. True religion enables us to advance ... from the material to the spiritual.[32]

Despite the challenges of modernism, Christian evangelicalism continued to thrive throughout the decade. At the outset of the Twenties, the most famous evangelist was William Ashley ('Billy') Sunday. A former janitor and, in the 1880s, a player for the Chicago White Sox baseball team, Sunday began evangelising in 1896 and reached the peak of his influence between 1906 and 1918. He replicated the 'hellfire-and-damnation' rhetoric of nineteenth-century circuit preachers, and adapted it to the urban environment of the early twentieth century. Sunday held rallies in auditoriums and sports stadiums in cities across the country. During one four-day 'crusade' in Michigan, in the fall of 1916, he claimed to have addressed two million people and to have converted 200,000.[33] The size of his congregations ensured he had no difficulty in raising funds. Enormous plates, two feet in diameter, would be passed amongst audiences and one rally alone, late in 1916, netted $50,000. Sunday kept audiences spellbound by mixing serious biblical messages with jokes and anecdotes but his message was, at heart, a deeply conservative one. He believed in the literal truth of the Bible, strongly supported Prohibition and was less concerned with social reform to help the disadvantaged than with the concept of *individual* salvation through Jesus Christ. This made him a particular bête noire of liberals. Some moderate Christians also found his message unpalatable. Sunday regularly excoriated 'wild-eyed socialists', who questioned American democracy and recommended them for the firing squad. He also displayed a certain insensitivity to women's issues, once advising, 'If some of you women would spend less on dope and cold cream and get down on your knees and pray, God would make you prettier.'[34]

Sunday's approach appealed to the already converted, but those with a more fragile or flexible faith were repelled by his brand of 'muscular' Christianity. Sunday was unrepentant. Churches in the Twenties, he argued, did not need an influx of *new* worshippers as much as they needed 'the old bunch made over'. 'Lord save us,' he boomed, 'from offhanded, flabby-cheeked, brittle-boned, weak-kneed, thin-skinned, pliable, plastic, spineless, effeminate, ossified, three-karat Christianity.'

Religious belief, of one sort or another, was alive and well in the Twenties, despite the new penchant for iconoclasm. What was changing were the ways in which faith was being expressed. Innovative techniques were increasingly employed to reflect the colourful, restless and commercial spirit of the age. The most notable of the new generation of evangelists was Aimee Semple McPherson. 'Sister Aimee' had been drawn to evangelism by her first husband, a Pentecostal preacher. After a failed second marriage, she began holding revival meetings across the United States and by the early 1920s, had neatly repackaged her evangelical message as the 'Foursquare Gospel' (the 'squares' being the literal truth of the Bible, divine healing, Christ's Second Coming and the saving of souls through conversion). Donations from the faithful paid for the building of an exotic 'Angelus Temple', which opened in January 1923 in Echo Park, Los Angeles and was renowned for the illuminated, rotating cross which topped its roof. Pentecostalism had always encouraged 'active' worship – singing, shouting and swaying congregations and the practice of 'speaking in tongues' – but Sister Aimee took the concept to spectacular new heights. Inside the Angelus, she enthralled congregations with slide-shows, dramatic enactments of the battle between Good and Evil, mass baptisms, choir singing and 'healing sessions'. A monthly magazine and radio station ensured that modern marketing devices would spread her message far beyond the Temple. Edmund Wilson, tongue firmly in cheek, described the 'good-natured but thrilling native angels' which perched at the base of:

> the big red radio-tower love-wand and see to it that not a tittle or vibration of their mistress's kind warm voice goes astray as it speeds to you in your sitting room and tells you how sweet Jesus has been to her ...[35]

McPherson's sheer stage presence and flair for dramatic entrances – she once rode into a service on a motorbike – carried an intoxicatingly upbeat message which stressed the celebration of life rather than fear of

Hell and forgiveness rather than condemnation. The simplicity and theatricality of the 'Foursquare Gospel' made it particularly attractive to the young and the rebellious who disliked the sombre, doom-laden themes of old-style religion. It also appealed to the thousands of migrants who flooded into California during the Twenties. By 1926, McPherson's sermons at the Angelus were attracting up to 5,000 a night and she had become one of the most wealthy and celebrated religious figures in the country.

If her brash style breathed of the 1920s, however, her decline was also an ironic reflection of her times. Rumours of an illicit liaison with a married man were followed by Sister Aimee's sudden 'disappearance' on 18 May 1926 and her equally unexpected reappearance on the Mexican border on 23 June. She claimed to have been kidnapped but police found no evidence to corroborate the story and indicted her for conspiracy to obstruct justice. Allegations of blackmail and rumours of furtive meetings in 'hot-pillow' motels caused a media frenzy until the Los Angeles District Attorney, without explanation, had the case against McPherson dismissed. Though claiming vindication, Sister Aimee never completely recovered her prestige. Her career embarked upon a long downward spiral which ended with her death, aged 54, in September 1944.

For women in general, the Twenties promised, but did not always deliver, radical changes in acceptable behaviour and gender roles. The widespread desire to break with the past was reflected in the revolution in hair and clothing styles. At the beginning of the decade, the entrenched preference for punishingly tight corsets and long skirts which reached down ten inches below the knee was still very much in evidence, despite their tendency to restrict freedom of movement. By the mid-Twenties, this decorative, billowing style had given way to straighter, slimmer skirt designs which cut off just below the knee. Younger women's hair was cut fashionably short in a Parisian-style 'bob'. As with the new, simpler clothing designs, 'bobbed' hair appealed to those seeking a faster pace and greater convenience in their lifestyles.[36] The simpler designs were often topped off by a tight-fitting 'cloche' (bell) hat. The bob hair style was the signature of the 'flapper' –the iconic representation of modern womanhood in the 1920s. The term 'flapper' had, in the nineteenth century, been a slang expression for a very young prostitute, but by the mid-Twenties it denoted a flighty young girl, usually in her early twenties, who wore lipstick and adhered to the latest fashions, in startlingly bright colours. The flapper smoked cigarettes and was often seen behind the wheel of a car, or travelling, unchaperoned, in one driven by her boyfriend. The expense of following the latest trends ensured that they were usually the daughters of upper middle-class and wealthy parents. The flapper epitomised not only the new, 'liberated' status of women but also the confident, energetic and highly materialistic society which was emerging in mid-Twenties America. Less content to sit demurely at home, reading 'appropriate' novels and awaiting male suitors, more women were entering full or part-time employment beyond the restricted range of jobs traditionally open to women – teaching, cleaning and shop work. Due to the disruption in employment patterns caused by the war, women now worked on factory production lines and in the offices of the burgeoning service sector as typists, telephonists and sales representatives. By 1929, nearly eleven million women were working either full or part-time outside the home, compared to around seven million in 1919.

Women's salaries, nonetheless, stayed below those of their male counterparts and despite press excitement at the arrival of the 'New Woman', female Americans found that the ingrained social attitudes of generations were still a bar to rapid advancement. As black Americans had discovered after the Fifteenth Amendment granted them the franchise, gaining the right to vote did not automatically place women on an equal legal or social footing with men. Increasingly, however, women's voices were being heard in debates over divorce laws, child labour laws, the minimum wage, birth control and education. They also began, slowly, to gain a higher profile in politics. Jeanette Rankin of Montana had been elected as the first female member of the House of Representatives in 1917. In the 1920s, the nation saw its first female state governors – Miriam A. 'Ma' Ferguson in Texas (1925–7 and 1933–5) and Nellie Tayloe Ross in Wyoming (1925–7).[37] By 1933, the first woman elected to the Senate, Hattie Caraway of Arkansas, would take her seat and Frances Perkins would become the first female member of a presidential cabinet.

As the decade reached its mid-point, some of its most bizarre 'crazes' were in full swing. In 1924, Alvin 'Shipwreck' Kelly climbed onto the roof of a hotel in Los Angeles, erected a pole and perched on top of it, using a small wooden platform, for 13 hours and 13 minutes. Crowds gathered below to hand up parcels of food and bottles of water or to yell questions or insults at Kelly. His feat was covered exhaustively by reporters and newsreel photographers and caused an outbreak of 'copycat' pole-sitting across the nation. Those with no head for heights could try 'marathon dancing' – a wildly popular pastime which began earlier in the decade and reached its peak in the early 1930s. Competing couples would swirl across the floor for days or weeks on end. McMillan's Dance Academy in Houston, Texas, held a 65-hour marathon in April 1923, a feat dwarfed by the June 1928 'Dance Derby of the Century' held in New York's Madison Square Garden, in which ninety-one couples danced for 481 hours. 'Bathroom breaks' and short rests for eating were allowed. Otherwise, the dancing continued until only one couple remained standing. Many dropped to the floor from sheer exhaustion and hospitals reported a rise in casualty admissions whenever a dance marathon was held in their vicinity. Although many such dances were held to attract sponsorship, with proceeds going to charity, the Los Angeles city authorities became so concerned at the health implications that they passed a city-wide ban on the craze. Tightrope walking became a popular spectator sport and was featured in the 1928 Charlie Chaplin film, *The Circus*.

The Twenties had begun to 'roar' as American society embraced excess and pushed at boundaries. The drive for *higher* and *longer*, for *faster* or, simply, for *more* became a national preoccupation. The crazes which swept the country throughout the 1920s were symbolic of the energy of a chronically restless nation. Returning prosperity and labour-saving innovations provided many with the time and the means to indulge their leisure pursuits to an extent not available to earlier generations. Media growth, looser social conventions and saturation advertising accelerated the changes. If American culture had become oddly 'faddish' and 'suggestible', it was because so much of the nation was now *open* to suggestion as never before.

Notes

1. Mencken, *A Carnival of Buncombe*, p. 64.
2. McAdoo was never convicted of any wrongdoing but the association with the oil scandals compromised his bid for the 1924 Democratic presidential nomination.
3. Sinclair, *The Available Man*, pp. 252–3.
4. Although the Coolidge administration made other attempts to lease Muscle Shoals, progressive opposition was insurmountable. In 1933, President Franklin D. Roosevelt's New Deal policies integrated Muscle Shoals into the state-run Tennessee Valley Authority hydroelectric power scheme.
5. This action had historical precedent in an 1882 Act of Congress which barred almost all Chinese immigration.
6. Samuel G. Blythe, 'And Then On The Other Hand', *Saturday Evening Post*, 30 October 1920, p. 4.

7. William Allen White, *A Puritan in Babylon: The Story of Calvin Coolidge* (New York: Macmillan, 1938), p. 307.

8. The original Klan was formed in Tennessee in 1866 by a group of ex-Confederate soldiers and headed by General Nathan Bedford Forrest. *Ku Klux* was a corruption of the Greek word '*kuklos*' or 'circle'.

9. Interestingly, Jews and Catholics were excluded from membership by the 1920s Klan but *not* by its 1860s predecessor.

10. John Hope Franklin and Alfred A. Moss Jr, *From Slavery to Freedom: A History of African-Americans*, 7th edn (New York: McGraw-Hill, 1994), p. 349.

11. Louis Francis Budenz, 'Indiana's Anti-Saloon League Goes to Jail', *The Nation*, 24 August 1927, 125: 3242, p. 177.

12. Similar techniques were being employed by the rising European fascist movements during the 1920s.

13. This view sat uncomfortably next to Underwood's role as one of the main organisers of the 1921 congressional filibuster of the Dyer anti-lynching bill.

14. The two-thirds rule was finally ditched by the party in 1936 at the instigation of President Franklin D. Roosevelt, whose own first nomination campaign in 1932 was nearly destroyed by it.

15. Politics had had its first lesson in the power of 'new technology'. As that technology developed further over the next thirty years, most of the spontaneity would be squeezed out of party conventions, reducing them to arid, over-rehearsed, one-ballot coronations.

16. LaFollette had also been the major motive force behind the creation of the National Progressive Republican League, in January 1911, which challenged President William Howard Taft for the Republican nomination and foreshadowed its disastrous electoral defeat at the hands of Woodrow Wilson the following year.

17. Donald R. McCoy, *Calvin Coolidge: The Quiet President* (New York: Macmillan, 1957), p. 258.

18. Schriftgeisser, *This Was Normalcy*, p. 213.

19. Sinclair Lewis, 'Publicity Gone Mad', *The Nation*, 6 March 1929, 128: 3322, p. 278. Charles Lindbergh, in his 1927 account of the historic New York-to-Paris non-stop flight, also mentioned, in passing, a deep emotional attachment to his 'Waterman' pen. Sinclair Lewis' views on this are unrecorded.

20. Frederick Lewis Allen, *Only Yesterday: An Informal History of the 1920s in America* (New York: Harper and Brothers, 1931), p. 233.

21. May, 'Shifting Perspectives on the 1920s', p. 407.

22. John Hope Franklin and Alfred A. Moss Jr, *From Slavery to Freedom: A History of African-Americans*, 7th edn (New York: McGraw-Hill, 1994), p. 376.

23. 'Crisis in Dancing Craze', *New York Times*, 25 September 1921, p. 75.

24. Ballistics tests and re-examination of available evidence later in the century appeared to confirm Sacco's role in the murder for which he was convicted but raised doubts about the validity of Vanzetti's conviction.

25. Leon Edel (ed.), *Edmund Wilson: The Twenties, From Notebooks and Diaries of the Period* (London: Macmillan, 1975), p. 266.

26. Allen, *Only Yesterday*, p. 239.

27. Thomas A. Bailey, *Woodrow Wilson and the Great Betrayal* (New York: Macmillan, 1945), p. 177. This particular advert accompanied an application form filled in, but never sent, by President Wilson himself.

28. 'Links Lawlessness to Lack of Religion', *New York Times*, 10 December 1928, p. 30.

29. Bryan lost to McKinley twice, in 1896 and 1900. He gained the Democratic nomination a third time in 1908, but was defeated by William Howard Taft. Five days after the end of the Dayton trial, Bryan died suddenly in his sleep.

30. White, *Masks in a Pageant*, p. 273.

31. 'Says Scopes Trial Will Help Religion', *New York Times*, 15 June 1925, p. 18.

32. 'Cardinal Assails "New Idea" of God', *New York Times*, 31 December 1928, p. 7.

33. Contemporary accounts in state newspapers put the figures closer to 1 million and 25,000.

34. Michael E. Parrish, *Anxious Decades: America in Prosperity and Depression, 1920–1941* (New York: W. W. Norton and Co., 1992), p. 132.

35. Edmund Wilson, 'The City of Our Lady, The Queen of the Angels', in Edmund Wilson, *The American Earthquake: A Documentary of the Jazz Age, the Great Depression and the New Deal* (London: W. H. Allen Co., 1958), p. 379.

36. This need was symbolised by the short-lived popularity of the 'one-hour dress' – a design produced by the Women's Fashion Institute which could be made at home in one hour.

37. Both, however, were the wives or widows of former governors.

CHAPTER 5

High Tide of Normalcy, 1925–8

Then go sit down, ye pessimists
Ye growlers of the glum
We've got a new apostle
And the Age of Youth has come.[1]

Coolidge and Congress

President Coolidge's 4 March 1925 inaugural address was a succinct restatement of the conservative economic and political philosophies which underlay the programme of normalcy. By 1925, these principles no longer represented a call for change, as they had done at Harding's inaugural, but a declaration of continuity and of the administration's intention to build upon the successes of the past four years. The President stressed the virtues of individual initiative and self-reliance and promised to continue the restraint of government spending and regulation. Tax levels would be reduced whenever possible. This relentless pursuit of economy was not simply obsessive penny-pinching. Coolidge declared, 'I favour the policy of economy not because I wish to save money but because I wish to save people.' Government extravagance and waste, he continued, were harmful both to the financial and to the moral and spiritual well-being of ordinary citizens.

> I want the people of America to be able to work less for the government and more for themselves. I want them to have the rewards of their own industry. That is the chief meaning of freedom. Until we can re-establish a condition under which the earnings of the people can be kept by the people, we are bound to suffer a very distinct curtailment of our liberty.

Perhaps sensitive to the accusations of progressives that the fiscal policies of the administration were dictated by Wall Street and lacked the ambitious idealism of Roosevelt's 'Square Deal' or Wilson's 'New

Freedom', the President offered up the novel proposition that, 'economy is idealism in its most practical form.'

The inaugural address was also notable for its emphasis on preserving national identity, although no direct mention was made of recent immigration legislation. Phrases such as 'distinctively American', 'more and more American' and 'candidly, intensely and scrupulously American' were deployed to satisfy nativist sentiment, which still ran high across the country, and, more subtly, to reassure isolationists that the administration's interest in international cooperation would not be allowed to threaten national sovereignty. Despite its '100 per cent Americanism' overtones, Coolidge's speech, like Harding's four years previously, was not a call for the United States to turn its back on active participation in world affairs. The 'common brotherhood of man', he argued, transcended national and geographic boundaries and the United States should commit itself to 'frequent conferences and consultations' with other nations. More specifically, he included another plea for active US involvement in the Permanent Court of International Justice. Whilst the nation could never compromise its independence, it should, he noted, 'bear its full share of the responsibility ... for the administration of evenhanded justice between nation and nation.'

Domestically, Coolidge could not have expected a greater degree of unity or cooperation from his party in the new sixty-ninth Congress than that which he had received from the sixty-eighth. The 1924 elections had produced a functional seventeen-seat majority for Republicans in the Senate and a sixty-seat majority in the House. Whilst not on the scale of the 1920 margins, they were comfortable enough to give members renewed confidence and plenty of scope for rebellion. Potential revolts would also be harder to head off after the death of Henry Cabot Lodge in November 1924 and his replacement as Republican Senate Floor Leader by the somewhat less authoritarian Charles Curtis. The isolationist Borah had assumed from Lodge the chairmanship of the Senate Foreign Relations Committee, ensuring that the State Department would now come under closer scrutiny from Congress. Additionally, few new pieces of legislation were being offered by the administration for congressional attention, thus creating more time for debate and dissection of specific policies and extra space on the timetable for members to pursue their own personal or constituency agendas.

Without a firm lead from the White House or the Senate Republican leadership, the President knew he would need to move with caution to avoid the dangers of drift and division. Both Coolidge and Curtis knew that progressive Republicans were likely to seize every opportunity to amend or defeat administration bills which they considered too conservative or pro-business. Despite the failure of LaFollette's presidential bid, progressivism remained a significant force in both House and Senate. Progressives held Coolidge, as they had held Harding, in barely concealed contempt. Believing that serious questions such as corporate power, the imbalance of wealth, environmental destruction and poor public health and education standards needed urgent attention, they could not understand why, as William Allen White wrote, 'in March 1925, the watchman on the tower was calling hour to hour, "All is well."'[2] In the political environment of the mid- to late 1920s, the progressive Republican faction constituted, to all intents and purposes, the main opposition to the pro-business administration and Republican congressional leadership, since the Democratic party itself was still a largely conservative force at this time. Most of the energy for social and political reform in the Coolidge years, therefore, was generated by the heirs of Roosevelt and LaFollette.

Under these conditions, most presidents would normally have relied upon the Vice-President, as presiding officer of the Senate, to negotiate compromises between the executive and rebel factions. Charles Dawes, however, had alienated senators on the morning of his inauguration by making an impatient, bad-tempered speech criticising time-honoured Senate procedures, particularly the use of the filibuster as a delaying tactic. As Coolidge watched, with evident disapproval, the new Vice-President systematically demolished the chance for close cooperation between Congress and the White House for the coming four years. Dawes had been in his element paring back the cost of government bureaucracy and constructing a rescue plan for the German economy. The vice-presidency, however, offered virtually no scope for independent action because most of its functions were ceremonial, leaving its occupant with little to occupy his time. The resentment generated by Dawes' remarks undermined his authority as the administration's principal spokesman in Congress and damaged his relations with Coolidge, which had, in any event, never been close.

When the lame-duck session of the sixty-eighth Congress met in December 1924, the Republican Senate leadership moved rapidly to punish Robert LaFollette for his insurgent presidential campaign, stripping him, Smith Brookhart and two other leading progressives, of their committee assignments and their membership of the Senate Republican Caucus. LaFollette's angry supporters in Congress promptly retaliated by sabotaging the President's appointment powers.

The retirement of Justice Joseph McKenna, late in 1924, provided them with their first opportunity. A vacancy now arose on the Supreme Court to which President Coolidge nominated his Attorney General, Harlan F. Stone (who had succeeded Harry Daugherty in 1925). The Stone nomination was opposed by progressives, led by George Norris, who contended that Stone was too conservative and too closely associated with Wall Street.[3] Although Coolidge handily won the Senate confirmation vote a gauntlet had been thrown down. When, on 25 March 1925, he sent the name of Charles Beecher Warren to Congress for approval as Stone's successor at the Justice Department, progressives argued that Warren, a former president of the Michigan Sugar Company, was tarnished by ongoing federal investigations into alleged manipulation of sugar prices. They secured the support of Democrats and the Warren nomination was rejected by a single vote.[4] This was a deep humiliation for Coolidge. For the first time since the Reconstruction era, a presidential cabinet nominee had been turned down by the Senate. Coolidge proceeded to dig himself deeper into the hole by resubmitting Warren's name, rather than offering a compromise choice, only to have it rejected a second time, by a more solid forty-six to thirty-nine margin. The White House accused progressive rebels of once more betraying their party but, arguably, Warren had been an ill-advised choice. It was only just over four years since the Senate had waved through the nomination of Albert Fall as Interior Secretary without even a formal vote. The exposure of Fall's corruption in 1923 was deeply embarrassing to the Senate and made it more likely that, in the short term at least, cabinet appointees' career backgrounds would be subject to much closer scrutiny. Warren's links to the sugar companies made him vulnerable to progressives who used the association to undermine the President's authority. Coolidge was eventually forced to withdraw the nomination. Having made their point, the rebels endorsed the President's second choice for Attorney General, John G. Sargent, whose nomination was carried unanimously.

Within months of the inauguration, the impression was growing in Congress and the national press that the President could not control his own party, despite his personal popularity with the electorate.

In December 1925, the annual Gridiron Dinner was hosted by the Washington press elite, with the President, Vice-President Dawes and

Speaker Nick Longworth as guests of honour. The Gridiron Club had been formed in 1885 and presidents since McKinley had attended the dinners, sometimes contributing a good-humoured speech of their own at the end of the evening. Satirical songs and sketches were performed by reporters, poking gentle fun at the major business and political figures of the day. In one sketch, reporters playing the roles of Republican congressmen sang, with malicious gusto,

> In a Congress of our own,
> We'll circumvent the President,
> We will rout him, we will flout him,
> Let the White House moan and groan.
> And if we like, we'll spend the last red cent
> We won't be bossed by any President.[5]

Presidential Style

Coolidge's concept of the role of Chief Executive was different, in some respects, to that of his predecessor. Whilst Harding sought a cabinet of 'best minds' in order to compensate for what he believed were his own intellectual deficiencies, Coolidge placed greater emphasis on self-reliance and distrusted unscripted displays of creativity from his cabinet officials. The difference was most noticeable in the two Presidents' dealings with Commerce Secretary Herbert Hoover. Harding openly admired Hoover's intelligence and efficiency, often calling him 'the smartest gink I know.' Coolidge, however, resented Hoover and snidely referred to him as 'the wonder boy'. He disliked Hoover's habit of empire-building – involving the Commerce Department in areas of policy making which were technically the responsibility of other departments such as Justice, Agriculture and State. This activism jarred with the President's personal belief in the virtues of restrained government. The difference between the Harding and Coolidge approaches also stemmed, at least partly, from a difference in temperament. The freewheeling Harding was always receptive to advice, solicited or otherwise. He delegated authority generously and was rarely offended by open disagreement with his own views. Coolidge disliked unsought views, particularly from Hoover, of whom he once acidly observed, 'That man has offered me unsolicited advice for six years, all of it bad.' Like Harding, he delegated power – but not generously. Coolidge treated the delegation of leadership responsibilities as a quid pro quo by which cabinet officers, in return for their place at the cabinet table, performed their tasks efficiently and refrained from involving the President unless absolutely necessary. An official from the Department of Labour, sent to the White House by Labour Secretary John Davis to seek Coolidge's opinion on a decision Davis was about to make, was brusquely dismissed with the instruction, 'You tell ol' man Davis I hired him as Secretary of Labor and if he can't do the job I'll get a new Secretary of Labor.'[6]

Coolidge shared the view of many conservative constitutional theorists of the day that the roots of presidential power lay in the symbolic status of the institution itself. As the only nationally elected public officer, he believed it was important for the President to distance himself from petty, factional rivalries and to focus, instead, upon articulating the nation's broader values and goals. The Chief Executive was elected, under this interpretation, to *preside* over the executive branch of government, not to dictate its every policy or second-guess every decision of its officers. In an age where political decision-making was becoming increasingly complex and inter-linked, the latter approach was both impractical and, for the physical and psychological health of the President, highly undesirable.[7] In Coolidge's view, the presidential office risked losing the respect of the nation if it were inextricably linked to every controversial decision made by senior or junior government officials. Harding had initially held similar views himself, but his conviction that Congress was failing to fulfil its side of the constitutional bargain by governing in the interests of the nation as a whole had caused him to modify his views. Coolidge's more rigidly constructed philosophy, however, was an ideal fit. He regarded the natural territory of the presidency as those powers *specifically* granted to it under Article II of the Constitution and disliked roaming into the grey regions of 'implied powers' – areas in which Roosevelt and Wilson had regularly pitched their executive tents. He relied upon his cabinet colleagues to interpret their roles in the same way and to do their jobs efficiently.[8] In so doing, they should also cooperate in protecting the prestige of the presidency. 'By involving me,' he once informed his cabinet, 'you have lowered the faith of the people in their government.'[9] This approach to presidential leadership was unpopular with progressives and liberals, who saw the executive branch as a vital counterweight to a faction-ridden Congress and as a vital source of moral and political inspiration. To their chagrin, however, it was perfectly legitimate as an interpretation of the presidency's constitutional position.

The thirtieth President was also more disposed than his predecessor to avoid open confrontations with Congress or the appearance of dictating to the congressional leadership. Here, as in his relations with the cabinet, Coolidge disliked 'grey' areas of overlapping authority, preferring to translate the constitutional theory of the 'separation of powers' as literally as possible. Lacking Harding's bonhomie, and his penchant for political horse-trading, he was often distant and uncommunicative with members of his own party – tending to leave them in the dark over his views or intentions. Over time, this weakened the Executive's ability to influence events in Congress and Coolidge, in his last years in office, resorted increasingly to the veto power. He had deployed it sparingly in the early period of his presidency, but used it twelve times in the final two years.

The President continued Harding's practice of twice-weekly press conferences with written questions to be submitted in advance. Direct quotation without permission was forbidden but important information could be attributed to 'a White House source'. Herbert Hoover's Commerce Department continued its habit, begun under Harding, of deluging reporters with fact sheets, press statements and statistical reports. Although less in the way of substantive news emanated from the White House itself, the administration's handling of the press was considered so effective that political scientist Lindsay Rodgers warned, in 1926, of an evolving threat to the constitutional balance of power. 'It is government by favourable publicity and Congress lacks the means to reply.'[10]

Part of this strategy involved the manipulation of 'photo opportunities'. As Vice-President, Coolidge had posed for photographers at his father's farm in Vermont, milking a cow, pitching hay or mending a maple sap bucket. He continued the practice as President – allowing himself to be photographed in the regalia of an Indian tribal chief, dressed as a cowboy or wearing a traditional New England farmers' smock. Despite his habitually dour expression, the President enjoyed these occasions and used them to nurture the mythology of 'Silent Cal', the puritanical Yankee farm-boy. Pictures and stories of Coolidge, set alongside Hollywood sex scandals, Sister Aimee's raucous sermons and the violence of Al Capone's Chicago, provided a refreshing contrast for the American public – a model of New England sobriety and, for some, a source of affectionate amusement. Of considerable help in the maintenance of the Coolidge 'mystique' was the President's wife, Grace Goodhue Coolidge, whose lively, unaffected nature made her one of the century's most popular First Ladies. Unlike Florence Harding, Grace Coolidge did not make her political opinions known or hold her own press conferences. Neither did she attempt to exert behind-the-scenes influence over her husband's political decisions. Coolidge, in fact, refused to discuss politics with his wife. Her presence, however, was an effective counterbalance to his introverted personality and probably made him more popular with the press than he might otherwise have been.

McNary-Haugenism

If images from Calvin Coolidge's farming roots helped to solidify his popularity with the American people, the crisis in agriculture itself was undermining his popularity with farmers and continuing to divide the Republican party. The measures undertaken by the Harding administration and the sixty-seventh Congress had alleviated some of the worst short-term difficulties through the extension of extra government credit, but the long-term outlook remained bleak. Overproduction continued to drive prices downwards and the most widely mooted solutions appeared too radical and unrealistic. Price-fixing was out of the question, as it interfered with the natural rhythms of the agricultural economy. Destruction of cotton and grain surpluses without compensation from the government was unthinkable, whilst destruction *with* federal compensation raised the spectre of socialistic, centralised planning, which was anathema to the White House. 'Simple and direct methods put into operation by the farmer himself are the only real sources for restoration,' Coolidge declared.[11]

It was not immediately clear what 'simple and direct' methods the President had in mind. Voluntary restriction of crop production by farmers themselves was considered impractical. Human nature being what it was, a minority of farmers were likely to publicly sign up for restriction but then maintain their existing production levels and conceal surpluses, releasing them onto the market once restraint by other producers had stimulated prices to rise.

Agriculture secretary, Dr William Jardine, an agronomist popular with the AFB, favoured the development of farming cooperatives as a solution to low prices.[12] The combined financial resources of multiple members would permit cooperatives to buy up surpluses, remove them from the market, thus allowing prices to float upwards. Jardine preferred this idealistic scheme, though it suffered from the same drawbacks as voluntary restriction, because he shared Coolidge's belief that more cash aid to agriculture from the central government would reduce the farmer's independence whilst doing nothing to address overproduction problems.

One of the most popular solutions with the farm bloc was a plan for dumping agricultural surpluses abroad, which became known as 'McNary-Haugenism' after its principal sponsors in Congress, Charles L. McNary (R-Oregon), chairman of the Senate Agriculture Committee, and Gilbert N. Haugen (R-Iowa).[13] The McNary-Haugen solution involved the establishment of a government corporation which would buy up farm surpluses, at an agreed price somewhat above the current low price levels, and then sell them abroad at a loss, which would subsequently be recovered through an 'equalisation' fee charged to producers. Whatever the final fee, the farmers would still receive more for their produce than if it had been sold on the home market or left to rot. Additionally, US tariffs would prevent cheap foreign produce being dumped on the domestic market. McNary-Haugen, its farm bloc supporters in Congress claimed, would 'make the tariff effective'. Farming organisations backed the plan, arguing that agriculture deserved the same assistance in selling its goods abroad as did the manufacturing sector.

The plan, popular in the mid-western farming states, was backed by the AFB and by public figures, including Illinois governor, Frank Lowden, General Hugh S. 'Ironpants' Johnson (the future head of Franklin D. Roosevelt's National Recovery Administration) and George N. Peek, who, with Johnson, had originated the idea in the early 1920s. Financial backing and moral support came from Bernard Baruch, the Wall Street financier, and helped offset the opposition of Andrew Mellon who thought the scheme too costly. Cotton producers in the South largely withheld their support of the plan until bad weather conditions and infestations produced a run of poor crops and sent cotton prices tumbling. The President, Mellon, Jardine and Secretary Hoover viewed 'McNary-Haugenism' as blatant price-fixing which set an unhealthy precedent for government interference in the natural operations of the market. Dumping the surplus, Mellon pointed out, would enable European markets to 'secure American commodities at prices below the American level.' The first effort by McNary and Haugen to pass a bill through Congress was soundly defeated in 1924 but the idea continued to gather momentum and was reintroduced, with modifications, in 1926.

This time, the congressional rivalry of the farm bloc and business and banking interests was aggravated by progressive Republicans in order to embarrass the White House. McNary-Haugen met stiff opposition from the business bloc, prompting Senator Robert M. LaFollette Jr to launch a retaliatory filibuster against a bill supported by business which extended the charters of the Federal Reserve banks.[14] Any attempt by the White House or its congressional supporters to prevent a vote on McNary-Haugen would thus lead to the loss of the McFadden-Pepper Banking Bill. Vice-President Dawes eventually negotiated a deal to break the deadlock and allow *both* bills to go to a vote. By so doing, he created the impression that he was working against the White House and incurred the displeasure of the President. Coolidge later complained that 'the McNary-Haugen people have their headquarters in the Vice-President's chambers.'

The bill passed the Senate on 17 February 1927, by a vote of forty-seven to thirty-nine but was vetoed by the White House.[15] In his veto statement, the President firmly reiterated his conviction that 'Government price fixing, once started, has no justice and no end,' and that McNary-Haugenism was 'an economic folly from which this country has every right to be spared.' Further efforts would be made to push the plan forward but Coolidge refused to consider a compromise. His resistance made the administration extremely unpopular in the farm-belt states but did not undermine the Republican vote in those areas. Farmers solidly supported Hoover in 1928, despite Democratic candidate Al Smith's promises to use more federal government money to resolve the farming crisis.

Problems of Prohibition

In his Annual Message to Congress, on 8 December 1925, President Coolidge maintained the themes of gradualism and continuity which had marked his inaugural speech nine months earlier: 'The country does not appear to require radical departures from the policies already adopted,' he said, 'so much as it needs a further extension of these policies and the improvement of details.'

One area, in particular, where improvement was badly needed was in the enforcement of Prohibition. Available evidence suggests that the President, like Harding, Mellon and William Howard Taft, doubted the wisdom of 'legislating morality' and considered the Volstead Act intrusive and unworkable. White House aide Colonel Edmund Starling claimed President Coolidge privately expressed the view that 'any law which inspires disrespect for the other laws – the good laws – is a bad law.'[16] The administration confined itself, as Harding's had done, to periodic calls for stronger enforcement of Volstead, but neither it nor the sixty-ninth Congress seemed in a hurry to achieve it. Harding himself had often enjoyed drinks during poker parties with friends at the White

House and Florence Harding was often on hand to mix them. Coolidge was generally abstemious but was occasionally prescribed alcohol by his doctor. Many other political, judicial, civic and cultural figures of the day privately flouted the law on a regular basis. Meanwhile, the deep divisions between wets and drys which split both the Republicans and the Democrats made any firm stand on the morality of drinking a dangerous political exercise.

After the first six years of the 'noble experiment', Prohibitionists were able to point to some successes. Thousands of saloons had lost their licences or now sold only soft drinks. Recorded levels of alcohol consumption had fallen sharply and, as predicted by the Anti-Saloon League, absenteeism at the workplace was down whilst individual productivity had risen. Even the liberal sceptics at *The Nation* admitted to some positive outcomes. Heywood Broun noted, 'The savings banks are just as full as are the jails.'[17] In Pennsylvania alone, 13,000 arrests for bootlegging were made between 1921 and 1925. Two Prohibition agents, Izzadore ('Izzy') Einstein and Moe Smith, became nationally known figures. Their success in capturing press and public interest stemmed not from their status as moral enforcers but from the devious methods they used to infiltrate speakeasies, adopting disguises and faking 'incidents' designed to trap unwary bartenders into dispensing alcohol from their hidden stores. On one occasion, Smith immersed himself in freezing water and was dragged into a bar by Einstein who pretended Smith had fallen into a frozen lake and begged for whiskey to save his friend's life. When the compassionate bartender produced it, they revealed their identities and shut down the bar. Together they made more than 4,000 arrests in New York City between 1920 and 1925, until the mounting embarrassment of the Bureau at their antics led to their enforced 'retirement' during an administrative reorganisation.

In some states, the Anti-Saloon League was not just a small pressure group but a formidable political force, exerting decisive influence in every aspect of politics and judicial decision-making. This was particularly the case in Indiana, where Edward S. Shumaker, leader of the Indiana branch of the Anti-Saloon League, pushed through a 'bone-dry' law banning even alcohol prescribed by doctors. Hoosier Prohibition agents employed blanket search and seizure warrants which covered entire residential or business districts in their determination to root out stocks of liquor until the state Supreme Court put a stop to the practice by ruling it a violation of the Bill of Rights.

Despite the propaganda efforts of the Prohibition Bureau, the battle to cut supplies of smuggled and home-manufactured alcohol was being lost, and lost badly. Alcohol was available to most citizens who were enterprising enough to seek it out. Almost overnight, whisky smuggling became a major growth industry, with thousands of barrels rolling into the country across 18,700 miles of vulnerable borders. Much of it came from Canada or from ships anchored offshore which ferried their cargo in motor boats, under cover of night, to unpatrolled beaches. The US Coast Guard budget averaged only $12 million a year during the Prohibition period.

The effectiveness of the smuggling operations ensured that, by the end of 1925, around 200 million gallons of hard liquor and 118 million gallons of wine were available for consumption and organised boot-legging was bringing in over $4 billion a year. By the Prohibition Bureau's own admission, only a fraction, perhaps 4 per cent, of the contraband smuggled over the borders was seized. Beyond smuggling, a variety of deceptions were employed to dodge the laws. Alcohol was still available on medical prescription and some doctors prescribed it liberally. Even the bourbon served at President Harding's poker parties was obtained through a friend of the Attorney General, who used Justice Department 'B' permits, granting alcohol to hospitals, to circumvent the law.[18] Wine for use in religious ceremonies was regularly acquired under false pretexts. In rural districts, 'moonshine' distilleries were commonplace. In cities, 'bathtub gin' slaked the thirsts of furtive customers. The fact that some of these home-made concoctions were potentially lethal merely added to hardened drinkers' thrill at flouting the law, a thrill which was already generating new cultural trends. Edmund Wilson, writing in 1927, observed that 'the vocabulary of social drinking ... seems to have become especially rich ... *fried, stewed* and *boiled* all convey distinctly different ideas; and *cock-eyed, plastered, owled, embalmed* and *ossified* evoke quite different images.'[19]

Cross-border smuggling and bootlegging were not the only forces undermining Prohibition. The Volstead Act gave legal muscle to the Eighteenth Amendment but required an enormous cash outlay and efficient organisation at both the federal and state levels. Neither was in place. Despite badgering both the Harding and Coolidge administrations, the Prohibition Bureau still had only 1,600 agents and a meagre budget. Under the terms of Volstead, each state was expected to appro-priate funds for the maintenance of its own branch of the bureau but many state legislatures bitterly resented paying. By 1927, a majority of states had followed the lead of the unrepentantly wet governor of New York, Al Smith, by refusing to contribute any funds at all.

The scarcity of cash inevitably affected the performance of bureau agents, who often had little or no training. Consequently, many were either incompetent or de-motivated. Others succumbed to temptation and took bribes. One Philadelphia bureau officer was found to have conspired with bootleggers to remove 700,000 gallons of whisky from the very government warehouses he had been assigned to protect.

H. L. Mencken, having admired the cunning of the San Francisco city authorities in 1920, was equally delighted at the easy availability of liquor on the streets of New York, where enforcement officers, for a predetermined fee, could be persuaded to look the other way.

> Very good beer is everywhere on sale, and nine-tenths of the Italian restaurants ... are selling cocktails and wine. Along Broadway the difficulty of concealing so bulky a drink as beer and the high tolls demanded by the Prohibition enforcement officers make the price somewhat high, but in the side-streets it is now only 60 per cent above what it was in the days before the Volstead act.[20]

Even if, at the outset, Prohibitionists had acknowledged that the corruption of local police and enforcement officers might become a problem, they could not have foreseen the degree to which elected political leaders would become complicit in the neglect and abuse of Prohibition which began after January 1920. A large proportion (probably the majority) of Congress members and their counterparts at state and local levels, had voted for the Eighteenth Amendment through fear of the electoral clout wielded by the temperance movement. They remained indifferent to the success or failure of the experiment once it had begun. At the state and local levels, mayors, sheriffs and police officials actively undermined Volstead, either by violating the law themselves or assisting others in its violation. The court system was inundated with around 50,000 prosecutions a year. As a result, a tacit agreement would sometimes be reached in order to speed up the judicial process, whereby exceedingly light sentences were handed down in return for guilty pleas.

The American entrepreneurial spirit, in degraded form, proved to be one of the toughest opponents of all. Racketeering, which had always existed in America's largest cities, where large populations were heavily concentrated, flourished in the era of Prohibition. Control of the illegal liquor supply offered a route not only to great wealth but to political power for those most adept at exploiting the opportunity. Here, as in other areas, the 1920s witnessed the birth of a new, better-organised and more dangerous version of an age-old practice. Prohibition agents and policemen, judges and local politicians were bribed or blackmailed to such an extent that some towns and cities came under the de facto control of criminal gangs. The structures of these gangs often resembled the corporate model, with stratified control, local representatives and team leaders, client groups and carefully managed investment of profits. The most notorious of the gang leaders was Alfonse Capone, who succeeded Johnny Torrio as head of Chicago's most powerful crime syndicate and who had accumulated a personal fortune estimated at $60–65 million by 1929. Capone controlled the city's liquor supply, in addition to revenues raised through prostitution and gambling. Speakeasy owners were either 'persuaded' or firebombed into accepting 'protection' from Capone against the attentions of the rival Chicago gang of Dion O'Banion. Capone eventually had O'Banion murdered but the two gangs continued to engage in street battles and assassinations for the rest of the decade.

Significantly, the principle force undermining Prohibition was not organised crime but the decade's antipathy towards 'big government' and taxation. It was this antipathy which aided bootleggers and motivated millions of normally law-abiding citizens to flout the law. Nothing, critics claimed, symbolised an over-mighty state more than the Prohibition Bureau, with its propaganda, its agents provocateurs, its demands for more taxpayers' money and its authoritarian zeal in seeking out and prosecuting 'immoral' citizens. In no other decade since the national temperance movement began could the 'noble experiment' have been more assured of failure. Bathtub gin sustained poorer citizens, whilst the rich relied upon their wine cellars, which they had ensured were well-stocked before Prohibition came into force. Andrew Mellon, whose Internal Revenue Bureau was expected to use its fiscal resources and legal powers to back up Volstead, detested the act and was half-hearted in helping to enforce it. In their distaste for 'legislated morality' the wealthy elites and labouring classes finally found common cause in the undermining of an unpopular law, from the first sip of illicit hooch to the final swing of the judge's gavel. Indiana's Shumaker himself eventually became the target of those who had grown resentful of the Anti-Saloon League's authoritarian attitudes. On the dubious pretext that his report to the national League offices had included 'veiled threats' to remove uncooperative judges at the next election and had shown 'contempt' for the state courts, Indiana's Supreme Court jailed Shumaker for sixty days and fined him $250.[21]

The declining popularity of the cause of temperance was most graphically demonstrated by the fall-off in electoral support for presidential candidates of the Prohibition party in the three elections of the decade. In 1920, shortly after the experiment with temperance began, the party's candidate, Aaron S. Watkins, polled 189,339 votes. Four years later, with the social and legal side-effects of Prohibition more readily apparent, Herman P. Faris garnered only 56,292. By 1928, when the Democrats felt confident enough to field an openly wet nominee, support for the Prohibition party and its presidential candidate, William F. Varney, had slumped to 20,101.[22]

In May 1929, the National Commission on Law Observance and Enforcement ('Wickersham Commission') would investigate the enforcement of Prohibition. The report of the commissioners, who included George Wickersham, President Taft's Attorney General and Roscoe Pound, Dean of the Harvard Law School, would reveal an extensive catalogue of corrupt practices within the police force linked to Prohibition and further undermine the long-term survival prospects of the 'noble experiment'.

Justice and Disarmament

President Harding had shown a considerable amount of interest in foreign affairs, partly due to his experience as a member of the Senate Foreign Relations committee, and partly because important issues such as League membership, disarmament, debt reduction and Soviet recognition had forced themselves onto his administration's agenda. Foreign policy was less of a preoccupation for his successor. Calvin Coolidge had no accumulated store of expertise in foreign policy, causing Frederick Lewis Allen to note, disparagingly, 'Neither he nor his intellect had ever ventured far abroad.'[23] Instead, the President relied heavily upon his Secretaries of State, Charles Evans Hughes and, after January 1925, Frank B. Kellogg.

In the early days of his administration, Coolidge's pledge to push ahead with the Harding programme meant, amongst other things, continuing to pressure the Senate to approve the protocol of the Permanent Court of International Justice, submitted to it by Harding shortly before his death. Coolidge's December 1923 message to Congress flagged the issue as an administration priority and the 1924 platforms of both the Republican and Democratic parties also called for membership of the World Court. Public opinion and the editorial opinions of a majority of the nation's newspapers appeared to show a solid consensus developing in support of the Court that had never formed behind the League. In March 1925, the House of Representatives adopted a resolution endorsing membership by 303 votes to twenty-eight. William Borah, however, in his new role as chairman of the Senate Foreign Relations committee, rallied isolationist support for a series of amendments when debate on the resolution opened in the Senate. These stipulated that US relations with the Court 'shall not be taken to involve *any* relation to the League of Nations'; that the level of financial contributions from the US would be set by Congress, not by the Court; that changes to the powers of the Court would not be made without American agreement; that the US would be permitted an equal role with other nations in electing members of the Court; and, finally, that America would not be 'bound by advisory opinions rendered without our consent.' This last proviso, which was aimed at preventing the alarming prospect of foreign 'meddling' in American immigration policy or challenges to the Monroe Doctrine, was the most important of the five conditions as far as isolationists were concerned. It was also, predictably, the one proviso which America's prospective partners on the Court could not accept. Isolationists claimed that Articles 12, 13 and 16 of the Covenant of the League of Nations left open the possibility that the Court's rulings might be enforced through military or other sanctions. This, they regarded as unacceptable. 'I am utterly opposed,' Borah declared, 'to the use of force or of economic sanctions in the enforcement of the decrees of an international court.' Those with pro-Court sympathies, such as Senator Thomas J. Walsh (D-Montana) argued that member states of the Court who were *also* member states of the League might be bound by League enforcement provisions but that since America was *not* a League member, she could be confident that those provisions would not be used against her. Senator Walter Edge, reflecting majority opinion, indicated that the language of the reservation proposed by Borah was, at any rate, 'sufficiently broad to cover any reasonable contingency.'[24]

On 26 January 1926, the Senate endorsed Court membership, *with* amendments, by seventy-six votes to seventeen. Coolidge immediately indicated that he would not seek to have the amendments overturned. To all intents and purposes, the vote brought an end to the prospect of US membership of the Court and Coolidge believed he had little alternative but to accept the Senate's decision. To openly oppose the amendments would have placed him in the politically embarrassing posture of arguing against specific safeguards for America's interests proposed by the people's elected representatives. His opponents would have an easier time arguing that the nation should not rely for its future strength and security upon the wording of a foreign covenant assuring it of US exemption from military or economic sanctions. Warren Harding had made a rather more energetic fight for the Court than his successor and it is questionable whether, when confrontation loomed, Coolidge's heart was really in the fight. Harding, however, had discovered to his cost that pursuing Court membership had the potential to re-ignite the whole League of Nations controversy, something which Coolidge certainly would not have wanted.

The administration also attempted to build upon another legacy of the Harding-Hughes period, in the field of disarmament. The Washington Naval Conference of 1921–2 had restricted production of the larger classes of naval vessel, such as aircraft carriers and battleships. This left the nations participating in the 1922 treaties free to continue naval expansion through the rapid production of smaller classes of vessel, such as sub-marines, cruisers and destroyers. Japan and Great Britain moved rapidly to boost production and by 1926, Britain had built, or was in the process of building, fifty-four new cruisers (weighing 10,000 tons – the maximum allowed under the guidelines laid down by the Washington Conference). Japan had twenty-five but the US had allocated funding for only eight new cruisers by 1924 and the Coolidge administration was not happy even with these. Appropriations for the army and navy had been reduced since 1921 as part of Andrew Mellon's drive to reduce the national debt, but the cost of arming and equipping the American army and navy continued to escalate (it would jump by $550 million dollars in the five years of Coolidge's presidency). The last thing the President now wanted was a costly new naval arms race. Just such a race now threatened to arise between the United States and Great Britain, much to the annoyance of the American government, which had attempted to show support for the impoverished British economy in negotiations over war debt repayments in 1923. During the Twenties, the Baldwin and McDonald governments in Britain authorised construction of nearly 150 new ships, compared to forty built by the United States. The total tonnage of Britain's output was almost four times greater than America's rather paltry 197,000 tons. Japan, too, was expanding its forces more rapidly than the United States and the administration came under pressure from naval chiefs to support a rapid and costly ship-building programme.

The President, encouraged by the privately expressed view of some British government officials that the cost of naval expansion was becoming prohibitive, decided the time was propitious for a new arms limitation agreement. A League of Nations Preparatory Commission had been meeting since 1926 in Geneva, to pave the way for a planned General Disarmament Conference. In February 1927, the administration issued invitations to those countries on the Preparatory Commission which had also attended the conference in Washington, to attend a new conference in Geneva to consider restricting construction of types of warship not covered by the 1922 agreements. France and Italy refused the invitations, arguing that they were already involved in disarmament plans drawn up by the League of Nations. This left only Britain, Japan and the United States at the table when negotiations opened on 20 June 1927. The American delegation proposed extension of the 1922 5:5:3 ratio to cruisers, destroyers, submarines and other smaller vessels but agreement could not be reached on the total tonnage of 'heavy' (10,000-ton) cruisers to be allowed to each nation. British negotiators were unwilling to sign up to an agreement which helped Coolidge's parsimonious domestic spending plans at the cost, as they saw it, of British security and naval power. The American delegates, for their part, suspected Britain of manoeuvering to prevent the Americans achieving naval parity. They were also sensitive to rising anti-British sentiment on Capitol Hill that precluded any significant concessions at the talks. After nearly two months of wrangling over exceptions clauses and total tonnage figures, the conference broke up without agreement.

Coolidge was vexed that he had failed in an area where his predecessor had so famously succeeded. His administration, however, had not invested as much time and effort in preparation for the Geneva conference as Harding and Hughes had done in Washington. Coolidge had not appeared at the conference in person, risking some personal capital by offering his formal seal of approval.

After Geneva, Coolidge bowed to the inevitable and requested a large increase in naval appropriations from Congress to fund construction of fifteen new cruisers and an aircraft carrier. Six submarines and another aircraft carrier were commissioned by the time he left office in 1929. The administration also sought to strengthen American commercial shipping, which had been in steady decline throughout the Twenties. Two-hundred and fifty million dollars was allocated to strengthening the commercial fleet and, in 1928, the Jones-White Act was passed by Congress, setting preferential railroad transport rates for goods to be exported on American ships.[25] Despite the allocations, expansion of American commercial shipping construction continued to lag behind that of its major competitors.

The failure of the Geneva initiative did not deter the American government from continuing to show interest in designs for a more stable international environment. Ironically, given prevailing American cynicism towards international agreements, it was the Coolidge administration which signed up to what was, perhaps, the most ambitious and unrealistic international agreement of the century. In 1925, France and Germany signed the Treaty of Locarno, under which they agreed to respect each other's Rhineland borders and to resolve any potential disputes through non-military means. Britain, Italy and Belgium, added their support and signatures, which seemed to underwrite a new era of stability in European affairs. In April 1927, French foreign minister Aristide Briand floated the possibility of a pact between France and the United States, built upon the apparent success of Locarno, which would remove the use of armed conflict to settle disputes between the two nations. A bandwagon of popular and political support quickly arose for a wider treaty outlawing war itself. The Federal Council of Churches of Christ issued a public statement, in late May 1927, drawing upon the symbolism of Lindbergh's crossing of the Atlantic to France and calling upon the nation's leaders to outlaw war for the sake of future generations. In a letter to the *New York Times* on 31 May 1927, the president of Vassar College, H. N. MacCracken, warned that the generation now in charge of American diplomacy would 'be held responsible for perversity and selfishness', if it failed to act on Briand's idea. Further, it would greatly assist the development of international law, he argued, if such a treaty, for the first time, gave definition to an acceptable notion of self-defence: 'it renders more difficult concealment, behind the pretense of defense, warfare for the purpose of real aggression.'[26]

In essence, though, the idea was gloriously impractical because no proper enforcement provisions were included in the draft of the treaty developed by Briand and Kellogg.[27] Even *with* these provisions, cynics found it hard to see how the United States could sign up to the agreement without becoming 'entangled' in precisely the kind of international policing framework it had been seeking to avoid since 1918. Secretary

Kellogg was known to prefer the flexibility offered by a system of one-off non-aggression agreements between different nations and it is likely Coolidge concurred in this view. Nonetheless, the President could not publicly oppose the pact without appearing negative and obstructionist. Borah's Foreign Relations committee, in a sudden burst of internationalist idealism, urged the administration to sign up and to encourage other nations to join in. Kellogg and Briand, somewhat reluctantly, broadened the scope of the original proposal and invited fourteen other nations to sign up.[28] The Kellogg-Briand Pact (also known as the 'Pact of Paris') was signed on 27 August 1928 and was quickly ratified in the Senate. President Coolidge, describing the pact as 'the most solemn declaration against war, the most positive adherence to peace ...' signed the agreement in a White House ceremony on 17 January 1929, almost a full decade after the failure of the League campaign.

Latin America

By the mid-1920s, America's exports were curving upward from a low point of $3.8 billion in 1922 to reach nearly $5.2 billion by the close of the Coolidge period. US investment abroad was also approaching a record $15 billion. Reflecting the change in the country's manufacturing base, cars, industrial machinery and petroleum-based products had become the nation's leading export items, whilst agricultural produce was sold abroad in ever-decreasing quantities. Trade with Europe declined from its pre-war levels whilst investment and trading links with Asia, Canada and Latin America increased. Oil corporations, such as Standard Oil and Sinclair-Doheny, expanded their operations in countries such as Mexico and Venezuela, where labour was cheap and competition from other countries substantially less, thanks to the Monroe Doctrine and the war-weakened economies of Europe. The increasing influence of American economic power on her poorer neighbours, however, continued to cause diplomatic difficulties.

President Coolidge had overseen US recognition of the Mexican government of President Alvaro Obregon, which had been arranged by Harding and Hughes, on 31 August 1923. Both the White House and State Department worked diligently, despite the apparent 'normalisation' of relations, to ensure the investments of American oil developers would be protected against possible future civil disturbances or revolutions. This was achieved, in part, by supplying Obregon's government with arms and munitions. In 1925, however, the newly elected government of

Plutarco Elias Calles adopted a radical set of leftist policies prioritising the improvement of living conditions for Mexican dirt-farmers and the 'liberation' of Mexico, as Calles saw it, from exploitation by foreign oil corporations and manufacturers. The Mexican legislature passed an 'Alien Land Law' in 1925, forbidding foreigners from buying up new land without first becoming Mexican citizens, and a 'Petroleum Law' offering only fifty-year leases to foreign oil companies who had acquired their oil lands before 1917. These acts, when combined with harsh anti-church rhetoric and the expropriation of church property, immediately raised American fears that the Calles government was preparing the way for a communist dictatorship. The White House came under pressure from sections of Congress and businessmen returning from Mexico to act against the new government. Secretary Kellogg warned Calles against the introduction or enforcement of laws which would 'either directly or indirectly ... deprive American citizens of their ... property.' Coolidge framed the issue in the same terms as those used by the Wilson administration when the question had arisen of diplomatic recognition of the Soviet government in Russia. 'The person and the property of a citizen,' the President stated, 'are a part of the general domain of the nation, *even when abroad*.' Mexico would not enjoy stable, non-threatening relations with her superpower neighbour whilst American property and investments remained vulnerable to seizure. Preferring diplomacy to sabre-rattling, however, Coolidge despatched a corporate lawyer and Amherst college classmate, Dwight W. Morrow, to open talks with the Mexican government in 1927. The result was the 1928 Calles-Morrow agreement, which quietly arranged for the Mexican Supreme Court to rule the more radical, confiscatory parts of the Petroleum Law unconstitutional. Standard Oil and twenty-one other American oil companies thus kept their rights and holdings. In return, Calles avoided the complete withdrawal of American goodwill and investment. This had suddenly become more vital as the Mexican economy moved into recession, caused partly by a precipitous drop of more than $40 million in investment by worried American oil corporations. Coolidge's 'dollar diplomacy' paid off, at least in the view of the oil companies, and relations between the two countries were placed, temporarily, on a more stable footing. Coolidge's tactic also revealed a similarity with the diplomatic practices of President Harding. Both men instinctively preferred to work behind the scenes in areas of potential confrontation, by sending personal emissaries who often had no connection with the State Department, or even with

Hoover's Commerce Department, which had its fingers in most foreign policy pies by the middle of the decade. Harding gained additional inside perspectives on foreign policy matters by sending Ryan, an oil executive, to Mexico and Cameron Forbes, a general, to the Philippines on 'fact-finding' missions, rather than relying upon the State Department for all his information. Dwight Morrow was not the last non-diplomat to be utilised by Coolidge in this way.

In 1925, the White House announced its decision to withdraw from Nicaragua the American marine detachment which had been stationed there since the days of the Taft administration. The move proved premature, since, within twelve months, the government in Managua had fallen to General Emiliano Chamorro. Although American pressure eventually saw the return of a civilian president – Adolfo Diaz – in November 1926, civil war engulfed the country soon after. The liberals fought to regain control of the government, which they had lost to Chamorro. The US supported Diaz, the conservative president, in the hope that he would protect American property and investments, which totalled around $32 billion by the mid-1920s. The Calles government in Mexico, however, recognised a fellow left-wing soul in Juan Sacasa, the liberal leader, and began sending arms to aid the liberal cause. Coolidge disliked the idea of further US intervention but ordered the Marines to return to Nicaragua and sent former Secretary of War, Henry L. Stimson, to negotiate a cease-fire between the Diaz government and its rivals.[29] The President instructed Stimson to 'clean up that mess'. A peace agreement was eventually hammered out whereby the warring factions agreed to surrender their weapons and submit to an election which would be closely monitored by US government representatives. Diaz served out his term as President but lost the election to Moncada in 1928. One rebel group, under the command of Augusto C. Sandino, refused to surrender its weapons and fought on until Sandino was killed in 1934. President Herbert Hoover was finally able to recall the US marine detachment in Nicaragua in 1933.[30] Overall, the administration succeeded in stabilising Nicaragua in the short-term but the disruption caused to the economic, communications and governmental infrastructure meant that the longer-term outlook was still uncertain. Significantly, neither Coolidge nor Kellogg were willing to contemplate further involvement, as suggested by American representatives in Managua, by sending in large quantities of aid and advisors to repair the damage. Such a venture, the administration claimed, would be too expensive, was not guaranteed a positive response from Congress and risked upsetting Nicaragua's neighbours as a renewed sign of 'Yankee imperialism'.

Coolidge's approach to Latin America, in summary, showed no strong divergence from that of Harding and Hughes. The foundations of Franklin Roosevelt's 'Good Neighbour' policy had been laid, although suspicion of America's economic and military intentions remained close to the surface of Latin American politics.

'Coolidge Prosperity'

In 1919, businessman Raymond Orteig had publicly offered a prize of $25,000 for the first airplane pilot to make a successful, non-stop flight across the Atlantic. The challenge was finally taken up by Charles Augustus Lindbergh, a twenty-five year-old former US mail pilot. Lindbergh had assisted in the design of his plane, the *Spirit of St Louis*, which had been financed by a St Louis business consortium. He took off from Roosevelt Field, New York, at 7.52 a.m. on 20 May 1927. The news that he had touched down at Paris' Le Bourget field the following day, after a flight of 33.5 hours, sparked an unprecedented outburst of national pride and celebration across the United States. Newspapers gave Lindbergh's triumph saturation coverage, including excruciating poetry from readers, lauding the young hero. Lindbergh was feted in France before returning to America on the *USS Memphis*. In New York City, he received the largest ticker-tape welcome ever bestowed as an estimated four million turned out to cheer him. 'Lucky Lindy' was awarded the Distinguished Flying Cross by the President, as well as New York's Medal of Valor and the Congressional Medal of Honour and embarked subsequently on a nationwide tour sponsored by millionaire Daniel Guggenheim. Thousands of American babies born that summer were named after the new national hero.

With this historic achievement, the confidence and optimism of the Twenties reached its apogee. Lindbergh's flight confirmed the nation's faith in its technological prowess and in its ability to defy all human and geographical limitations. More importantly, perhaps, the achievement revived enthusiasm for the 'frontier spirit'. Since Frederick Jackson Turner had first presented his 'frontier thesis', in Chicago in 1893, academics had discussed the effect of ever-expanding geographical horizons on the strength of American individualism and democracy. Jackson, however, had also announced the frontier's 'closure' as the United States spread outwards to its geographical limits. Lindbergh's

daring flight seemed to point America's way to the new, limitless frontier
of the skies and promised to reinvigorate the nation's flagging 'pioneer
spirit', producing new explorer-heroes and fresh confrontations between
the American spirit and the laws of nature. Americans of the Twenties
needed no further encouragement. Air travel became increasingly
popular after May 1927 and transcontinental distances, already eroded by
road and radio, shrank even further. In 1928, Amelia Earhart would
become the first woman to fly solo across the Atlantic.

From 1925, the pattern of economic recovery from the slump of 1920–
1 became stronger and more consistent. Steady growth in government
revenues enabled Andrew Mellon to reduce the national debt and prepare the ground for further tax cuts. In real terms, the economy grew 59
per cent between 1921 and 1929, and annual economic growth averaged
more than 6 per cent. Although wage rises were not uniformly spread
across all sectors of industrial, agricultural or commercial employment,
average annual income was improving steadily. The result, according to
some economic historians, was the unusual phenomenon of the gap
between rich and poor in American society widening *without* the poor
becoming still poorer.[31] By the end of the Coolidge presidency, around
28,000 families in the highest income bracket were outstripping the
earnings of the 11,000,000 who brought in less than $1,500 a year. The
potential problem arising from this phenomenon was that consumer
purchasing power was neither as strong nor as broadly based as it needed
to be in order to ensure the long-term continuation of prosperity.

Rising productivity encouraged firms to expand their operations and
hire more workers. Stocks and shares began to climb, reflecting nationwide confidence that the economic course set by Harding and Mellon,
and continued under Coolidge, was the correct one. A notable exception
to the improving conditions, one later regarded by economic historians
as a warning of hazards to come, occurred in Florida in 1926. The state
had experienced a major boom in land development beginning in the
aftermath of the post-war economic slump and partly fuelled by wartime
restrictions on travel abroad, which caused more Americans to take their
holidays at home. The attractions of Florida as a desirable place to live
were aggressively promoted by the state government and before long
thousands of Americans were buying homes. This, in turn, caused a
major boom in land clearance projects and new building work to meet
demand. Speculators, sniffing the possibility of fast and substantial
profits, moved in. House prices soared between 1921 and 1925, with one

plot of land in the Miami area recording a 766-fold increase in eleven years. Houses were bought and sold rapidly, with buyers often not bothering to move in before selling their newly acquired properties on again. This speculative frenzy was encouraged by the lax lending policies of the banks. In early 1925, the number of loans granted for house purchase doubled. Later that year, however, prices levelled off as the market became saturated and then began to fall as investors realised en masse that it was time to quit the game. Those who had bought land and houses for profit had relied on the expected profits to meet their mortgage payments. The Miami Real Estate Board estimated that 75 per cent of speculative purchasers had defaulted on payments by late 1925. A substantial number of small banks, which had been equally confident that the boom would continue and loaning heavily as a result, failed in 1925–6. Building work also fell off, with the value of contracts falling from $4,486,316 in July 1925 to $1,518,630 a year later, The final blow was dealt by two powerful hurricanes in September 1926 which killed one hundred people and injured many more, ending hopes of a swift recovery. The *New York Times* commented, 'As a word, "boom" is obsolete.'[32]

The experience of Florida's great land boom and subsequent dramatic bust was a salutary lesson, not only for investors themselves but for the banks and for government economists in Washington. Where investment appeared to carry no financial risk whatsoever and where large profits appeared a certainty for those with the energy and initiative to dig them out, there was an ever-present danger of a speculative orgy in which market prices would lose their connection with reality. When the institutions most relied upon to counsel sound borrowing practices abandoned restraint and fuelled the speculative boom, poorly resourced investors would be drawn in. An inverted economic pyramid would result, with enormous amounts of buying and selling at the top based upon a dangerously small amount of capital at the bottom. One gust of nervousness in the markets, enough to release a hurricane of panic selling, would send the pyramid toppling to the ground, leaving many banks as destitute as the speculators they had encouraged.

Despite a brief slowdown in the first half of 1927, when corporate income fell by over $1 billion from its 1926 total, the economy entered upon a phase of rapid growth in the last quarter of the year which would last until October 1929. During this period, almost all economic indicators pointed to the robust condition of industry and commerce, with continually rising productivity, and improving standards of living for average Americans encouraging further commercial expansion. Not all areas of the economy were faring well. Farming income continued to drop, as the McNary-Haugenites had feared, from $22 billion in 1919 to $8 billion by 1928 and there appeared to be no end in sight to the problems of declining prices and product surpluses. In the rest of the economy, however, average earnings between 1927 and 1929 climbed by around 11 per cent. Unemployment continued to fall from its 1921 peak to around 2.5 million at the end of 1928. The nature and scale of the country's industrial might, meanwhile, was being transformed. America's gross national product soared from $72.4 billion in 1919 to $104 billion by 1929. The number of manufacturing companies rose from 183,900 to 206,700 between 1925 and 1929. Industrial production, which had registered a fairly healthy 12 per cent increase in the ten years leading up to 1920, rose a phenomenal 64 per cent between 1920 and 1929. Improvements in technology during the same period stimulated an estimated 72 per cent increase in the individual output of the manufacturing employee. The Federal Reserve index of industrial production averaged 67 in 1921 but stood at 110 in July 1928 and 126 a year later.

Behind this array of impressive statistics, however, lay some disturbing trends. The banking system of the United States continued to show signs of instability. Only around 30 per cent of the nation's banks formed part of the Federal Reserve system, the remainder being 'independent' institutions which were often badly run or corrupt and which often indulged in unwise lending and speculative ventures. Of these banks, 5,000 failed during the 1920s, 669 in 1927 alone. Despite this, bank lending rose sharply throughout the Twenties. The level of public debt also rose as a result of the new popularity of 'hire purchase' agreements, which permitted customers to acquire goods before they could afford to pay for them in full. Many such agreements were signed by those on average or below-average incomes. The dangers inherent in these trends were publicly acknowledged by relatively few financial analysts at the time. Around 60 per cent of the national total, 16,350,000 families, earned less than $2,000 a year in the late 1920s. A further 21 per cent earned under $1,000. These income groups could sustain debt repayments only while interest rates remained low and share prices stayed steady. Any significant rises in one or falls in the other would mean bankruptcy for thousands and trigger a marked downturn in consumer spending. This, in turn, would have harmful consequences for the manufacturing sector, which depended upon healthy sales for the maintenance of profit, investment and employment levels.

Compounding the danger was the fact that much of the money loaned by the banks went to finance speculation on the stock markets by millions of small-scale investors – ordinary citizens who, though completely inexperienced in the ways of Wall Street, decided to take the plunge and buy stocks and shares in a market which seemed to have no ceiling. The number of shareholders had been increasing since the war, a trend accentuated by big corporations such as US Steel and DuPont, who encouraged workers to buy shares as part of their workforce welfare schemes. Individual stock ownership in US Steel multiplied fivefold through the Twenties, a modest increase compared to that of some other corporations. By 1926, every popular magazine carried articles recommending share purchase as a way of augmenting regular earned income and buying power. The holding of a 'portfolio' of investments became a new status symbol. Around 1.5 million small investors were active by 1928, a large enough number to have a significant influence on prices in the event of a panic.

Stock purchase, like everything else, was made easier for amateur investors by lax credit facilities. Having little hard cash for investment, they used borrowed money to buy 'on the margin' – paying for stocks with a bank loan which would, theoretically, be paid off by the profits from the investment, leaving a tidy sum left over for reinvestment or spending on new luxury items. The downside to this practice was that small investors were more vulnerable than larger ones to fluctuating market conditions and more likely to panic sell, since they often could not afford to sit out a 'bear market' and wait for values to climb again.

From late 1927 to the autumn of 1929, the performance of stock values on Wall Street seemed to justify the confidence of those who believed America stood on the edge of a new era of permanent prosperity. The *New York Times*' average of the price for twenty-five leading industrial stocks had registered 106 in May 1924. By the close of 1927 it had already reached 245 and no immediate end to the rise was in prospect.

With most business forecasts projecting long-term growth and with more tax cuts in the pipeline, confidence amongst economic analysts was high. Secretary Mellon, a devotee of the theory of natural 'boom' and 'bust' economic cycles regarded the latest boom as an inevitable follow-on from the deep recession of 1920–1 and saw no reason for alarm. Indeed, cautionary statements from the Treasury, or serious public discussion of the possibility that the foundations of the boom were unstable, were discouraged by the leaders of big business, for fear of halting the surge of confidence in its tracks.

Instead, published articles in newspapers and financial journals theorised upon the possibility that the low cost, mass-output industries of the new consumerist era may have created a system almost impervious to recession. America's industrial and economic infrastructure and practices had changed to such an enormous degree, some suggested, that even if growth slowed to a crawl, the nation would simply rest for a while on a 'golden plateau' before resuming its upward climb to undreamed of prosperity.

Some remained sceptical. Early in 1925, H. L. Mencken predicted of the second Coolidge term,

> there will be song and praise services wherever ... profits run to 50 per cent. There will follow, for a year or two, a reign of mirth in Washington, wilder and merrier, even, than that of Harding's time. And then there will come an explosion.[33]

Notes

1. From *The Young Chevalier* – a poem by Robert Underwood Johnson, commemorating the 1927 solo flight across the Atlantic by Charles Lindbergh. Published in the *New York Times*, 27 May 1927, p. 2.
2. White, *A Puritan In Babylon*, p. 318.
3. Norris later publicly admitted that he had underestimated Stone, who was a more liberal Justice and, later, Chief Justice than he had foreseen.
4. The vote was a 40–40 deadlock which would have been broken by Vice-President Dawes' casting vote, had Dawes not been taking a nap at the time in Washington's Willard Hotel.
5. Harold Brayman, *The President Speaks Off-the-Record: Historic Evenings With America's Leaders, the Press and Other Men of Power at Washington's Exclusive Gridiron Club* (Princeton: Dow Jones Books, 1976), p. 168.
6. Sugrue and Starling, *Starling of the White House*, p. 209.
7. A good deal of discussion abounded in current affairs magazines and political science journals during the 1920s on the possibility that the presidency had become too large and complicated a job to be undertaken by one man. The paralysis of Wilson and the death of Harding, both caused by overwork, added to this view. Interestingly, Herbert Hoover's immense public popularity as a presidential candidate derived from his image as the 'Great Engineer' – a technical and administrative 'wizard' who, more than any other man, was capable of shouldering the burdens of office with ease. His deep unpopularity as President during the Depression reflected the extent to which voters felt their unusually high expectations had been dashed.
8. Herbert Hoover's frequent interference with the jurisdictional territories of other government departments was, almost certainly, one reason for Coolidge's baleful view of his Commerce Secretary and successor.
9. Robert Sobel, *Coolidge: An American Enigma* (Washington, DC: Regnery Publishing Co., 1998), pp. 242–3.

10. Ponder, *Managing the Press*, p. 123.
11. Sobel, *Coolidge*, p. 250.
12. Jardine's predecessor, Henry Wallace, died in 1924.
13. McNary also lent his name to the 1924 Clark-McNary Act which encouraged the establishment of State forestry agencies in cooperation with farmers, and the 1928 McSweeney-McNary Act which set in motion the first comprehensive survey of American forestlands.
14. The son of the firebrand progressive senator who died in 1925.
15. Coolidge was also compelled to veto a third McNary-Haugen bill in May 1928.
16. McCoy, *Calvin Coolidge*, p. 303.
17. Heywood Broun, 'It Seems to Heywood Broun', *The Nation*, 6 March 1929, 128: 3322, p. 275.
18. It is unclear if President Harding was aware of the source of his alcohol supply. The friend of the Attorney General was Jess Smith, who committed suicide in May 1923.
19. Edmund Wilson, 'The Lexicon of Prohibition', in Wilson, *The American Earthquake*, p. 91.
20. Mencken, *A Carnival of Buncombe*, p. 77.
21. Louis Francis Budenz, 'Indiana's Anti-Saloon League Goes to Jail', *The Nation*, 24 August 1927, p. 178.
22. Interestingly, the Prohibition vote would rise again in the 1930s and 1940s, possibly as a reaction to the twin emergencies of depression and war. In the 1950s, it declined once again. The Prohibition party remains politically active and ran candidates in the 2004 presidential elections.
23. Allen, *Only Yesterday*, p. 242. During his term in office, Coolidge left the country only once – to attend a conference in Cuba.
24. 'Ten Senators on the World Court', *The Nation*, 30 December 1925, 121: 3156, p. 751.
25. The 1920 Merchant Marine Act set similar preferential rates but the Wilson and Harding administrations had viewed them as contrary to existing international trading agreements and had been lax in enforcing them.
26. 'Time Ripe for Treaty', *New York Times*, 31 May 1927, p. 20.
27. Although provisions were built in permitting nations under military attack to respond militarily in their own self-defence.
28. The final number of signatory nations was sixty-two. Kellogg received the Nobel Peace Prize for his efforts though, oddly, Briand did not.
29. Stimson had been Secretary of War under President Taft and would serve as Herbert Hoover's Secretary of State (1929–33) before heading the War Department once again under President Franklin D. Roosevelt (1940–5).
30. Sandino's death provided a cause and an iconic figure for the left-wing 'Sandinista' rebel movement which fought the dictatorship of the Somoza family in Nicaragua from the 1930s until the overthrow of the last Somoza in 1979.
31. For an analysis of this phenomenon, see George Soule, *Prosperity Decade* (New York: Macmillan, 1947).
32. 'New, Lasting Boom Expected in Miami', *New York Times*, 29 September 1926, p. 8.
33. Mencken, *A Carnival of Buncombe*, p. 105.

CHAPTER 6

Normalcy Looks Ahead, 1928–9

The country can regard the present
with satisfaction, and anticipate the
future with optimism.[1]

The 1928 Elections

Political pundits, surveying the condition of the United States as the President and First Lady departed for their summer vacation in July 1927, agreed that the re-election of Calvin Coolidge in 1928 was a 'racing certainty'. Much of the country was reaping the rewards of 'Coolidge prosperity'. Farmers, progressives and Democrats, predictably, were not moved to contribute to the paeans of praise now being showered upon the President, but Wall Street and the electorate appeared willing to extend his White House tenure to a record ten years.[2]

On the morning of 2 August 1927 – the fourth anniversary of his accession to the presidency – Coolidge drove to his temporary office in the Black Hills of South Dakota and instructed his secretary to type multiple copies of a twelve-word statement. In one of the more bizarre scenes of American political history, the President cut the paper into strips himself, called waiting reporters into the office and announced, 'The line forms on the left.' Each journalist received a strip of paper, after which Coolidge departed without further comment. The statement read, 'I do not choose to run for President in nineteen twenty-eight.'

The press and political establishment were taken by surprise. Officials of the Republican National Committee, not notified in advance of Coolidge's decision, were stunned at the loss of their greatest electoral asset. Some hypothesised that the statement had been carefully worded to suggest he would not *seek* re-election but would accept a *draft*. Consequently, 'Draft Coolidge' clubs sprang up in towns and cities across the country in an effort to persuade the President to run again. White House aide, Colonel Starling, did not regard the statement as ambiguous, explaining that 'I do not choose', in Vermont parlance, meant simply, 'I ain't gonna do it and I don't give a dern what you think.'[3]

Coolidge's reasons for refusing another term remain a mystery. The death of his son in 1924 may have contributed to his decision but speculation also persists that the President saw calamity ahead for the nation's economy and sought to escape it. Grace Coolidge is reputed to have told a relative, 'Poppa says there's going to be a depression.' As with many Coolidge anecdotes, it is impossible to discern whether this story was genuine or apocryphal. Despite his reassuring public statements, Coolidge's *personal* views on sound economic management did not sit comfortably with the speculative frenzy which was in full swing by summer 1927. Also, given his belief in the natural 'boom-bust' cycles of a capitalist economy, it is feasible the President foresaw that any future bust might match, in scale and ferocity, the wild boom now underway. Historian Isabel Leighton notes, 'It is quite possible that Calvin Coolidge saw the hurricane coming.'[4]

After some months, the Republican party reluctantly took Coolidge at his word.[5] Candidates for the nomination began jockeying for position. The clear favourite was Commerce Secretary Hoover, whose national popularity as the 'Great Engineer' was reaching its peak. To the general public, Hoover's name was associated not only with administrative efficiency, through his handling of the expansion of radio and his successful tenure as Commerce Secretary, but also with humanitarianism. This latter strand of his reputation derived from his wartime duty as President Wilson's food relief director and, more recently, from his widely admired handling of the relief effort for victims of the 1927 Mississippi Valley floods. Other presidential hopefuls were Governor Frank Lowden of Illinois, Senator Charles Curtis of Kansas and Indiana's senator, James Watson. Hoover won on the first ballot of the 12–15 June convention in Kansas City. The now-familiar list of policies – high tariff barriers, low taxes, aid for agriculture through increased food exports, improvement of the nation's inland waterways to cut agricultural and industrial transport costs and more effective enforcement of Prohibition – were included in the party platform, together with a denunciation of McNary-Haugenism, approved over the protests of farm-state delegates.

The Democratic convention met in Houston from 26 to 29 June and proved as uneventful as the Republican gathering. To the relief of party managers, the withdrawal of William McAdoo from active contention left a clear run for Al Smith, the stogie-chewing, four-times Governor of

New York, with whom McAdoo had deadlocked in 1924. Smith, like Hoover, won on the first ballot. Having nominated a wet northern Catholic, Democrats balanced the ticket by selecting the dry southern Protestant, Joseph T. Robinson of Arkansas, for Vice-President. The party platform lambasted the Coolidge administration for failing to resolve the farm crisis and promised to create a Federal Farm Board to assist farmers in selling their crops. It called for the exemption of organised labour from antitrust laws, along with federal building projects to provide work for the unemployed and promised federal aid to education. The platform echoed the Republicans, however, in supporting low taxes and protective tariffs for American industry. On foreign policy, the Democrats chose to endorse the concept of international association but did not commit themselves irrevocably to membership of the World Court. Many Democrats considered that the historic choice of a Catholic nominee was controversial enough. Beyond that, the party attempted to play safe.

The 1928 presidential campaign was dominated by three main issues – the economy, Prohibition and religious faith. On the first, Smith faced the almost impossible task of convincing the nation's voters that improved living standards, technological advances, rising value of stocks and budget surplus were, in some way, 'unsatisfactory'. The problem was compounded by Smith's conservatism on economic issues, which prevented his campaign from carving out a set of fiscal policies distinct from those already on offer from Hoover. The appointment of millionaire businessman John J. Raskob as campaign manager was, in part, an effort by Democrats to reassure Wall Street that their economic policies followed the same basic lines as those pursued by Andrew Mellon. Not all businessmen were convinced by the ploy. Smith, as a New York assemblyman and governor, had demanded tighter regulations of working conditions and safety standards, after witnessing the horrendous aftermath of the fire in the Triangle Shirtwaist factory in which 146 women died because the building had too few fire exits. He also pursued extensive and costly welfare schemes. Consequently, business feared that Smith's conservatism and commitment to free enterprise was skin-deep.

Republican campaign slogans urged, 'Let's keep what we've got' and promised 'a chicken in every pot, a car in every garage.' These slogans reflected the confident, forward-looking spirit of the times, as the Republican nominee, in his speech accepting the nomination, declared, 'We in America today are nearer to the final triumph over poverty than ever before in the history of the land.' This statement, which eventually came back to haunt Hoover, encapsulated the dilemma confronting his opponents in 1928. As a political goal, the abolition of poverty was generally regarded as the terrain of ambitious liberals and progressives but Hoover, the new captain of normalcy, could now make a credible effort to commandeer the issue for Republicans and big business. From a progressive perspective, he was the hardest candidate to beat. His reputation for humanitarianism was coupled with his consistent support for better work and safety regulations on the factory floor. He had strongly supported President Harding in his battle with steel bosses for the eight-hour day in 1923.

Smith and the Democrats were on the back foot in other ways throughout the election. On the issue of Prohibition, the party called for 'honest enforcement' of Volstead, even though it was not made clear exactly what this meant. Moreover, the Smith-Robinson ticket was derided by pro-Republican sections of the press as 'a wet head wagging a dry tail.' Critics questioned how the party pledge could be squared with Al Smith's known contempt for Prohibition and his tendency to undermine its implementation in New York. Party activists tried to reassure voters, particularly those in the South who already doubted their nominee for other reasons, that decisions on enforcement would be left up to the separate states. This sop to states' rights sympathisers succeeded in keeping most party workers from the South and Mid-west on board throughout the campaign. Hoover faced an easier task than Smith, simply restating the Republicans' existing commitment to the 'great social … experiment, noble in motive and far-reaching in purpose.' His party's platform promised 'observance and vigorous enforcement' of Prohibition.

To historians, the 1928 election is most memorable for the central role played by religion in the campaign. The Democrats had taken a brave step in nominating a Roman Catholic candidate and although Hoover refrained from attacking Smith's faith (a tactic which would have been entirely out of character), Republican activists and sympathisers in the press saw no reason why they should be quite so scrupulous. Voters were warned that a Smith administration would turn over direction of American foreign policy to the Vatican, that ways would be found to annul Protestant marriages as 'unlawful in the sight of God', or that Roman Catholicism would be declared the established religion of the United States, in violation of the First Amendment. These preposterous claims were sometimes made outright but often simply inferred. A number of

Protestant preachers, in their pre-election sermons, presented homilies on the evils of drink, 'alien' influences and city life, leaving their congregations to ponder the relative merits of Smith and Hoover in those contexts. In the southern and mid-western farm states, Smith's faith, his stance on Prohibition and his connections to New York 'machine politics', blurred into one, over-arching, negative image. This served to undercut the impact of the Democratic candidate's pledge to aid destitute farmers in ways the Harding and Coolidge administrations had refused to contemplate. Roland Jones, of the *New York Times*, recorded, 'What the farmers and their wives talked was rum, Romanism respectability ... these things were all so inextricably tied in with each other that it is hard to tell where one left off and the other began.'[6] In 1928, therefore, forces were at work against the Smith-Robinson ticket which, in combination, could not be overcome. Confidence in the nation's economic prospects, meanwhile, made rejection of the Republican party seem unnecessary, even illogical, to voters.[7]

On 6 November 1928, the Republican party achieved a third successive electoral landslide – the last great victory of the era of normalcy. The Republicans would not regain the White House until the victory of Dwight Eisenhower in 1952.[8] Herbert Hoover won 58 per cent of the popular vote to Smith's 41 per cent and 444 electoral votes from forty states to Smith's eighty-seven. Smith lost his home state of New York, as well as Tennessee, Kentucky, North Carolina, Florida, Texas and Virginia in the South – states not won by the Republicans since Reconstruction. This was a fair indicator of the attitudes of southern voters to the Smith campaign. The new seventy-first Congress would again come under Republican control, with a seven-seat gain for the party in the Senate and a thirty-seat gain in the House. Although the Democratic party scored well in cities such as Detroit and Chicago, they lost Michigan and Illinois to the Hoover-Curtis ticket. Wall Street recorded a 15-point rise in share prices to celebrate the continuation of normalcy in the White House.

The 'Great Bull Market'

The value of stocks and shares on Wall Street had been moving upwards since 1925, with periodic pauses and slippage as investors and speculators paused for breath or reacted to the occasional set of ambiguous corporate returns. After the spring of 1928, however, they embarked upon a last, seemingly relentless, upward march. The new 'bull market' was unlike anything which experienced brokers and bankers had witnessed before.

In the period 1925–7, stock prices had risen to reflect corporate growth and rising profits. By the summer of 1928, this area of growth had levelled out and, in some cases, had slipped slightly, but stock market prices failed to adjust accordingly. Wall Street was no longer in touch with, or was choosing to disregard, economic indicators which suggested the need for restraint. Speculators, seeking quick and effortless profits, bought and sold with increasing rapidity, pushing prices still higher. Amateur investors also threw caution to the winds after hearing or reading tales of lucky share-buyers who had seen the value of their investments double or triple overnight. Only the very poor or the very timid, it seemed, could resist taking advantage of the golden eggs Wall Street was now laying. The price of shares in DuPont rose from 310, at the start of 1928, to 525 by the end. Shares in Radio Corporation of America rose from 85 to 420 in the same period, while General Electric and Westinghouse tripled their value. The *New York Times* average of the price for twenty-five leading industrial stocks moved upwards from 245 in 1927, reaching 449 by mid-1929. What J. K. Galbraith termed, 'The mass escape into make-believe' had begun.[9]

The foundations of the bull market, as noted earlier, were insecure. They relied upon the expectation that the economy would continue to expand but a number of factors militated against this. The domestic market for consumer goods such as cars, radios and refrigerators, was temporarily sated. Most of those with the purchasing power to buy such goods had now bought them and were not likely to replace them in the immediate future. Those on lower incomes either did not buy them at all or bought them on hire-purchase, thus raising their levels of personal debt. In the face of weakening demand, factories producing these goods would have seen no justification, under normal conditions, in maintaining high productivity rates. Output and profit levels would thus have tailed off accordingly. Under the conditions of the 'Great Bull Market', however, the companies whose stocks were recording the greatest rises, including Sears and Roebuck, Chrysler and General Electric, simply redoubled their efforts to *boost* output. To the minority of cynics willing to speak out, this strategy seemed ill-advised, but, as one financial analyst explained,

> as a practical matter, executives feel called upon to justify market valuations of their securities through building up business profits. This pressure from the Stock Market, which is partly only psychological, intensifies the mad race for heightened volume.[10]

Thousands of investors were now buying 'on the margin' with wild abandon. Millions of dollars worth of stocks and shares were bought up at inflated prices by purchasers who could not realistically afford to pay for them, let alone sustain losses should their value suddenly decline. If prices fell, they would be expected to produce more 'margin' but most small investors had little or no capital left over to protect themselves. Some had invested so heavily, with the expectation of making a small fortune, that even a fairly modest loss could bankrupt them.

The weak foundations of the 1928–9 market were also apparent in the amount of brokers' loans made to investors. In 1927, these loans had totalled $3.5 billion. In early 1928, the figure had risen to $4.4 billion. By September 1929 it would reach $8 billion. In its last year, 'Coolidge prosperity' resembled nothing so much as the contemporary craze for tightrope-walking, as investors wobbled precariously along the high-wires strung out for them over the deep canyons of Wall Street. Beneath them lay a long drop.

The reaction of the Coolidge administration to this frenzy of specula-tion has often been criticised by historians. The President was privately uncomfortable with the easy credit facilities being offered by banks and of the conversion of millions of ordinary Americans to deficit spending. He gave no public indication of disapproval, however, and unwittingly hampered chances for a moderate taming of the bull market when, in a press conference, early in 1928, he disagreed with the suggestion that the steep increase in brokers' loans was a worrying trend. Coolidge, un-doubtedly prompted by Mellon, attributed the record amounts to larger bank deposits and the availability of more securities for sale on the Stock Exchange. In his remarks, the President also confessed, to the surprise of some in his audience, that he was 'in no position to judge accurately' the activities of Wall Street. The recollections of various officials who conferred with the President in 1927 and 1928, suggest that although Coolidge's puritan soul disapproved of 'gambling' on the stock market, he firmly believed that his personal views on sound fiscal management, reflected in the frugality of his own lifestyle, should not be imposed upon Wall Street or the nation. This view, baffling to some observers of the presidency before and since, reflected his broader philosophy of govern-ance, touched upon in the preceding chapter. The President, when asked for comment on 'technical matters' which he considered beyond his expertise, adopted the habit of farming the queries out to relevant govern-ment departments, bureaus or individual experts. After absorbing the information received in response, he would relay it to his interlocutors. This was not an unusual, or entirely inappropriate, practice. Few presidents are fully conversant with every detail of administration policy and most rely, to a greater or lesser extent, upon advice from subordinates. In the case of Coolidge's handling of the overheating American economy in 1927–8, however, a consensus among historians holds that the President was either completely unaware of, or did not realise the importance of, a potentially dangerous economic trend. To these critics, 'his untimely utterance' (on the subject of brokers' loans), 'was the most unfortunate blunder he ever made.'[11] Reporters relayed his optimism to the nation, renewing speculators' confidence that their activities carried the President's blessing. Apart from the flap over the brokers' loans issue, Coolidge restricted his comments on market activity to bland, non-committal observations on the virtues of expanding output and rising wages. At the height of 'Coolidge Prosperity', it is important to note, a broad consensus of political, financial and public opinion supported the President's approach, which they identified as a positive influence on the economy. Former President Taft noted approvingly Coolidge's decision to allow the American people to 'work out for themselves the prosperity they deserve.'

Economic confidence was further stimulated by the action of the Federal Reserve Board in lowering the rediscount rate from 4 per cent to 3.5 per cent in August 1927. This move was largely the consequence of negotiations between Andrew Mellon, Benjamin Strong, chairman of New York's Federal Reserve Bank and representatives of British, French and German banks who were pushing for a cut in American interest rates to stem the large amounts of capital investment flowing from these countries and into the USA which was impeding economic recovery in Europe. If returns on US securities were smaller, the Europeans believed the flood would slow to a steady trickle. Since the Federal Reserve and the US Treasury did not believe a half per cent cut would pose problems for the economy, indeed it could stimulate consumer purchasing, the reduction was made. Wall Street prices reacted with another upward surge.

The 'New Era'

To contemporary observers, the impending transition from a Coolidge to a Hoover administration offered the reassurance of continuity with the past – a change of personnel, rather than of policy. To the delight of Wall Street, Hoover announced that Andrew Mellon would remain as

Treasury Secretary. The extension of his term was interpreted as yet another signal that the administration in Washington saw no need to alter its long-term economic strategy.

Coolidge, however, was not entirely sanguine about the nature of the legacy which he was to hand to his successor in March 1929. Federal spending, despite the cost-cutting of the Harding era, had resumed its upward trajectory after 1925. The budget for the fiscal year 1928, approved by the President and Charles Dawes' successor as Director of the Budget Bureau, Herbert M. Lord, in August 1927, was $3,316,000,000. This larger-than-expected sum included $20,000,000 in extra appropriations for Mississippi flood relief, more money for the Veterans' Bureau and funds for the additional ships and aircraft ordered up after the failure of the Geneva talks. Limited expenditure cuts could not offset the overall increase in federal spending. Although the overall budget surplus was healthy (around $212,000,000), the upward curve deeply disappointed Coolidge and made it harder for Mellon to push the administration's next proposed $225,000,000 tax cut through Congress. Reed Smoot, chairman of the Senate Finance Committee, and William Borah opposed further reductions until it was clear that enough revenue was flowing into the Treasury to pay for them.

The steady rise in spending, it has been suggested since, indicated the ultimate failure of the normalcy programme. A study of per capita expenditure levels, omitting spending on the military and interest payments on the national debt, reveals a total of $22.75 per person spent by the federal government in 1916. The war pushed this level up dramatically to $477.53 by 1919. It fell away immediately after the war ended, in the Wilson administration's final year, to $170.15. President Harding's budgets had massaged the figure down to $70.36 by 1924. Under Coolidge, ironically, levels began floating upwards again, rising each year after 1924 and reaching $79.89 by 1928.[12] Clearly, although the policies of normalcy succeeded in making reductions, they never returned government spending to its pre-war levels. Although the expenditures of 1918–19 dwarfed those of the Harding-Coolidge years, the latter period only temporarily succeeded in restraining government spending. Non-military expenditure recorded a 27 per cent *increase* under Coolidge. Included in this total is an annual increase of 11.4 per cent in agricultural spending, a 10.2 per cent rise in yearly expenditure on education and a 17.5 per cent annual growth rate in law enforcement funding.[13]

The budget figures may have reinforced Coolidge's determination not to seek another term in office. They may also have sharpened his conviction that the economic and political tide was beginning to turn against normalcy, which became more evident to his colleagues in the last months of his presidency.

The significance of the Coolidge-Hoover transition has often been played down by historians. There were, in fact, some sharp differences between the outgoing and incoming administrations. Most histories of the 1920s lump the three Republican presidents into one broad 'conservative' category, ignoring the subtle important differences. As has already been suggested, Coolidgean conservatism differed, in key respects, from the conservatism practiced by Warren Harding. Even greater differences existed between Coolidge and Herbert Hoover. Coolidge's disdain for the 'wonder boy' is indicative of the fact that the President mistrusted Hoover's preoccupation with administrative structures and processes and his energetic pursuit of efficiency and results. As a result of this preoccupation, the Commerce Department, under Hoover, had become one of the most powerful and active offices of the federal government. This fact did not endear him to the President. Coolidge favoured *less* government action. The question of its efficiency was an important consideration, but a *secondary* one. Coolidge's conservatism existed on an instinctive and human level. It drew its strength from small communities and revered traditions and resented the aggressive modernism of flow charts, performance indicators and statistical analyses.

In 1928, Herbert Hoover was 'modernism' incarnate. His reputation as the 'Great Engineer' was very much in tune with the *zeitgeist* of the late 1920s, which admired activism in government if it was expertly managed and embraced technological progress. Hoover was popular precisely because he personified the 'can-do' spirit of a restless age, with its eyes fixed on the horizon and its faith resting more in business and technology than in politics or religion. The contrast with Calvin Coolidge, the tight-lipped farmer's son who had taken his oath of office in the glow of a kerosene lamp, could not have been more stark.

Hoover was not the first political neophyte to enter the White House. Washington, Jackson, W. H. Harrison and Zachary Taylor had all moved directly from military careers to the presidency without first holding elective office or undergoing any political training.[14] Hoover was, however, the first *technocrat* to make the leap. American voters after 1918 had not responded to military leaders such as Pershing and Wood with the same admiration as they had shown for Jackson or Taylor. In the Twenties, however, managerial or business acumen attracted adulation.[15] In 1922–4, efforts had been made to organise a 'Ford for President' campaign. Henry Ford, like Hoover, was admired for his achievements outside the political sphere and his supporters believed his managerial and entrepreneurial skills would be as effective in directing the nation's affairs as they had been in transforming industry. In mid- to late 1923, Ford held a substantial lead over President Harding in public opinion polls and some Republicans even considered a 'draft Ford' campaign to force the President into retirement.[16] The Ford-for-President boom died down, partly because the motor manufacturer was distracted by business concerns, but also because Harding's death and Ford's anti-Semitism made success increasingly unlikely.

Through the recollections of his aides, it is clear that Coolidge regarded his successor as the herald of a new political age, in which active government and large budgets would become the norm. In this environment, the President's own particular skills would lose their relevance. He confided to a cabinet official in 1928, 'Perhaps the time has come when we ought to spend money. I do not feel that I am qualified to do it.' Coolidge had learned his parsimonious fiscal habits in nineteenth-century rural New England and was never truly at ease with the fast-moving decade over which he presided. As Frederick Lewis Allen observed, 'Calvin Coolidge still believed the old American copy-book maxims when almost everybody else had half-forgotten them or was beginning to doubt them.'[17] These old maxims included thrift, caution and gradualism. Calvin Coolidge seemed to sense that his philosophy of governance was out-of-step with the times. As it 'roared' to its climax, the 1920s had finally outgrown normalcy.

The coming of the 'Great Engineer' did not fill every politician with confidence for the future. In late December 1928, Franklin D. Roosevelt, on the eve of his inauguration as Governor of New York, confessed, in a private letter, to entertaining doubts about the new occupant of the White House. FDR wondered, 'whether his type of ability could coordinate all of the one hundred and one simultaneous tasks that fall to the lot of a President.'[18]

Roosevelt's doubts were shared by many professional politicians, particularly Calvin Coolidge. The President-elect had no grounding in party politics and showed little interest in acquiring one. Warren Harding had been particularly proficient in the manipulation and channelling of public sentiment and understood the need for barter and compromise with Congress. Hoover preferred to leave the 'basics' of politics – the identification of group needs, the calibration of messages to suit particular audiences, the favours bestowed upon constituents, the sensitive ear required to gauge changes in the mood of the town meeting hall – to his aides or to professional politicians. In only one area – the management of publicity – did Hoover display an interest, albeit a limited one.

Hoover's political skills were regarded by many of his political contemporaries as weak because he had not worked his way up from the political grass-roots as Harding, Coolidge and most members of Congress had done. Harding and Coolidge had succeeded, in different ways, in transferring their state-learned political skills to the arena of national politics. Hoover had no such assets to transfer, a point not missed by members of his party in the seventy-first Congress. The President-elect, they warned, would soon learn that the tree of politics grew from the roots up, not from the canopy down.

As President, Hoover would be compelled to work with Congress in the kind of close relationship he had often avoided during his tenure at Commerce. Harding had been disillusioned and Coolidge frustrated by their frequent clashes with Congress, but both were career politicians and understood that neither the Constitution, nor Congress permitted the President to govern alone. Hoover, on the other hand, took a dim view of Congress' ability to function as the 'efficient' articulator of the nation's needs and aspirations. He also had little confidence in its ability to differentiate between partisan goals and the national interest. Patronage, horse-trading and coalition-building – the staples of congressional life – were of little interest to the new President. Hoover sometimes gave the impression that he expected the sheer force of public opinion, weighing in behind the President, to stir Congress into united, altruistic action.

The President-elect, as mentioned earlier, shared one talent with Harding and Coolidge – an ability to manipulate the press. As Commerce Secretary, he had ensured that materials publicising the work of the department were freely available to newspapers and magazines as well as to other government offices. Journalists were rarely short of information on the latest projects undertaken at Commerce, even though Hoover tried to ensure that his name was not included in the bulletins released. He also held press conferences and hired professional publicity consultants. These actions made the Commerce Department appear to be a hive of innovation and activism throughout Hoover's tenure, though they also provoked jealousy and resentment from some cabinet colleagues. A sophisticated public relations strategy had the potential to serve him well as President but reporters did not warm to Hoover personally. Many felt unable to swap jokes with him as they had with Harding and were well aware of the Quaker President's disapproval of gambling. Coolidge was hardly garrulous and rarely stirred himself to assist reporters in gathering information, but he had provided a bottomless well of amusing anecdotes and his odd mannerisms had inspired affection. 'We kinda liked the old coot', one White House correspondent later recalled. Hoover's rather cold public personality had the potential to cause him problems as President if the Washington press corps turned against him. *The Nation*, reviewing the outlook for the new regime in March 1929, made a passing mention of the clouds scudding across Hoover's presidential horizons,

> it is known that he is unpopular with ... press correspondents; that he has never been beloved in Congress, sometimes for reasons entirely to his credit. His shyness with strangers is recorded, likewise the occasions when he has lost his temper when badgered before committees ... he deeply resents criticism ...[19]

Expectations of the new President were so great, the article observed, and the opportunities and potential pitfalls of the approaching 1930s so numerous that, 'Mr. Hoover's Administration will either be one of the most memorable in our history, or ... he will be one of the greatest failures in the Presidency.'[20]

Rising confidence and prosperity were accelerating the pace of social and cultural change, stimulating the imaginations of builders, designers and manufacturers. Grandiose schemes were enacted for new dams, airports, aircraft, power plants and highways. Immense new concrete sports arenas appeared, altering the face of American sport and assisting in its conversion into a multi-million dollar business. Giant supermarkets dotted the landscape, symbols of the increasing dominance of the chains over smaller retail outlets. Commissions were formed, bringing together representatives of government and private industry, to plan the building of the Boulder Dam in Colorado (later renamed the Hoover Dam), the St Lawrence Seaway, connecting the Great Lakes to the Atlantic Ocean and a host of other large-scale projects. President Coolidge gave them his executive benediction but their cost and sheer scale probably discomfited him. Business, by 1929, was moving towards greater consolidation

and the development of an 'oligopoly', in which markets were dominated by a handful (usually three or four) of powerful corporations. These
giants had arisen by swallowing up smaller enterprises. The pattern of
merger and takeover which had such a profound impact on the development of the film industry was replicated across the country. Between
1920 and 1929, more than 6,000 manufacturing companies closed down,
whilst chain stores such as F. W. Woolworth and Walgreen's forced
many smaller retail outlets to sell out, unable to compete with their larger
rivals' ability to sell everything from food and drugs to clothes and books.
At the end of the Coolidge era, around 200 corporations controlled 45
per cent of the nation's corporate assets.

A new America was emerging, one which Calvin Coolidge and most
of his generation would have neither recognised nor welcomed. The
greatest symbols of the wealth and confidence of the new dawn were the
'skyscrapers', which had altered American city skylines beyond recognition by 1929. Buildings of between ten and twenty stories first began
appearing in New York and Chicago as long ago as the 1880s and taller
constructions appeared in the early 1910s, such as the fifty-eight-storey
Woolworth Building, completed in 1913, which was, for a time, the
world's tallest building. The skyscrapers of the Twenties were, typically,
bigger and brasher than their predecessors and used more eye-catching
designs. In 1925, work was completed in Chicago on the thirty-storey
Wrigley Building, notable less for its height than for it's exotic 'Spanish
revival' architectural style, its terra cotta exterior tiling (for easy
cleaning) and its giant clocks, each of which had second hands measuring
over six feet in length. The original Madison Square Garden in New
York, where the forces of Smith and McAdoo had clashed so violently in
1924, was demolished the following year to make way for the forty-
storey New York Life Insurance Company headquarters, a neo-gothic
structure with a golden pyramid roof. Work on the projected seventy-
seven-storey, art deco Chrysler Building had been started in New York
but its supremacy would soon be challenged by the 102-storey Empire
State Building, plans for which were taken out in 1929.

Despite their often attractive design features, some critics expressed
doubts about their 'dehumanising' impact. Hundreds of thousands of
office workers now scurried along vast, shadowy canyons to work in
box-like rooms or open-plan offices which seemed designed to remind
them of their anonymity and insignificance. So powerful had the corporations become that these steel-and-concrete monoliths hardly seemed to

do them justice. Fritz Lang, director of the memorable and stylish 1926 film, *Metropolis*, later claimed that the inspiration for his nightmarish vision of the future had come from his first sight of the Manhattan skyline.

The ever-increasing price of real estate was one reason for the skyscraper explosion, although Irwin S. Chanin, president of the Chanin Construction Company, also attributed it to the fact that 'man is a social animal with a herding instinct'. This, he added facetiously, was why New York had a 'theatre district'.[21]

The entertainment industry continued to thrive in the late Twenties. Around 250,000 radios were sold in 1927, permitting an audience of over 5,000,000 to listen in to the 'fight of the century' between Jack Dempsey and Gene Tunney on 22 September which ended with Tunney controversially retaining the title he had taken from Dempsey the previous year. Rapid technological strides had been made in Hollywood since the early Twenties, leading to the introduction of 'talking pictures'. *The Jazz Singer*, starring Al Jolson, was released in 1927. It featured sound in some scenes and for Jolson's blackface rendition of *Mammy*. Although only a limited number of theatres could install a sound system in time for the movie's release, *The Jazz Singer* was the most popular film of the year. Shortly afterwards, *The Lights of New York* became the first all-talking movie and doomed silent films to a rapid extinction. Some established Hollywood stars failed to make the transition from 'silents' to 'talkies' but the careers of others, including Greta Garbo, Laurel and Hardy and Charlie Chaplin, flourished. Another watershed innovation came on 18 November 1928, with the release by the Disney Corporation of *Steamboat Willie*. This cartoon, just over seven minutes in length, was the first cartoon feature to boast a soundtrack synchronised with the animation. As the Harding-Coolidge era drew to its close, Mickey Mouse made his entrance on the world stage.

Notes

1. Calvin Coolidge, 'Message to Congress', December 1928.
2. Comprising Harding's unexpired term (1923–5), Coolidge's elected term (1925–9) and a prospective second full term (1929–33).
3. Sugrue and Starling, *Starling of the White House*, p. 259.
4. Isabel Leighton (ed.), *The Aspirin Age: 1919–1941* (New York: Simon and Schuster, 1949), p. 150.
5. Lillian Rogers Parks offered an interesting account of Coolidge's reaction to Hoover's nomination in her memoirs. She claimed that Coolidge had secretly hoped to be

drafted in 1928 and spent the entire day sulking in his room, refusing food, when the Republican convention failed to oblige. See Lillian Rogers Park, *My Thirty Years Backstairs at the White House* (New York: Fleet Publishing, 1961), pp. 196–7.

6. 'Prejudice Killed Smith in the Corn Belt', *New York Times*, 18 November 1928, p. B2.

7. The force of this last argument is underlined by the fate of the Republicans in 1932, when the economic bubble had burst. Had he gained the Democratic nomination a second time, the chance was high that Al Smith would have been elected, despite his Catholicism.

8. The Republicans did keep control of the House of Representatives in 1930s midterm elections but lost forty-seven seats and had a technical majority of only seven. They also lost overall control of the Senate.

9. J. K. Galbraith, *The Great Crash 1929* (Boston: Houghton Mifflin, 1961), p. 16.

10. Merryle Stanley Rukeyser, 'Wall Street's Speculative Optimism', *The Nation* 127: 3306, p. 514.

11. Schriftgiesser, *This Was Normalcy*, p. 239.

12. After 1928, the Depression and the New Deal policies of Franklin Roosevelt caused per capita spending to skyrocket past the $300 mark.

13. Randall G. Holcombe, 'The Growth of the Federal Government in the 1920s', *Cato Journal*, Fall 1996, 16: 2, pp. 5–6.

14. Dwight Eisenhower is, to date, the last man to become President without previously holding political office.

15. The trend continued throughout the twentieth century with Lee Iaccoca, Ross Perot and Steve Forbes all touted as potential presidents due to their success in business and management. None won a major party nomination, however, and only Perot became, temporarily, a significant political force.

16. It has been claimed that the article being read to President Harding by his wife at the moment of his death was not, as most writers claim, Samuel G. Blythe's favourable review of the Harding presidency, 'A Calm Review of a Calm Man', but a profile of Henry Ford which examined, amongst other things, his presidential prospects.

17. Allen, *Only Yesterday*, p. 242.

18. Elliott Roosevelt (ed.), *The Roosevelt Letters, Volume 3, 1928–1945* (London: George G. Harrap and Co., 1952), p. 25.

19. 'The Thirty-First President', *The Nation*, 3 March 1929, 128: 3322, p. 272.

20. Ibid.

21. 'Says Skyscraper is Public Benefit', *New York Times*, 16 December 1928, p. RE1.

Conclusion:
Looking Back at Normalcy

The Perspective of History

Retrospective analysis of any historical period is, inevitably, influenced by two key factors: (1) the political and economic conditions prevailing when the assessment is made and (2) the ideological viewpoint of the assessment's authors, or what historian Thomas Bailey calls, the 'ticklish question of political prejudice'.[1] With these factors in mind, students of American politics and society in the 1920s should exercise particular caution.

Historians have long been in the habit of treating the Twenties as a period characterised by greed and isolationism. This is primarily because the years from 1919 to 1929 are topped and tailed by two epochs of conflict and change – the progressive era and World War One on the one hand and the Great Depression and World War Two on the other. Against these periods of great human drama, the Twenties appear, to many writers, as an irrelevant interlude in the ongoing liberal-internationalist historical narrative. The Depression and Second World War changed the shape of American society and the priorities of American politics so completely that the 1920s became, almost overnight, a strange and distant land. Henry May comments, 'the Twenties shot into the past with extra-ordinary suddenness.'[2] By the mid- to late 1940s, a powerful and costly federal government, an 'imperial' presidency, Keynesian economics and internationalist foreign policies dominated the political landscape. A new generation of liberal-progressive historians rummaged around in the wreckage of the 'era of normalcy' for the lessons to be learned from the mistakes of a non-liberal past which had, apparently, brought calamity upon the nation at home and abroad.[3]

If the Twenties were not excoriated, they were brushed over. Later American history texts tended to focus upon Prohibition, flappers, jazz and the Great Crash before moving quickly on to the New Deal era. The presidencies of Harding and Coolidge usually received cursory treat-ment, with the focus mostly on the presidents' personalities rather than their policies. An American student recalled, 'We never paid any attention to what the books said about Harding and Coolidge because we knew the professors were in a hurry to get to Roosevelt.'[4]

More in-depth histories presented the Twenties as a classic morality tale in which small-minded conservative leaders, failing to learn from the past, ignored their duty to the nation and the world. Social reform was rejected and hedonism infected all levels of society, while powerful corporations dominated politics and drove the American economy into the ditch. Second-rate politicians shuffled around in, but failed to fill, the over-sized shoes of Teddy Roosevelt and Woodrow Wilson. The United States turned its back upon the world and embarked upon what F. Scott Fitzgerald termed, 'the greatest, gaudiest spree in history.'

An air of 'inevitability' pervaded these works. Few historians bothered to assess policies on their individual merits, take account of socio-economic or political *context* or modify the liberal consensus that the era of normalcy had been a colossal mistake.

What Normalcy Was and Wasn't

It is unlikely that Warren Harding ever intended that his use of the word 'normalcy', during a speech in Boston in 1920, should be regarded as a cohesive political programme. As with Franklin Roosevelt's use of the term 'new deal', the term 'normalcy' implied a projected *end*, without specifying the *means* by which it would be reached. It is important, therefore, to try to understand exactly what normalcy did, and did not, represent, both in socioeconomic and political terms.

Normalcy did not possess the tight ideological coherence of a political doctrine. It was rooted in a set of key conservative principles – smaller government, lower taxes, cost-cutting and a reduction in government regulation of industry and the economy. These certainly represented a break from the Wilson era but were more or less in line with traditional Republican policies of the late-nineteenth and early-twentieth centuries. Normalcy undoubtedly reflected a yearning for the past, but it would be a mistake to claim, as many later historians did, that Harding attempted to roll back twenty years of progressive reform. It never adopted the radical language of an ideological crusade, such as that used by the Republican party's 'Contract with America' in the mid-1990s. The twenty-ninth President was no Newt Gingrich and had neither the ambitious energy nor the political inclination to attempt such a bold move. It is worth noting that progressivism, whilst temporarily losing the political initiative, remained popular in many western states and made its presence felt in Washington during both the Harding and Coolidge presidencies.

The essence of normalcy was its effort to facilitate a period of national 'convalescence' in response to an overwhelming public demand. It was a reflexive political reaction to the traumas and disappointments of the past four years, not a carefully concocted plot to dismantle the legacy of progressivism. Harding recognised what the public wanted and tried to provide it. Liberal Democrats and progressives, on the whole, failed to understand the electorate. Their mystification over the Harding-Coolidge victories of 1920 and 1924 demonstrates the degree to which reformers had lost touch with grass roots public opinion, which was growing markedly more conservative.

Perhaps this failure is not surprising. Between 1913 and 1917, progressives had become accustomed to using the power of the federal government in Washington to introduce national socioeconomic and political reforms. The 1917–18 war period spread this influence still further through emergency wartime powers which escalated spending and regulated economic and social behaviour. By war's end, most progressives believed the momentum of government-directed reform was unstoppable and was driving America into a new, enlightened, liberal era.

In just over eighteen months, these hopes were dashed – first by the rout of the Democrats in the 1918 mid-term elections, then by the paralysis of Wilson and the death of Theodore Roosevelt and, finally by the loss of the Versailles Treaty debate and the election of Harding. The swiftness of the collapse left reformers embittered at what they saw as a conservative 'counter-revolution'. This reaction helps to explain the biting, personal contempt which many expressed towards Harding and the popularity of the myth that the President was 'controlled' by Lodge, Standard Oil, Mrs Harding or a combination of the three. The 'counter-revolution' theory was, in some ways, preferable to the alternative explanation – that voters were tired of upheaval and deeply sceptical of efforts to bring about 'social justice' through government programmes.

No counter revolution had, in fact, been necessary. Progressivism's hold on the electorate had always been tenuous. Wilson's victory in 1912 had been achieved only through a split in the Republican party. His 1916 re-election margin was extremely narrow and the Republicans had made gains in both the 1916 and 1918 mid-terms, suggesting that the electorate's conservative instincts remained strong.

Harding's normalcy, as earlier stated, had only limited counter-revolutionary ambitions, most of which were open to compromise. Economically, normalcy mandated cuts in taxation but these were, at least initially, less radical than they appeared. Even the Wilson administration felt taxes were too high, whilst the scale of the Mellon cuts of 1922 and 1924 was reduced by progressive and Democratic opposition in Congress. It is certainly true that the distribution of wealth during the 1920s moved disproportionately towards upper-income earners, but so did the overall tax burden, as more low-income earners were removed from the tax rolls – a practice of the Wilson era continued by Andrew Mellon.

Government regulation of industry and the economy was scaled back in some areas but expanded in others. Federal spending dropped back for the first few years of the Twenties, but never to pre-1916 levels. Government funding for the care of wounded veterans, for improved standards of maternity care and for highway, radio and airplane development all increased in the same period. By 1926, both the size and the cost of government were rising, not falling.

Normalcy succeeded in fostering a calmer, more upbeat, national mood and in restoring free political dialogue. Harding's release of jailed antiwar protestors, heartily approved by progressives, had been blocked for over two years by Wilson himself.

In foreign policy, normalcy adopted the only approach realistically open to it – that of qualified internationalism. It recognised that the League of Nations aroused either disinterest or antipathy amongst voters. Moreover, the League, after Wilson and Lodge had finished with it, could not attract sufficient congressional support. Other forms of international association, however, were encouraged and Harding, in particular, pressed for US membership of the World Court. In the case of the Court, when normalcy was forced to choose between isolationism and modified internationalism, it opted for the latter.

One important caveat to the above points should be made. Although the Coolidge administration proclaimed continuation of the 'normalcy programme' as its first priority, changes to foreign and domestic policy inevitably occurred after August 1923. These changes, which reflected the differences in personality between Harding and Calvin Coolidge, altered the nature of normalcy itself. The differences between the 1921–3 and 1923–9 administrations are more significant than most histories of the period allow and are examined, briefly, below.

Warren Harding

The sharp decline of Warren Harding's reputation set in well before the end of the 1920s. Revelations that he had entertained a mistress in the White House and had been deceived by his corrupt associates broke in the mid- to late Twenties. Alice Roosevelt Longworth's comment that, 'Harding was not a bad man, he was just a slob,' quickly became the twenty-ninth President's epitaph. Republican politicians distanced themselves from the mess, for obvious reasons, and Harding became a soft target for the critics of normalcy. Following the lead set by Sinclair Lewis and H. L. Mencken, the twenty-ninth President was posthumously subjected to an unusually high level of personal abuse, in which his judgement and morals, his dress sense and leisure pursuits, his intellect and rhetoric and even his choice of wife, were disparaged. This assault soon lost all sense of proportion and Harding's place in history became that of a tragi-comic figure, a slovenly presidential buffoon. Although other presidents, notably Jefferson, Pierce, Lincoln, Arthur and Clinton, suffered similar treatment, Harding's case was unique. Since his presidency was considered a historical irrelevance, few serious scholars bothered to separate the public and private spheres of his life. Most accounts of his presidency rushed through the Washington conference, the eight-hour day, the bonus battle, Latin America and the World Court in order to spend more time with Nan Britton, Jess Smith, spittoons and poker parties. The picture which therefore emerged was that, 'The country ran itself with the president content to sit back and watch.'[5]

Part of the reason for this lack of balance was the delayed release of the Harding presidential papers until 1963, but unbalanced, negative or trivialised accounts continued to appear into the 1980s. These works took their cues from William Allen White's *Masks in a Pageant* (1928), as well as Frederick Lewis Allen's *Only Yesterday* (1931) and Samuel Hopkins Adams' *Incredible Era* (1939). These works set the stereotype for later treatments of the 1920s as a bizarre and trivial period and, for the most part, for the contemptuous dismissals of Harding and Coolidge. Their political analysis was, however, less than reliable. White, for example, had a progressive axe to grind against normalcy.

As liberal dominance of American politics started to decline, in the late 1960s, low taxation, small government and a 'de-imperialised'

presidency attracted more public support. Harding's political achievements began to attract more serious attention from scholars in works
such as Robert K. Murray's *The Harding Era* (1969), Kenneth Grieb's
The Latin American Policy of Warren G. Harding (1976), Eugene Trani
and David Wilson's *The Presidency of Warren G. Harding* (1977) and
John Dean's *Warren G. Harding* (2004). A modest revisionist wave also
spread through the broad-brush histories of American politics. In his
1997 survey, Paul Johnson claimed that Harding had been 'an honest and
shrewd President, prevented by his early death from overwork from
becoming, perhaps, a great one.' Johnson attacked most of the pre-1960s
Harding literature as 'an exemplary exercise in false historiography.'[6]
The rehabilitation of President Harding is an overdue, though currently
little-noticed, trend in modern American historical writing.

Calvin Coolidge

Calvin Coolidge fared better than Harding on a personal level, although
his *political* legacy is more controversial. Aside from occasional allegations of vindictiveness, depression and even latent sadism, accounts of
Coolidge published after the early 1930s tended to focus upon the
thirtieth President's stewardship of the American economy. Perspectives
here are mainly negative, arguing that Coolidge's failure to intervene as
the economy overheated led directly to the crash of 1929. Coolidge is
presented, like Harding, as a lazy Chief Executive whose 'hands-off'
approach to the presidency had become outdated by the 1920s. This
claim has a fairly solid foundation. The gap between Coolidgean myth
and reality has been narrower than that marring the literature on Harding.
Historians have more accurately summarised Coolidge's approach to
government and it is harder, though by no means impossible, to dispute
their conclusions that the thirtieth President was unusually reluctant to
direct, or interfere with, the economic policies of his own administration.
For Coolidge, unlike Harding, non-intervention was 'a state of mind,
almost a physical compulsion.'[7]

More determined conservative revisionists after the early 1980s did
attempt to burnish Coolidge's reputation by crediting his 'hands-off'
approach with sparking the great economic boom of the mid- to late
Twenties. They also suggest that the origins of the Depression lay as
much with European economic instability as with the recklessness of
Wall Street. Whilst these reassessments do not entirely exempt Coolidge
from responsibility for the economic calamity which befell America,

they do suggest that a severe recession was unavoidable, whatever the White House said or failed to say. Since President Ronald Reagan shocked Washington's liberal press elite in 1981 by bringing Coolidge's portrait out from storage to hang in a prominent position in the White House, some efforts to reappraise the 1923–9 administration have been made. Most notable have been Robert Sobel's *Coolidge* and Robert Ferrell's *The Presidency of Calvin Coolidge*. Mostly, however, they stress the President's success in steering the Republican party clear of the Teapot Dome scandal and presiding over strong economic growth. Suggestions that Coolidge (like Dwight Eisenhower in the 1950s) governed more actively than has been supposed, through 'hidden-hand' leadership, are rarely made and are not wholly credible.

Harding and Coolidge

As mentioned earlier, few historians have bothered to distinguish between the 1921–3 and 1923–9 periods in American politics. Instead, they are generally presented as the 'Harding-Coolidge' era. There were, however, important differences between the two men. Although both were conservative, Harding's conservatism was pragmatic. He displayed, on many occasions, an inclination to intervene or to guide through consultation and compromise. His policies and pronouncements on race, the World Court, shipping subsidies, disarmament and the veterans' bonus often disappointed hard-line conservatives as much as progressives.

Coolidge's conservatism, on the other hand, was undisturbed by changing political and social realities. Although he, too, had his problems with conservatives and Republican progressives, Coolidge avoided open confrontations. After clumsily handled efforts at compromise failed, he was inclined either to wash his hands of the issue or resort to the presidential veto.

Harding quickly abandoned his early faith in a strong legislature, operating with independent authority and minimal direction from the White House. Despairing of rampant factionalism in the House and Senate, he tried to assert greater control over national policy and often appeared to court controversy. Coolidge was piqued by setbacks but showed no desire to storm congressional trenches. In the effort to 'out-McKinley McKinley', he succeeded where Harding failed.

Coolidge's ability to pursue this path, however, owed much to the economic recovery of 1924–9. Harding was forced to contend with economic recession, labour unrest, progressive discontent and an almost unprecedentedly hostile and disorganised Congress. Faced with the wreck of his normalcy agenda, he was compelled to adopt a tougher, more interventionist stance. Most of these negative influences, however, had either diminished or disappeared by the mid-point of the Coolidge administration, making it feasible for the presidency to 'change down' into a lower gear. It is possible to speculate, therefore, that normalcy might have assumed a different character had Harding served his term and, Teapot Dome notwithstanding, been re-elected in 1924.

The battle over the World Court would almost certainly have been a politically bloody one, had Harding lived. Calvin Coolidge, however, refused to force the pace of debate, to confront Johnson and the irreconcilables or to stake the prestige of the presidency upon the issue. It is also possible that a second disarmament conference under Harding would have been more fruitful than the exploratory Geneva talks of 1927 proved under Coolidge. Contemporary observers sharply criticised Coolidge and Secretary of State Kellogg for failing to prepare adequately for the negotiations, a weakness which Harding and Hughes never displayed. It is also questionable whether Congress would have been able to steamroller a second Harding veto of the veterans' bonus quite as easily as they overrode Coolidge's in 1924. Although nothing tangible arose from Harding's 1921 denunciation of racial discrimination, it takes a considerable leap of the imagination to envisage Coolidge making the same address. Nor is it likely that the Coolidge White House would have badgered the steel industry to reform working hours with the grim determination exhibited by Harding and Hoover. Finally, Harding's April 1921 legislative agenda may have disgruntled progressives, but it was a positive whirlwind of activism in comparison with the Coolidge agenda presented to Congress in 1925.

In making these distinctions, it is important for students of the politics of the Twenties to be clear as to their *objectives*. An interesting trend in 'revisionist' literature, of the Harding presidency in particular, has been to suggest that this conservative President was more successful and competent than his reputation allows because he possessed latent *activist* inclinations. In other words, Harding's willingness to consider intervention and qualified internationalism – tendencies favoured by *liberal* schools of political thought – are regarded by some revisionist scholars as a reason for upgrading history's judgement of Harding. Post-Reagan historiography continues, ironically, to be affected by the liberal interpretation of history which it set out to correct. New perspectives on

Herbert Hoover, for example, attempt to credit the thirty-first President with laying the foundations for Roosevelt's New Deal – hardly a legacy which Hoover himself would have wished to embrace.

In Harding's case, though not in Coolidge's, the picture is confusing. Although his intentions in engaging in international political dialogue were partly motivated by a capitalistic urge to expand American commercial power, it cannot be denied that the twenty-ninth President genuinely sympathised with the idea of using international institutions to prevent armed conflict. Similarly, although he sought cuts in armaments for *budgetary* reasons, the President's desire to forestall an arms race was a key motivating factor. In economic and industrial relations matters, Harding held fast to his conservative principles but also displayed a pragmatic flexibility. Thus, the Wilkerson injunction was watered down, a veterans' bonus was deemed acceptable *with* a new sales tax and the first round of Mellon's tax cuts were pared back in deference to congressional hostility. This pragmatism ensured that the 1921–3 administration maintained a coherent agenda, despite reversals, and that the conservative President retained public confidence, to the chagrin of his opponents, throughout his tenure. In these features, rather than in 'latent liberalism', lay the key to Harding's quite creditable performance as President.

The 1920s represented a transitional stage between the old America and the new. In this transition lay the roots of the decade's schizophrenia – it looked ahead with hope but backwards for reassurance; it embraced change but experienced deep uncertainty as to where the changes might lead. The nation may have *voted* conservatively but most of its major cultural trends marched in the opposite direction. It admired the traditional family and rural values depicted in Norman Rockwell's covers for the *Saturday Evening Post*, but flocked to the cities to work in factories, purchase electrical goods and dance to the rhythms of jazz. It enacted, and then flouted, Prohibition. Through all of its struggles and contradictions, the Twenties emerged as the first 'modern' decade. It introduced the United States, and much of the world, to the consumer capitalist society in which it lives today. If it erred in its boundless confidence in economic expansion, its cavalier attitudes towards debt, its belief in regional solutions to regional problems or its cynicism towards international intervention, such errors were, to some extent, predictable, given the times through which the nation had recently passed. The Twenties was by no means the only decade to place faith in the notions of 'states' rights' or 'America First'.

Socially, culturally and economically, the Twenties witnessed revolutionary changes unmatched by most previous decades. Class barriers weakened as rising prosperity brought cars and the latest fashions and labour-saving devices within the reach of ordinary consumers. Pressure for social equality between the races began spreading *downwards*, from the intellectual heights of political and civil rights organisations to the cities of the North, where white and black cultures had begun to intermingle. Similarly, though the Nineteenth Amendment finally gave women *political* status at the end of the Wilson era, it was in the 1920s that changing work patterns and family relationships began to offer women a greater variety of lifestyle choices. Many such changes were tentative and vulnerable to sudden reversals, but they had, undeniably, begun. Despite their cataclysmic climax, many of the defining trends of the 'Roaring Twenties' resumed, at a still faster pace, after the intervening years of depression and war. In various ways, the 1950s and 1980s carried distinct echoes of the confidence and doubts of the years of normalcy – years which, though long gone, continue to shape and to haunt modern America.

Notes

1. Thomas A. Bailey, *Presidential Greatness: The Image and the Man from George Washington to the Present* (New York: Van Rees Press, 1966), p. 26.
2. May, 'Shifting Perspectives on the 1920s', p. 409.
3. This was a perfectly natural exercise and was repeated towards the end of the twentieth century, as conservative revisionist writers poked around for signs and sins in the ashes of Great Society liberalism, to explain and justify the 'Reagan revolution'.
4. Paul A. Carter, *The Twenties In America* (New York: Thomas Y. Crowell Company, 1968), p. 38.
5. Trani and Wilson, *The Presidency of Warren G. Harding*, p. 191.
6. Paul Johnson, *A History of the American People* (London: Weidenfeld and Nicolson, 1997), p. 592.
7. Johnson, *A History of the American People*, p. 596.

Select Bibliography

Abels, Jules, *In the Time of Silent Cal* (New York: G. P. Putnam, 1969).

Adams, Samuel Hopkins, *Incredible Era: The Life and Times of Warren Gamaliel Harding* (Boston: Houghton-Mifflin, 1939).

Adler, Selig, *The Uncertain Giant 1921–1941: American Foreign Policy Between the Wars* (London: Collier-Macmillan Ltd, 1965).

Allen, Frederick Lewis, *Only Yesterday: An Informal History of the 1920s* (New York: Harper and Brothers, 1931).

Anonymous, *The Mirrors of Washington* (New York: G. P. Putnam's Sons, 1921).

Anthony, Carl S., *Florence Harding: The First Lady, the Jazz Age and the Death of America's Most Scandalous President* (New York: William Morrow and Company, 1998).

Bailey, Thomas A., *Woodrow Wilson and the Great Betrayal* (New York: Macmillan Company, 1945).

Bailey, Thomas A., *Presidential Greatness: The Image and the Man from George Washington to the Present* (New York: Appleton-Century, 1966).

Bailey, Thomas A., *Probing America's Past: A Critical Examination of Major Myths and Misconceptions*, vol. 2 (Lexington: D. C. Heath and Co., 1973).

Bamford Parkes, Henry, *The American Experience* (New York: Vintage Books, 1959).

Barck, Oscar Jr, and Nelson Blake, *Since 1900: A History of the United States in Our Times* (New York: Macmillan, 1959).

Behr, Edward, *Prohibition: The 13 Years that Changed America* (London: BBC Books).

Bernstein, Barton J. (ed.), *Towards a New Past: Dissenting Essays in American History* (New York: Vintage Books, 1969).

Blythe, Samuel G., *A Calm Review of a Calm Man* (New York: Cosmopolitan Book Co., 1923).

Brayman, Harold, *The President Speaks Off-the-Record* (Princeton: Dow Jones Books, 1976).

Britton, Nan, *The President's Daughter* New York: Elizabeth Ann Guild, 1927).

Bryson, Bill, *Made in America* (London: Secker and Warburg, 1994).

Burner, David, *Herbert Hoover: A Public Life* (New York: Knopf, 1979).

Carroll, Peter N., and David W. Noble, *The Free and the Unfree: A New History of the United States*, 2nd edn (London: Penguin Books, 1988).

Carter, Paul, *The Twenties in America* (New York: Thomas Y. Crowell Company, 1968).

Cashman, Sean Dennis, *America in the Twenties and Thirties* (New York: New York University Press, 1989).

Chalmers, David, *Hooded Americanism: The History of the Ku Klux Klan* (Durham, NC: Duke University Press, 1987).

Chapple, Joe Mitchell, *Warren G. Harding – The Man* (Boston: Chapple Publishing Company Ltd, 1920).

Chapple, Joe Mitchell, *Warren G. Harding: Our After-War President* (Boston: Chapple Publishing Company Ltd, 1924).

Clark, Norman H., *Deliver Us from Evil: An Interpretation of American Prohibition* (New York: W. W. Norton, 1976).

Cooke, Alistair, *The Vintage Mencken* (New York: Alfred A. Knopf Inc., 1955).

Cooper, John Milton, *The Warrior and the Priest: Woodrow Wilson and Theodore Roosevelt* (Cambridge, MA: Belknap Press, 1983).

Daugherty, Harry M., *The Inside Story of the Harding Tragedy* (Boston: Western Islands, 1975).

Dobson, John, *A History of American Enterprise* (Englewood Cliffs: Prentice-Hall, 1988).

Dray, Philip, *At The Hands of Persons Unknown: The Lynching of Black America* (New York: Random House, 2002).

Dumenil, Lynn, *The Modern Temper: American Culture and Society in the 1920s* (New York: Hill and Wang, 1995).

Ferrell, Robert H., *The Strange Deaths of President Harding* (Columbia: University of Missouri Press, 1996).

Ferrell, Robert H., *The Presidency of Calvin Coolidge* (Kansas: University Press of Kansas, 1998).

Franklin, John Hope, and Alfred A. Moss, *From Slavery to Freedom: A History of African Americans*, 7th edn (New York: McGraw-Hill, 1994).

Galbraith, John K., *The Great Crash* (Boston: Houghton-Mifflin, 1955).

Gatell, Frank, and Allen Weinstein (eds), *American Themes: Essays in Historiography* (London: Oxford University Press, 1968).

Goldberg, David J., *Discontented America: The United States in the 1920s* (Baltimore: Johns Hopkins Press, 1997).

Grieb, Kenneth J., *The Latin American Policy of Warren G. Harding* (Fort Worth: Texas Christian University Press, 1976).

Henry, Laurin L., *Presidential Transitions* (Washington, DC: Brookings Institution, 1960).

Hicks, John D., *Republican Ascendancy, 1921–1933* (New York: Harper and Row, 1960).

Johnson, Paul, *Modern Times: The World from the Twenties to the Eighties* (New York: Harper and Row, 1983).

Johnson, Paul, *A History of the American People* (London: Weidenfeld and Nicolson, 1997).

Jones, Maldwyn Allen, *American Immigration*, 2nd edn (London: University of Chicago Press, 1992).

Kennedy, David M., *Freedom from Fear: The American People in Depression and War, 1929–1945* (New York: Oxford University Press, 1999).

Kitano, Harry H. L., and Roger Daniels, *Asian Americans: Emerging Minorities*, 2nd edn (Englewood Cliffs: Prentice Hall, 1995).

Lears, Jackson, *Fables of Abundance: A Cultural History of Advertising in America* (New York: HarperCollins, 1994).

Leighton, Isabel (ed.), *The Aspirin Age: 1919–1941* (New York: Simon and Schuster, 1949).

Leuchtenburg, William E., *The Perils of Prosperity: 1914–32* (Chicago: University of Chicago Press, 1958).

Lewis, David Levering, *When Harlem was in Vogue* (Oxford: Oxford University Press, 1989).

Lynd, Robert and Helen Lynd, *Middletown: A Study in Modern American Culture* (New York: Harcourt Brace and World, 1956).

McCoy, Donald R., *Calvin Coolidge: The Quiet President* (New York: Macmillan Company, 1967).

McNeil, William C., *American Money and the Weimar Republic: Economics and Politics on the Eve of the Great Depression* (New York: Columbia University Press, 1986).

Mee, Charles L. Jr, *The Ohio Gang: The World of Warren G. Harding. An Historical Entertainment* (New York: M. Evans and Co., 1981).

Mencken, H. L., *A Carnival of Buncombe: Writings on Politics.* (Baltimore: Johns Hopkins University Press, 1956).

Miller, Nathan, *New World Coming: The 1920s and the Making of Modern America* (New York: Scribner, 2003).

Morello, John A., *Selling the President, 1920: Albert D. Lasker, Advertising and the Election of Warren G. Harding* (Westport: Praeger, 2001).

Mowry, George C. (ed.), *The Twenties: Fords, Flappers and Fanatics* (Englewood Cliffs: Prentice Hall, 1963).

Murray, Robert K., *The Harding Era: Warren G. Harding and his Administration* (Minneapolis: University of Minnesota Press, 1969).

Murray, Robert K., *The Politics of Normalcy: Governmental Theory and Practice in the Harding-Coolidge Era* (New York: Norton, 1973).

Nye, R. B., and J. E. Morpurgo, *The Growth of the USA* (London: Penguin Books, 1970).

Parks, Lillian Rogers, *My Thirty Years Backstairs at the White House* (New York: Fleet Publishing, 1961).

Parrish, Michael E., *Anxious Decades: America in Prosperity and Depression, 1920–1941* (New York: W. W. Norton and Company, 1992).

Perret, Geoffrey, *America in the Twenties* (New York: Touchstone, 1982).

Ridings, William J. Jr, and Stuart B. McIver, *Rating the Presidents* (New York: Citadel Press, 2000).

Roosevelt, Elliott (ed.), *The Roosevelt Letters. Volume Three (1928–1945)* (London: George G. Harrap and Co. Ltd, 1952).

Ross, Ishbel, *Grace Coolidge and Her Era* (New York: Dodd Mead and Company, 1962).

Russell, Francis, *President Harding: His Life and Times 1865–1923* (London: Eyre and Spottiswoode, 1969).

Schlesinger, Arthur M. Jr, *The Crisis of the Old Order: 1919–1933* (Boston: Houghton-Mifflin, 1957).

Schriftgiesser, Karl, *This Was Normalcy: An Account of Party Politics During Twelve Republican Years: 1920–1932* (New York: Oriole Editions, 1973).

Sinclair, Andrew, *The Available Man: Warren Gamaliel Harding* (New York: Macmillan, 1965).

Smith, Gene, *When the Cheering Stopped* (London: Hutchinson, 1964).

Sobel, Robert, *The Great Bull Market* (New York: Norton, 1968).

Sobel, Robert, *Coolidge: An American Enigma* (Washington, DC: Regnery Publishing Inc., 1998).

Soule, George, *Prosperity Decade* (New York: Harper Ltd, 1947).

Starling, Edmund W., with Thomas Sugrue, *Starling of the White House* (New York: Simon and Schuster, 1946).

Stevenson, Elizabeth, *Babbitts and Bohemians: The American 1920s* (New York: Macmillan, 1967).

Trani, Eugene P., and David L. Wilson, *The Presidency of Warren G. Harding* (Kansas: University Press of Kansas, 1977).

Warren, Harris Gaylord, *Herbert Hoover and the Great Depression* (New York: W. W. Norton Inc., 1967).

White, William Allen, *Masks in a Pageant* (New York: Macmillan, 1928).

White, William Allen, *A Puritan in Babylon: The Story of Calvin Coolidge* (New York: Macmillan, 1938).

White, William Allen, *The Autobiography of William Allen White* (New York: Macmillan, 1946).

Wilson, Edmund, *The American Earthquake: A Documentary of the Jazz Age, the Great Depression and the New Deal* (London: W. H. Allen, 1958).

Wilson, Edmund, *The Twenties* (London: Macmillan, 1975).

Newspapers and Newsmagazines

The New York Times
The Nation
The Outlook
The World's Work

Selected Articles

Bates, J. Leonard, 'The Teapot Dome Scandal and the Election of 1924', American Historical Review, 60: 2, January 1955, pp. 303–22.

Cornwell, Elmer E. Jr, 'Coolidge and Presidential Leadership', Public Opinion Quarterly, 21: 2, Summer 1957, pp. 265–78.

Grabiner, Judith V., and Peter D. Miller, 'Effects of the Scopes Trial', Science New Series, 185: 4154, 6 September 1974, pp. 832–7.

Hawley, Ellis W., 'Herbert Hoover, the Commerce Secretariat and the Vision of an "Associative State", 1921–1928', Journal of American History, 61: 1, June 1974, pp. 116–40.

Kettleborough, Charles, 'Soldiers' Bonus', American Political Science Review, 18: 3, August 1924, pp. 559–65.

Maddox, Robert James, 'Keeping Cool with Coolidge', Journal of American History, 53: 4, March 1967, pp. 772–80.

May, Henry F., 'Shifting Perspectives on the 1920s', Mississippi Valley Historical Review, 43: 3, December 1956, pp. 405–27.

Ngai, Mae M., 'The Architecture of Race in American Immigration Law: A Reexamination of the Immigration Act of 1924', Journal of American History, 86: 1, June 1999, pp. 67–92.

Padelford, Norman J., 'The Veterans' Bonus and the Constitution', American Political Science Review, 27: 6, December 1933, pp. 923–9.

Rogers, Lindsay, 'American Government and Politics: The First (Special) Session of the Sixty-Seventh Congress April 11, 1921–November 23, 1921', American Political Science Review, 16: 1, February 1922, pp. 41–52.

Rogers, Lindsay, 'American Government and Politics: The Second, Third and Fourth Sessions of the Sixty-Seventh Congress', American Political Science Review, 18: 1, February 1924, pp. 79–95.

Rogers, Lindsay, 'American Government and Politics: First and Second Sessions of the Sixty-Eighth Congress', American Political Science Review, 19: 4, November 1925, pp. 761–72.

Sherman, Richard B., 'The Harding Administration and the Negro: An Opportunity Lost', Journal of Negro History, July 1964.

Weinstein, James, 'Radicalism in the Midst of Normalcy', Journal of American History, 52: 4, March 1966, pp. 773–90.

Whitaker, W. Richard, 'Harding: First Radio President', Northwest Ohio Quarterly, 45: 3, 1963, p. 43.

Index

The British Association
for American Studies (BAAS)

The British Association for American Studies was founded in 1955 to promote the study of the United States of America. It welcomes applications for membership from anyone interested in the history, society, government and politics, economics, geography, literature, creative arts, culture and thought of the USA.

The Association publishes a newsletter twice yearly, holds an annual national conference, supports regional branches and provides other membership services, including preferential subscription rates to the *Journal of American Studies*.

Membership enquiries may be addressed to the BAAS Secretary (see *www.baas.ac.uk* for contact details).